Doing Politics

T0383698

Aimed at politics students in their final year of secondary education or beginning their degrees, this highly readable book is the ideal introduction to politics.

Doing Politics is a detailed guide to both the study and the activity of politics, which explores why we study politics, what is involved in a politics degree, and the skills and mindset that are needed to tackle the subject.

Key questions are answered, including:

- Just what is politics and how does it affect us?
- Why does politics, and why do politicians, get a bad press?
- How do we study non-traditional forms of politics?

Assuming no prior knowledge, this lively and engaging guide is the perfect introduction to the academic study of politics.

Jacqueline Briggs is the Head of the School of Social and Political Sciences at the University of Lincoln and Vice Chair of the Political Studies Association UK (2011–2014).

Also available from Routledge

International Relations: The Key Concepts (3rd edition)
Steven C. Roach, Martin Griffiths, Terry O'Callaghan
978-0-415-84494-9

Politics: The Basics (5th edition)
Nigel Jackson, Stephen D. Tansey
978-0-415-84142-9

Politics: The Key Concepts
Lisa Harrison, Adrian Little, Ed Lock
978-0-415-49740-4

Doing Politics

Jacqueline Briggs

Routledge
Taylor & Francis Group

LONDON AND NEW YORK

First published 2015
by Routledge
2 Park Square, Milton Park, Abingdon, Oxon OX14 4RN

Simultaneously published in the USA and Canada
by Routledge
711 Third Avenue, New York, NY 10017

Routledge is an imprint of the Taylor & Francis Group, an informa business

British Library Cataloguing in Publication Data
A catalogue record for this book is available from the British Library

Library of Congress Cataloging in Publication Data
Briggs, Jacqui.
Doing politics / Jacqui Briggs.
pages cm
1. Politics, Practical–Study and teaching (Secondary)
2. Political science–Study and teaching (Secondary)   I. Title.
JF2051.B74 2014
320–dc23

2014018219

ISBN: 978-0-415-67806-3 (hbk)
ISBN: 978-0-415-67805-6 (pbk)
ISBN: 978-1-315-75048-4 (ebk)

Typeset in Times New Roman
by RefineCatch Limited, Bungay, Suffolk

Contents

Acknowledgements

I would like to express my sincere thanks and deepest gratitude to my colleagues within the School of Social and Political Sciences at the University of Lincoln for their aid, advice and assistance. Particular thanks to Bernie Russell from the School of Journalism and to Marie Nicholson, academic subject librarian, for their invaluable research support; and to Sara Mann and Tom Kirman, for their help and advice with regards to data presentation. Special thanks too to everyone at the Political Studies Association of the United Kingdom, especially my wonderful colleagues Professor John Benyon, Professor Paul Carmichael and Professor Charlie Jeffery. Thank you to Iram Satti at Routledge for her guidance and expertise.

Last, but not least, thanks to my partner, John, daughter Imogen, Mum and Dad for their support and sacrifice.

Introduction to
Doing Politics

Those of us stimulated by the infectious nature of political debate and the ebb and flow of power within the political spectrum will find this chapter thought-provoking. For the converts amongst us, there can be nothing more exciting than to 'do politics'. This chapter introduces the book and the topic of *Doing Politics*. This first chapter highlights how the book constitutes a detailed guide to both the study of politics and the activity of politics. The text within provides a penetrating insight into what is involved in studying politics at university. Explanation is given as to whom the book is for. What is the book intended to achieve? How to use the book? Why should we study politics? What is involved in a politics degree? What topics and areas do you study as part of a politics degree? What sort of careers might be open to you if you study for a politics degree? Examination is made of the kinds of topics and areas that you would expect to study as part of a politics degree. In addition, reference is made to the kinds of skills you can be expected to acquire as part of your politics degree. This book gets behind the mindset needed to study politics at undergraduate level. This involves asking questions rather than just accepting what one is told. The creation and development of a 'critical thinker' is important here.

As stated, the book comprises a critical appraisal of what is involved in the study and activity of politics. It forms a practical guide for those wishing to study politics at university. Organised into ten chapters, the book outlines why politics is important and why politics gets such a bad press before moving on to look at the key areas that the student of politics will investigate as part of their studies. Written in a lucid and accessible style, this book is an easy to read guide for those new to the study of politics. Many young people choose to study politics at AS level and also at A-level. In addition, they may choose to continue their political education by studying politics at undergraduate level too, either as single honours or as part of a joint degree (as a major or minor subject combination). Some undergraduates may choose to study politics at university without having studied it prior to coming to university. Those who have studied the discipline at AS or A-level will obviously have covered the key topic areas and so will, initially at least, be at a slight advantage in comparison with those coming to the subject afresh at undergraduate level. University lecturers are used to this dichotomy in terms of background knowledge and the competent tutor is well versed in ensuring that those who have not covered the subject at A-level are quickly brought up to speed during the first year of an undergraduate degree. In addition, the topics covered at undergraduate level will soon deviate from those covered at AS and A-level, as well as going into much greater depth than hitherto. As the contestants on the television programme 'University Challenge' state when they introduce themselves, undergraduates are 'reading' for a degree. To study politics, therefore, involves reading in detail about the key topics, concepts and themes involved in the discipline of politics.

The book is intended to be used as an introductory guide to studying politics at university. The author is passionate about political study and political education *per se*. Having taught politics since 1986 in a further education establishment and then in the higher education sector since 1992, the author is well versed in the requirements of political education at GCSE, A-level and undergraduate level. In addition, her research into young people and politics provides added insight into the notion that young people need and deserve to be educated politically. The introduction of citizenship classes goes some way towards achieving that goal but there is still a long way to go before young people have a thorough and comprehensive grounding in politics. Citizenship classes are now compulsory but, even so, they have been criticised for focusing upon issues other than politics. Drugs awareness, anti-bullying lessons and discussion of personal relationships have been cited as topics covered in citizenship classes. These are all laudable topics and aims but not the original idea envisaged by the late Professor Bernard Crick when citizenship classes were first mooted. Evidence reveals that, relatively recently, citizenship lessons in schools have played more of a role in encouraging young people to take an interest in the political system and to become more aware and knowledgeable of political issues. In addition, recent changes, such as the fact that young people at the age of 16 and 17 were able to vote in the Independence Referendum vote in Scotland, which took place on 18 September 2014, may have the added effect of encouraging more young people to 'do' politics. It will be interesting to ascertain whether the numbers choosing to study politics at A-level and at undergraduate level increase in the near future and, if so, whether this can be attributed to increasing levels of political awareness stimulated by changes such as the lowering of the voting age in certain elections.

These are certainly exciting times as far as the student of politics is concerned. Global issues such as environmentalism and poverty mean that politics is of interest and concern to many. Politics governs the way we live our lives and, indeed, whether we live at all – if examination is made of certain political regimes. The rise of mass communications with the development and proliferation of the internet and of mobile technology means that politics ought to be of increasing importance. No longer does the ordinary citizen need to simply rely upon what politicians and media moguls tell us is the truth – often a particular and partial version – mobile technology can often provide a direct, immediate, countervailing force to the more official versions. The so-called Arab Spring of 2011 provided a clear illustration of people power and how this can impact upon politics and sometimes bring about regime change. *Doing Politics* remains, therefore, as pertinent and as exciting as it ever was, if not more so.

As stated, the book is divided into ten chapters. After this introductory chapter, Chapter Two examines the importance and relevance of politics. It highlights key definitions of politics before moving on to assess the all-pervasive nature of politics and how it impacts upon our lives. Broader definitions of politics, such as those encapsulating sexual politics, office politics, etc. are also examined. Rather than simply focusing upon mainstream politics, this broader approach highlights the breadth, scope and reach of politics. Chapter Three involves analysis of what studying politics today involves and what the student of politics is likely to encounter. The focus here is upon the academic study of politics. The issue of bias is raised and the ability to differentiate between fact and opinion. This chapter also looks at how politics is studied in terms of using new technology and media as part of the teaching and learning process. Moving on to Chapter Four, attention turns to why politics sometimes gets a bad press and the negativity that often surrounds politics and politicians, in particular. This perception of politics and politicians, although exacerbated by the recent expenses scandal, has a long history. As will be shown, Shakespeare, in King Lear, refers to the 'scurvy politician'.

Likewise, Samuel Johnson, the eighteenth century writer and poet, was equally scathing about politics, so the negativity is not a new phenomenon. Chapter Five looks at policy making and power; different models of policy making and differing types of power are assessed. The sixth chapter focuses upon the key actors and institutions involved in politics, investigating whether these actors change over time and, again, assessing where power lies in relation to these key players. Chapter Seven concentrates on civil society by examining new social movements and less formal methods of political activity and political participation. Seeking to redress the balance in terms of the formal and informal political arena, this chapter looks at whether new social movement activity appeals to differing sectors of society. In Chapter Eight, debate centres on comparative politics and how the comparative approach can help the student of politics to have a greater understanding of political regimes and cultures. The penultimate chapter, Chapter Nine, focuses upon the linkages between politics and international relations, looking at synergies and scope for collaboration between these two distinct but related disciplines. Finally, Chapter Ten draws the overall conclusions from this text about *Doing Politics*. It assesses the lessons to be learned and highlights the interest to be gleaned through a study of politics.

What is the book intended to achieve?

The aim of *Doing Politics* is to provide a general overview for those who are relatively new to studying politics. It is, therefore, particularly suited to those studying politics at A-level but also for those in their first year of undergraduate study. It flags up the importance of politics both in terms of it being an academic subject, a discipline that is both fascinating and challenging, but also in terms of its practical applicability. As well as highlighting specific subject-relevant careers, reference is also made to other pathways whereby a degree in politics can provide a less-obvious passport to a rewarding and satisfying vocation. Following on from an explanatory chapter looking at what politics entails, and what it is like to study politics in the twenty-first century, there is also exploration of why politics gets such a bad press. It is a divisive subject area and has suffered, certainly over the last few years, from less than favourable media coverage. Through such explanatory approaches and by providing examples of what the student of politics can expect to encounter, the text provides a useful academic foundation stone for the budding political scientist. In a sense, the book aims to further whet the appetite of those who have already succumbed to the power of political study.

Studying politics at university

Many changes have taken place relatively recently in respect of study at higher education level. For example, the increase in tuition fees to £9,000 per annum has made many people think deeply about what to study at university and, indeed, whether to attend university in the first place. As Adam Roberts, former president of the British Academy, points out, '. . . teachers and students in the humanities and social sciences feel threatened by the new fees regime, cuts in teaching funding and a general atmosphere of uncertainty' (2011: 28). On a positive note, however, he goes on to point out that 'Our subjects are flourishing [and that all] the indicators are that UK research in these subjects is world class' (*Ibid.*). Certainly, these are changing times with respect to studying any subject at university. Students of politics, therefore, need to be assured that they have chosen to read for a valuable and worthwhile degree. In part, the aim of this book is to reassure potential applicants, students and parents that there is genuine merit and currency in a politics degree. For some, there may still exist the luxury of studying the discipline for its own sake. These are probably the lucky few. For most, however, the love of studying politics has to be weighed alongside the demonstrable gains that its economic power provides. In these austere times, few can study a subject solely for education *per se*. Parents too demand increasing reassurance that the three years of intensive study and a debt of circa £30,000 will be a passport to a fulfilling career and economic recompense. *Doing Politics* will, hopefully, provide that parental and applicant reassurance in terms of conveying a passion for politics but also depicting its practical application.

What is involved in a politics degree?

How you study for a politics degree is equally as important to the topics that you cover. There are many examples of innovative teaching and learning practices taking place in a politics degree. Dr Annabel Kiernan, for example, teaches politics with a focus upon the practical aspect. Her students learn how to carry out a protest and how they would organise a campaign. In addition to learning about the theory of politics, students are, therefore, learning about the practical aspects too. As Annabel points out, it's not about instigating a revolution, it's about helping people to participate (see Richardson, 2009). Annabel states,

> Praxis is key; it's important to know how as well as why. Having not just political knowledge but also the tools and confidence to apply that knowledge is where real empowerment lies. In that sense, the development of creative and subversive space or inserting 'active' space into the curriculum is essential as a means of meeting the challenges of political participation which, in turn, is essential for democracy, freedom and social and political transformation.
>
> (interview with author, 28 February 2014)

Kiernan's method of teaching politics is innovative and thought-provoking. Other examples of innovative teaching and learning practices include Steven Curtis and colleagues' work in relation to politics placements. This is where the focus was upon enabling politics students to be able to undertake a work-related placement as part of their politics degree. Since Curtis *et al.* produced their study of politics placements and their value to a politics degree, many higher education establishments have gone down the route of emphasising the practical side of a politics degree and links with the real world. In these days of an extremely competitive jobs market anything that students of politics can do to make themselves more marketable and to stand out from their peers is to be encouraged and applauded. A third innovative approach to the teaching and learning of politics is the case study approach. Academics at the University of York, for example, produced a number of case studies designed to aid the teaching and learning of the discipline. More recently, John Craig, formerly of the University of Huddersfield and now at the Higher Education Academy, was involved in producing a number of detailed case studies that would benefit the student and teacher of politics.

Another project that has pioneered innovation in the teaching and learning of politics is the PREPOL Project centred around a consortium of academics and universities and led by Dr Rose Gann, Head of Politics and International Relations at Nottingham Trent University. The project was aimed at encouraging young people to consider studying for a degree in politics by providing them with information about what politics entails, how they would study politics at university and what they could potentially do with a degree in politics in terms of possible career options that they might wish to consider upon graduation. The PREPOL project conducted in-depth interviews with lecturers and students to ascertain their views on these topics and produced a bank of materials to help potential applicants to consider studying politics. These materials included a website and an interactive DVD. According to the report on the PREPOL project, the

. . . aim of the project is to provide a pre-entry guidance package for the study of Politics and International Relations for prospective university students. . . The key output of this project is a DVD entitled 'Politics and You', which provides a student-led perspective on what the study of Politics and International Relations at University entails.

(see www.politicsatuniversity.com for further information about the PREPOL project)

Indeed, Professor Vicky Randall, a former chair of the Political Studies Association UK described the accompanying DVD as

. . . an excellent DVD, fresh and lively, which uses the voices of students themselves to demonstrate why politics is so relevant for our lives, the wide variety of insights and skills that Politics and IR degree courses offer and the career opportunities that they open up.

(*Ibid.*)

Discussion with the PREPOL Lead, Dr Rose Gann, helps to flesh out the value and relevance of the PREPOL project,

One of the main challenges of the PREPOL project – Developing pre-entry guidance for the study of Politics and International Relations at University (2005–2009) – was to find a way of broadening young people's views of what studying Politics at university entails and enabling young people to question what are often very stereotypical views of Politics as an academic discipline. The PREPOL project sought to address this challenge by using the student voice – via the production of a DVD – in which current cohorts of Politics students could explain to other young people why they found studying Politics and IR interesting, relevant and exciting to study. This proved to be very successful and popular.

(email exchange with Dr Rose Gann, March 2014)

Dr Gann proceeds to explain how the project was disseminated in a novel and engaging manner,

Another approach was a series of short regional workshops on the study of Politics – run by a small theatre company – which enabled young people to engage in detailed discussion and debate about the study of Politics and thus helped to widen views and perspectives on the discipline.

(*Ibid.*)

This use of a theatre company to convey the message regarding studying politics is an interesting departure from more usual educative processes.

A plethora of learned societies (such as the Political Studies Association of the United Kingdom; the British International Studies Association; the European Consortium for Political Research; the American Political Science Association, to name but a few) are also involved in the promotion of political study. As well as providing a focus and forum for academics and their research, such organisations also seek to help lecturers and teachers of politics not just with research into the discipline but also in terms of how to teach and convey the subject to students. Increasingly, such organisations provide a network of support and a wealth of materials to help lecturers and students in their pursuit of political study. Learning resources banks supply ideas for seminars on specific topics, such as pressure groups or the constitution, for example. Tutors and students can converse with like-minded peers in discussion groups. Case studies of alumni provide role model material and inspirational career trajectories. Conferences permit a dialogue between political scientists, and increasingly, graduates and undergraduates are encouraged to join these debates – with dissemination strategies, such as via poster presentations, becoming a favoured way of welcoming those new to the discipline into the fold.

What topics are involved in a politics degree?

There are many and varied politics degrees that the student of politics can pursue. In terms of similarities across institutions, quite often level one will involve a focus upon institutions and a preliminary introduction to key concepts. This may mean that students will examine the legislature, the executive, the judiciary, the media, the electoral system, pressure groups, amongst other aspects. At level two, there tends to be more of an emphasis upon political theories. Quite often students will study a history of political thought module or a module examining modern political thought or key political concepts. At level three, there is often a move to greater specialisation. Research engaged teaching often comes to the forefront at level three, with politics academics being able to teach modules centred on their own research specialism. Examples include tutors teaching specific area studies or particular topics such as political participation with an emphasis upon the youth vote or whether or not there is such a concept as grey power with an older cohort of voters able to have an impact upon the policy making system. In addition, at level three the student of politics will often have the opportunity, or perhaps be compelled, to produce a dissertation. These are extended, in-depth projects focusing upon a specific area. In terms of length, they vary in size but can be anything from around 10,000 to 20,000 words long. Clearly, the skills needed to write such an extended piece differ slightly from those required to write, say, a 2,000 or 3,000-word essay. Rather than having lectures or seminars on this topic area, dissertation students are expected to research and investigate their chosen topic area themselves, under the guidance of an allocated supervisor. Most institutions require students to produce a dissertation proposal or plan beforehand whereby they outline their chosen topic area, why they have decided upon this area, how they intend to conduct their research, i.e. will it be primarily library-based, will it have some primary research such as any in-depth qualitative interviews, questionnaires or survey material? Usually, there will be an expectation that the student produces an indicative reading list or bibliography in order that tutors are persuaded that the student intends to locate information in the most appropriate places using the most relevant and up-to-date source material. The student of politics at level three will often have periodic, say weekly or fortnightly, meetings with their supervisor whereby they report back on achievement to date, upon what they have been working on and what they intend to do next. This is a useful way of working as it familiarises the student of politics with the research process and, often, provides an extremely useful training ground for those who wish to proceed to further study – such as at Master of Philosophy (MPhil) or Doctor of Philosophy (PhD) level. There is less emphasis upon the creation of or adding to knowledge then there is at postgraduate level, but the dissertation student is still expected to research widely and to produce a detailed study of one specific area. The key to success, at dissertation level, quite often centres on whether or not the research question or hypothesis is sharply focused. A relatively narrow area of investigation means it is easier for students to highlight what they intend to do. In turn, it is easier for the tutor to assess whether they have actually achieved their aim(s). Have they done what they said they were going to do?

Politics, as will be shown in subsequent chapters, can be studied either on its own as a single honours subject or it can be combined with other subjects and disciplines. This can be on an equal footing as a major/major subject or as a major/minor combination, with politics forming either the greater or the lesser part of that degree combination dependent upon personal preference. Sometimes politics might be chosen as a third subject. This can be the case at level one, with students often choosing to specialise in subsequent years. This can be a useful way of those new to the discipline ascertaining the extent of their interest in the subject area. Having said this, politics can be studied at degree level by those who have studied it at A-level or it can be taken by those new to the subject who are taking it from scratch. As will be revealed later, politics can be studied with a whole host of other subjects. Some of these, such as International Relations, constitute logical and relatively common degree combinations. Others, such as degrees combining, say, Politics with Theatre Studies, or Politics with Arabic, are more unusual pairings but presumably just as riveting for those choosing to proceed down this route of study.

Studying politics involves a focus upon particular topics. One of the key areas that the student encounters is differing political ideologies. This is examined in greater depth in subsequent chapters but, suffice to say at this juncture, politics cannot be studied without at least some reference to how ideology underpins debates, discussions and actions. The contested nature of ideology as a concept will be examined, followed by analysis of specific ideologies. It is fascinating to note the importance of ideology even to the extent that people may be prepared to die for their political beliefs. As Charles Funderburk and Robert Thobaben put it,

> Beliefs so compelling that multitudes fight and die for them; ideas so powerful that leaders can use them to transform societies; principles that bring order out of chaos and make reality readily comprehensible – these are some of the themes and issues of ideological analysis.
>
> (1994: 1)

Likewise, Roy Macridis reiterates the importance and relevance of ideology:

> Whether we know it or not, all of us have an ideology, even those who claim openly that they do not. We all believe in certain things. We all value something – property, friends, the law, freedom, or authority. We all have prejudices, even those who claim to be free of them. We all look at the world in one way or another – we have 'ideas' about it – and we try to make sense out of what is going on in it. Quite a few of us are unhappy, discontented, critical of what we see around us compared to what we would like to see. Some become alienated – rejecting the

society and its values, sulking into their separate and private tents but ready to spring forth into action.

(1992: 1)

It is fascinating to contemplate the fact that these are, quite literally, ideas but some people may be prepared to lay down their life for these, such is the strength of their conviction. Similarly, there is the notion that even people who believe that they are not ideological hold certain beliefs and ideas that are dear to them. The power and all-pervasive nature of ideology are part of the appeal of political study. The strength of feeling evoked by ideology merits in-depth investigation. *Doing Politics* involves analysing the rationale under-pinning that passion.

In terms of how politics is studied, the usual process is that a student would expect to take three or four modules per semester or term. It is often the case that each module would have a one-hour lecture and a one-hour seminar per week. Lectures often involve anything up to one or two hundred students listening to the lecturer giving a talk on a specific topic area. The skills required are active listening and note-taking, knowing what to write down and what not to jot down and, hopefully, being inspired by an enthusiastic lecturer. These are very much tutor-led with students playing more of a passive role. Seminars, on the other hand, usually entail a great deal of student participa-tion. Often student-led, they may involve students giving a presentation or discussing a series of questions before sharing their responses with the group as a whole. In terms of class-contact, this may appear relatively minimal. This is, however, indicative of how much time the student of politics is expected to spend on self-directed study, reading and researching by themselves. More innovative ways of learning may involve the use of simulations or role play, with students expected to immerse themselves into a part or character in order to gain a greater understanding of a particular institution, such as the European Union or the United Nations, or to have a thorough grounding in how policies emerge. This might be, for example, by taking part in a cabinet committee simulation or by playing the role of a pressure group spokesperson campaign-ing against a particular proposed or actual action of central or local govern-ment. There is a burgeoning literature on the usage of role play exercises in the teaching and learning of politics. Some students may find they are out of their comfort zones when initially asked or compelled to participate in a role play exercise. Others, especially those of a more theatrical bent or inclination, may discover that they are in their element when asked to assume a particular position or characteristics. This notion of immersion in a role can, however, be indispensable for facilitating understanding of specific arguments or positions. This is especially the case when asked to research a stance that is contrary to one's own views or opinions. Students who have taken part in role play and simulation exercises often report, with the benefit of hindsight, that their initial reluctance was soon dispelled and that, aside from the fun element of the exercise, they actually learned a great deal!

What careers can you pursue with a degree in politics?

As with any degree, there are many different career paths and career options that the student of politics can pursue. Simply by virtue of having a degree, it opens the door to a whole host of graduate level jobs, many of which are not directly related to politics. This aside, there are some jobs that are more suited and directly relevant to a degree in politics. Opportunities in local government, for example, working for the civil service or within certain public bodies, have a definite link to politics. Likewise, careers in, say, political journalism or as a practical politician, either at national, local, regional or even transnational level, would suit the politics graduate. Politics alumni, therefore, can be located in many different jobs and roles. Some of these are obvious, some less so. Learned societies such as the Political Studies Association of the United Kingdom (PSA), or the British International Studies Association (BISA) have built up their alumni databases and are a useful tool for the student of politics to use in search of career ideas and role models. In addition, individual higher education establishments are making increasing use of their alumni links to demonstrate the practical applicability and real-world relevance of their degrees, with many holding alumni evenings, live web chats, podcast profiles and written testimonies from their ex-students. The aforementioned changes to the fees regime have meant that it is increasingly important for the 'value' of a politics degree to be constantly flagged up for both potential applicants and their increasingly savvy parents. Individual institutions and the learned societies often work together to drum home the message that, aside from being a fascinating subject with real-world consequences, politics is a valuable degree to possess and opens up a whole host of career opportunities to the graduate. The marketability of a politics degree should not be underestimated. Alumni, therefore, are a valuable commodity. In addition, it is always worthwhile booking a careers interview whilst studying politics. University careers teams constitute a valuable source of information about contemporary, real-world opportunities. They can provide one-to-one interviews but often also run seminars and workshops on topics such as writing one's CV and interview techniques. Working alongside the Politics departments, they can tailor their advice to politics undergraduates and/or social science students *per se*. They often advise of upcoming vacancies, so much so that some graduates are ready to walk into employment immediately upon graduation.

What skills will you acquire as part of a politics degree?

Studying politics at A-level, and, more so, at undergraduate level, enables the scholar to acquire numerous transferable skills in addition to enhanced knowledge and understanding of key political facts and concepts. This is why a degree in political studies furnishes more than mere knowledge of the subject matter. Key skills acquired include the ability to think critically. The development of critical thinking is an aspect that many undergraduates highlight when questioned about what they have gained from their degree in political studies. Students are encouraged and taught to be more questioning and probing in terms of any information that they receive. A challenging and questioning approach is vital as far as the student of politics is concerned. Not taking information at face-value is crucial. This involves questioning sources, asking difficult and challenging questions and recognising that, as is often the case, there is no such aspect as the 'truth', only particular and partial versions and interpretations of the truth.

Other skills include generic, transferable skills such as working as a team. Group work, and quite often assessed group work, can be found on many political studies degrees. Working alongside a team of three or four colleagues is not as easy and straightforward as it may sound. Negotiation, co-operation and compromise are often required as ways of ensuring that the group makes progress. Problems such as how to deal with the 'free-rider' or the person who is not pulling their weight, whether the group will have a leadership figure, all have to be addressed. Such skills can be difficult to teach and are best learned through action. To quote that ancient Chinese proverb, 'I hear and I forget. I see and I remember. I do and I understand'. Group work is all about facilitating understanding and a deeper level of learning. By being action-oriented, working as part of a small group fosters skills that will be useful in the world of work. Team-building and working together are vital attributes in most places of employment. The notion of a solitary employee, working alone on a project, is alien to many workplace situations. More likely, the employee needs to closely and co-operatively work with colleagues in order to bring a particular task to fruition.

Other competencies include presentational skills. This is increasingly important in the world of work and also in terms of interview techniques, which often form part of the gateway into the aforementioned employment sphere. Many employers, in order to differentiate between a large pool of applicants/interviewees, request that a short presentation is given as part of the interview process. For many, this can represent a potential stumbling block if they are unable to perform in front of the interview panel. No matter how knowledgeable they are, if they are unable to present in a confident, knowledgeable and engaging manner, they may lose out to a less subject-savvy but more skilled rival. Possession of key skills may, in fact, tip the balance in favour of one particular candidate over and above the competition. Having said this, public-speaking ranks highly as one of the key phobias for many people. Alongside such perils as fear of spiders or of flying in an aeroplane, the dread encountered by some people in anticipation of talking to an audience knows no bounds. Many A-level and undergraduate politics courses require students to present findings to their lecturers and to their peers. Initially, it may be hard to accept that presentational skills can be acquired or taught. Certainly, there is a degree of subjectivity in presentations. Akin to the idea that one's favourite actor may, for example, be Bradley Cooper whilst a friend prefers Jude Law, there will be a certain amount of personal preference in presentations. It can be difficult to articulate why one presentation rates more highly than another on a certain level. Yet, it is evident that presentations can be assessed and that a checklist of criteria can be cited. This checklist should include factors such as: subject content – is the presenter knowledgeable and able to display familiarity with the key aspects of the subject matter; structure of presentation – i.e. does it have a definite introduction, main body and conclusion and is it set out in a logical manner; use of audio-visual resources – this is to say, does the presenter(s) use a range of ways of conveying their message to the audience using, for example, relevant video clips (YouTube™ is often a preferred source), PowerPoint™ slides or a Prezi™ delivery format? Body language and mannerisms are also important in terms of delivery. It's not simply what the presenter is saying but also how they are delivering their message that matters. It is necessary to try to avoid or at least minimise distractions such as annoying tics or habits such as ritualised hand-wringing! It is often the case that the person charged with speaking in public is unaware of any strange or repetitive body movements. Their audience will, however, hone in on such habits to the detriment of listening to and absorbing the message that their presentation seeks to convey. Those who advise presenters often suggest that, rather than hands flapping about and gesticulating like a human windmill, hands should be clasped with the two index fingers in a pointing motion – seen as a useful device for emphasis as part of a speech. Likewise, annoying and repetitive phrases such as the ubiquitous 'like' or others such as 'at the end of the day', 'to be honest', 'does that make sense', 'you know what I mean', etc., all detract from the performance. Speakers are often taught to make points in a series of three so that these verbal bullet points can be prefaced with, 'Firstly . . ., secondly, . . .' and, by the time the third point is reached, the audience is ready to provide a crescendo of applause. These techniques are often used by politicians when making a speech in public. In addition to body language and speech patterns, the key to a perfect presentation is, in part, the notion that the presenter should make everyone in the room feel that, at that particular moment in time, they would not prefer to be anywhere else, such is the extent of their enjoyment. Vocal coaches talk about the 'I'm happy to be here, I'm happy you're here' approach. An approach possibly particularly suited to a more outgoing American mindset but, nonetheless, encapsulating part of what any public speaker ought to strive to attain. Part of this mindset involves making eye contact with everyone in the room, even if it is only for a few brief seconds. This can be quite difficult if you are speaking in a large lecture theatre in front of a huge audience. In this scenario, the advice is to make eye contact with sections of the room, moving from one side to the other, rather than remaining static and just talking to a particular section. Other tips and techniques include the renowned imagining your audience naked approach or focusing upon a fixed point at the rear of the room, such as a clock at the back. Delivering a speech or making a presentation is, therefore, a key skill that those *Doing Politics* need to acquire. There is a degree of subjectivity but, this aside, there are certainly tips and techniques that the student of politics will acquire as part of their studies.

Another, more obvious, transferable skill that the student of politics will acquire or hone is the art of writing. Writing forms the basis of the majority of the forms of assessment encountered by those studying politics. Examples include examinations, where the skills lies in answering specific questions in a sharply focused manner, or essays, dissertations and suchlike. More innovative writing exercises may include such assignments as writing a review – such as a book review or a review of a journal article – or a requirement to produce a short blog. The rise of online assessments means that politics students have to familiarise themselves with new technology. Different writing tasks require slightly differing approaches. The ability to write in a lucid and articulate manner is, however, common to all forms. Writing needs to be crisp and concise, as opposed to flowery, hyperbolic and full of colloquialisms.

Feedback on assessed work can help the student to perfect their writing skills and ensure that they, for example, know how to utilise the correct discipline-specific jargon and that they are able to answer specific questions in a direct and focused approach. More recently, several lecturers of politics have sought to expound the virtues of good feedback. Alasdair Blair *et al.* (2013) highlight the benefits of feedback for the student of politics. There is a burgeoning literature in this area. In order for maximum benefit to be gained from feedback, it needs to be detailed and timely. This ensures that students are able to learn from comments on their work and this can be then used to improve subsequent assessments.

Guidance in relation to what the student of politics does and ought to cover can be found in the subject benchmark statements for politics. These are published by the regulatory body, the Quality Assurance Agency for Higher Education. Subject benchmarking statements are published for most academic disciplines. They provide a detailed guide as to what the student can expect to cover in any given discipline. In addition, they also highlight key skills that students will encounter and learn as part of their degree. As well as being of interest to students, parents and employers, they provide a useful guide for academics when they are reviewing, updating and amending their programmes as they provide general guidance in relation to programme level learning outcomes. The benchmarking statements are subject to regular review, revision and update in order to ensure that they have continued relevance and that they provide a clear expose of the key aspects of that particular discipline. The original subject benchmarking statements for politics were first produced in 2000; they were reviewed in 2007 and have just been reassessed in 2014 to ensure continued currency. Academics involved in curriculum review look to the subject benchmarking statements for guidance in terms of what should be included in that particular degree. The statements provide a useful reference point against which to position or benchmark any new degrees. Some critics believe that statements can be rather woolly and vague. A more realistic interpretation is that they probably have to remain deliberately vague in order to permit differing interpretations. Not to be confused with a sort of pseudo-national curriculum at undergraduate level, they constitute a useful guide as to the content of a politics degree. They provide a detailed summary of the key focus of the discipline. To quote the benchmark statement for politics and international relations,

> Politics is concerned with developing a knowledge and understanding
> of government and society. . . analyses of who gets what, when, how,

why and where are central, and pertain to related questions of power, justice, order, conflict, legitimacy, accountability, obligation, sovereignty, governance and decision-making.

(QAA, 2007: 3)

It is interesting to note the recognition, within the benchmark statements, of how the contemporary and changing nature of the discipline contributes to its attractiveness. As stated, 'Perhaps in no other academic discipline are the subject matter and approaches so much in contention and in flux. This contributes to the challenging yet captivating nature of the discipline' (*Ibid.*: 4). As will be shown in subsequent chapters in *Doing Politics*, this dynamism inherent in the discipline furnishes a huge part of its appeal.

Conclusion

This initial chapter sets out the scope of *Doing Politics* and the parameters of the discussion. As well as emphasising the value and merits of a politics degree, the chapter has expanded upon what the study of politics entails, including discussion of some of the more innovative and unusual ways of studying politics. The key topics encountered when studying politics are illuminated, as are the key transferable skills that the student of politics is likely to acquire en route. Typical and more unusual careers proffered by a degree in politics were flagged up in this chapter. It has also been shown how the learned societies, both UK-based and those residing further afield, contribute to the promotion of the discipline. Subject benchmarking statements are illuminated as providing a valuable reference tool/yardstick for ensuring that key topics and skills are covered and conveyed in a politics degree. Chapter One has also scoped out the rest of the book, providing a chapter by chapter breakdown of the structure of *Doing Politics*. It has, hopefully, also explained, in part at least, the fascination and appeal of politics to so many scholars and people at large.

It is interesting to note that the value of a politics degree is recognised in various quarters, some less predictable than others. As Andrew Heywood explains, 'Politics is exciting because people disagree' (2007: 3). He clarifies,

. . . the disagreement that lies at the heart of politics also extends to the nature of the subject and how it should be studied. People disagree about both what it is that makes social interaction 'political', and how political activity can best be analysed.

(*Ibid.*)

Likewise, Gerry Stoker flags up the appeal and importance of politics thus:

> ... when it works politics delivers one great benefit: it enables you to choose, within constraints, the life you want without fear of physical coercion and violence being used against you. Politics creates space for human choices and diverse lifestyles. Politics, if done well, creates the positive context and stable environment for you to live your life. That's why politics matters.
>
> (2006: 7)

Both Heywood and Stoker capture the essence and attraction of politics. Similarly, as John Craig points out, part of the appeal lies in the fact that there are differing approaches to the discipline:

> ... Political Studies is a rich and diverse discipline so the types of learning experience that students will engage with on a Politics degree should also be rich and diverse. The plurality of the discipline should be reflected in the plurality of the pedagogy.
>
> (Craig, 2012: 34)

As far back as 1969, Derek Heater's edited collection flagged up the value of studying politics. Heater stated, 'There are many varieties of ways of teaching about matters political; many competing demands for the construction of syllabuses and methods of teaching' (Heater, 1969: ix) before proceeding to spotlight the '... belief that constructive debate about the teaching of Politics urgently needs to be revived' (*Ibid.*: x). One more recent yet unusual example of a belief in the inherent value of a politics degree emanates from the broadcaster Janet Street-Porter who, in her self-help book, *Life's Too F***ing Short*, advises,

> Nowadays, I tell women to stay on at university for as long as they can, not to waste their time by getting a degree in media studies, but to hone their brain by getting to grips with serious stuff like politics, history or English.
>
> (2009: 100)

She also recommends that people should 'Read an intelligent newspaper every day, think about politics and how they impact on you' (*Ibid.*: 209). Street-Porter is an unwitting ambassador for degrees in political studies. This book, hopefully, will prove to be a more explicit and overt ally of the Street-Porter school of thought!

Chapter bibliography

Asal, V. (2005) 'Playing games with international relations', *International Studies Perspectives*, Vol. 6, No. 3: 359–73.

Blair, A. (2013) 'Democratising the learning process: the use of Twitter in the teaching of politics and international relations', *Politics*, Vol. 33, No. 2: 135–145.

Blair, A, Curtis, S., Goodwin, M. and Shields, S. (2013) 'What feedback do students want?', *Politics*, Vol. 33, No. 1, February: 66–79.

Blair, A., Curtis, S. and McGinty [Shields], S. (2012), 'Is peer feedback an effective approach for creating dialogue in politics?', *European Political Science*, Vol. 12, No. 1: 102–115.

Briggs, J. E. (2012) 'Teaching politics to small groups', chapter five in Lightfoot, S. and Gormley-Heenan, C. (eds), *Teaching Politics*, Basingstoke, Palgrave: 65–77.

Craig, J. (2012) 'What (if anything) is different about teaching and learning in polit-ics?', chapter two in Lightfoot, S. and Gormley-Heenan, C. (eds), *Teaching Politics*, Basingstoke, Palgrave: 22–37.

Curtis, S. (2012) 'Politics placements and employability: a new approach', *European Political Science*, Vol. 11, No. 2: 153–163.

——(2012) 'How relevant are other ways to learn?', chapter six in Gormley-Heenan, C. and Lightfoot, S. (eds), *Teaching Politics and International Relations*, Basingstoke, Palgrave: 78–90.

Fox, R. and Ronkowski, S. (1997) 'Learning styles of political science students', *PS: Political Science and Politics*, Vol. 30, December: 732–736.

Funderburk, C. and Thobaben, R. G. (1994) *Political Ideologies: Left, Center, Right*, second edition, New York, HarperCollins.

Heywood, A. (2007) *Politics*, third edition, Basingstoke, Palgrave Macmillan.

Heater, D. B. (ed.) (1969) *The Teaching of Politics*, London, Methuen.

Macridis, R. C. (1992) *Contemporary Political Ideologies: Movements and Regimes*, fifth edition, New York, HarperCollins.

Nicholls, G. (2002) *Developing Learning and Teaching in Higher Education*, London, Routledge.

Obendorf, S. and Randerson, C. (2013) 'Evaluating the model United Nations: diplo-matic simulation as assessed undergraduate coursework', *European Political Science*, Vol. 12, No. 3: 350–364.

Quality Assurance Agency (QAA) (2007) *Subject Benchmark Statement for Politics and International Relations*, Gloucester, The Quality Assurance Agency for Higher Education.

Richardson, H. (2009) 'Students learn how to protest', http://news.bbc.co.uk/1/hi/education/8386885.stm, accessed 10 May 2012.

Roberts, A. (2011) 'The end is not nigh', *Times Higher Education*, 3 March: 28.

Shellman, S. M. and Turan, K. (2006) 'Do simulations enhance student learning? An empirical evaluation of an IR simulation', *Journal of Political Science Education*, Vol. 2, No. 1: 19–32.

Simpson, A. W. and Kaussler, B. (2009) 'IR teaching reloaded: using films and simulations in the teaching of international relations', *International Studies Perspectives*, Vol. 10, No. 4: 413–427.

Stoker, G. (2006) *Why Politics Matters: Making Democracy Work*, Basingstoke, Palgrave Macmillan.

Street-Porter, J. (2009) *Life's Too F***ing Short*, London, Quadrille Publishing Limited.

Websites

http://www.politicsatuniversity.com for further information about the PREPOL project, accessed March 2013.

2

Politics is key[1]

Having examined the overall scope of *Doing Politics*, attention now turns to what is meant by politics and studying politics in general. Chapter Two focuses upon *'You don't do politics? What do you do?'* This chapter examines the importance and the relevance of politics. It encapsulates the key definitions of politics, including that politics is about conflict, before moving on to examine the broader definitions. What does politics mean? How does politics affect you? This chapter involves analysis of the all-pervasive nature of politics, to make us understand how politics impacts upon our lives in numerous different ways. In addition to highlighting the usual components of politics, examination is made of the broader definition of politics. This can be subsumed under the catch-all phrase of 'politics is everything' but it will also involve a focus upon sexual politics, office politics, etc. Widening our definition of politics so that we are aware that what goes on behind closed doors could be regarded as politics. The feminist mantra of the 'personal is political' is highlighted here.

Studying politics

It is necessary to outline what politics is and why it is has continued importance. It has been and, indeed, remains a very popular subject at both A-level and undergraduate level. Data obtained from the examination boards and the Universities Central Admissions System (UCAS) reveals the continued and growing popularity of Government and Politics at both A-level and degree level. The key examination boards at A-level that offer Government and Politics are OCR, AQA and Edexcel. Figures reveal growing numbers of young people opting to study the subject at A-level. With regards to the study of politics at undergraduate level, numbers have risen steadily and the predicted freefall in numbers with the increase in tuition fees in 2012 has not materialised. Numbers remain buoyant and the subject continues to be a popular choice amongst undergraduates. Russell Group universities and, likewise, those in other higher education groupings, such as Million+, recognise the value and kudos of continuing to offer the discipline of politics as part of their undergraduate and postgraduate portfolio. The subject is well respected by employers and educationalists alike. Politics alumni proceed to a wide range of careers and further study. Some careers are closely aligned to the discipline, such as proceeding into practical politics, working in local government or working for the civil service. Other avenues are less clearly aligned to the discipline itself but nonetheless rely upon the skills and knowledge acquired as part of a degree in politics. These include working as a journalist, working in the public sector, and moving into the legal profession, by way of example. Politics alumni, therefore, occupy a range of interesting and varied positions. Learned societies, such as the Political Studies Association of the United Kingdom, and the British International Studies Association, alongside umbrella organisations such as the Campaign for Social Science, regularly produce profiles of politics alumni and publish these both in their publicity materials and on their websites as a way of demonstrating the value of a degree in politics and illustrating the wide range of career options open to the student of politics. It pays to think widely when focusing upon what can be done with a degree in politics and not to be limited by a narrow range of options.

Choosing the right political studies course/university is a difficult decision in some senses simply because of the sheer number of institutions offering a degree in political studies and also the wide variety of degrees and degree combinations on offer. There are, for example, around ninety institutions offering degrees in politics. Just looking at the five years between 2007 and 2011, there was the continuation of an existing trend with a year-on-year increase in the number of applications to study politics, culminating in 36,118 applications for 2011 entry. As stated, the subject remains buoyant despite the introduction of increased tuition fees in 2012. There remain many grounds for optimism in terms of applications for Political Studies. Interest remains very strong, despite the threefold fees increase. Studies show that young people are very interested in politics and in the study of politics. Politics' demand is affected by the global and national picture but we also have excellent teaching and learning taking place in schools, colleges and universities. It is true that global events have certainly fostered interest but, no doubt too, national happenings such as more women in politics, general elections coverage, and coalition politics have also garnered attention. Ironically, the issue of increased tuition fees appears to have contributed to the increasing politicisation of a generation of teenagers.

In terms of those considering studying politics at undergraduate or postgraduate level, there is an exciting and wide array of courses and institutions from which to choose. Some students may wish to focus upon certain countries – such as a focus upon British, American, Chinese or Russian politics; others may wish to concentrate upon political theory, election studies or area studies. Relatively newer areas of focus such as gender politics, environmental politics or race and politics are all proving increasingly popular. Indeed, there are a whole host of specialist routes within the overall discipline of politics. Politics can be combined with a huge array of other subject areas. Some are fairly obvious combinations, such as Politics and Law; Politics and Journalism; Politics and Social Policy. Other linkages are less so, for example students may opt to study Politics and Television Studies, Drama and International Politics, or Politics with Creative Writing. There is certainly a lot of choice for those intending to study politics.

The student cohort varies; many students choose to study politics straight after A-levels (young adults going to university for the first time). Others opt to study politics as a mature student and, in these instances, they are often thinking about studying politics as means of developing a new career. Perhaps they are returning to study after a career break or taking time out to raise a family.

Tuition fees are now generally in the region of £9,000 per year (this may vary slightly and, for example, be slightly lower if students opt to study for a degree via a college provider). Generally, however, students will expect to pay circa £9,000 per annum. This is a significant long-term investment on the part of the student. As with those studying other degrees, however, the students do not pay themselves and they do not begin to back pay the fees until they are earning £21,000 per year. Many choose to see it almost as a graduate tax in this sense. In terms of what students get for their money, the Key Information Set data that each university has to provide on its website outlines details in relation to class contact time, employability, salary data, accommodation costs, etc. Most students can expect to study four or five modules/ units each week. On average, they are likely to have at least an hour lecture and an hour seminar per week, per module. In addition, students are expected to 'read' for their degree and will be expected to devote a substantial amount of additional time to researching and reading around their subject area. Class sizes vary but lectures might be in the region of 100+, with some huge courses being significantly larger than this. They are tutor-led with, usually, relatively little student participation. Essentially, the skills that students need to acquire are those of active listening and note-taking. There may be some limited inter-action such as a show of hands on a particular subject or even voting with electronic devices (such as Optivote™), which operate along the lines of 'Ask the Audience' in *Who Wants to Be A Millionaire*. Lecturers can instantan-eously show the results of the participation on the screen. Seminars are much smaller, size varies but it is fair to say that, in many institutions, average seminar size is between sixteen and twenty-four. Here, there is a much greater degree of student interaction and participation. Students are usually directed to read certain books and journal articles prior to seminars and this will form the basis of the ensuing debate. Quite often, the seminar group may be broken up into smaller groups of, say, four or five people and asked to discuss a par-ticular issue or question and then to relay their responses back to the whole seminar group in a plenary session. There might be individual or small group presentations within the seminars. The usual expectation is that seminars are very much student-led whilst the lectures are tutor-led. Other forms of classes might be working in IT labs on quantitative data analysis – electoral statistics, for example – or participating in simulations or role play exercises (Model UN courses or Cabinet Committee Simulations are usually very popular in terms of encouraging students to critically engage with the subject matter). Increasingly, work experience, placements and internships are offered as part of a degree in political studies. These might be at local level with organisa-tions such as local authorities and various other public bodies or they might be at national or even international level (such as working with a Member of Parliament or for a non-governmental organisation). Increasingly, students studying for a degree in political studies are able to combine this with study abroad – be this for a semester or for a whole year. These various initiatives help students in terms of their employability, providing invaluable experience in real-world situations and facilitating the development of key skills – such as presentational skills, time-management and team working.

Applications to study politics and international relations at undergraduate level were examined in-depth by the Political Studies Association and by the British International Studies Association in September 2012's *PSA News* (Briggs and Curtis, 2012). Additional data, released by UCAS in 2013, was subject to further scrutiny and revealed the continuation of a number of note-worthy trends. It is interesting to assess these trends with regards to recent comments in the national media – for example, Ros Coward (2013) in *The Guardian*, who highlights a 'gendered dimension' with regard to the decline in university applications, which, she argues, is four times greater among male applicants. Coward also points out that there has been a '. . . massive decline in part-time applicants, invariably mature students' (*Ibid.*).

Whilst the trends highlighted by Coward are an accurate reflection of university applications in general; a more granulated analysis of the data released by UCAS suggests that applications for politics and international relations degrees do not rigidly follow these trends. For example, whilst there was a slightly higher decline in male applicants than female applicants to study politics degrees between 2011 and 2012 – 9.1 per cent and 7 per cent respectively – the 'gendered dimension' was certainly not as great as highlighted by Coward. In addition, applications to study international relations appeared to buck this trend with the decline in applications slightly higher amongst females (7.25 per cent) than males (6.71 per cent). Nevertheless, the UCAS data revealed there was a decline of 11.8 per cent in applications from mature students (25+) to study politics degrees and 10.8 per cent to study international relations degrees, and whilst this does not correspond to the 'massive decline' highlighted by Coward, the figures are a cause for concern.

Whilst it is evident that some of the observations made by Coward in relation to university applications more generally do not necessarily correspond to application trends for politics and international relations degrees, it is true

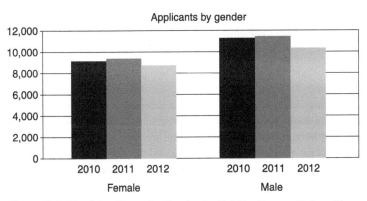

Figure 2.1 Total Applicants by Gender for Politics (*Source:* Universities and Colleges Admissions Service).

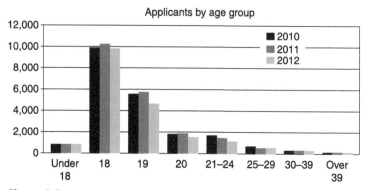

Figure 2.2 Total Applicants by Age for Politics (*Source:* Universities and Colleges Admissions Service).

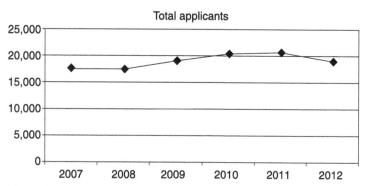

Figure 2.3 Total Applicants for Politics (*Source:* Universities and Colleges Admissions Service).

that there was a significant decline in applications, and correspondingly acceptances, to study both courses in 2012. This 8.21 per cent decline in applications and 5.40 per cent decline in acceptances, whilst not as high as some may have predicted, suggests that potential applicants were dissuaded from applying to university in 2012 by the new fees regime. It is to be hoped that, once the new regime becomes embedded, this decline may be halted and possibly reversed. The prospect of £9,000 per year in tuition fees, regardless of the value of a degree in political studies, has undoubtedly and unsurprisingly impacted negatively upon applications to study politics and international relations, particularly by mature students.

Having said this, preliminary data in relation to applications to higher education for the 2013 cycle showed a rise of 3.5 per cent and, specifically for politics, 7.0 per cent (see http://www.ucas.com/about_us/media_enquiries/media_releases/2013/20130130c) when compared with the same point the previous year. Obviously, these are applications only and may be subject to an increase in applications through late submissions and clearing; in addition, conversion rates may tell a different story. In reference to the fact that application data generally has not gone into meltdown, Liam Burns, former President of the National Union of Students, is quoted in the *Times Higher Education* as saying, '. . . as we stare a triple-dip recession in the face, as youth unemployment remains high and as swingeing public funding cuts begin to bite, it is hardly surprising that demand appears largely strong' (Burns, 2013: 28). Optimists amongst us will look at this data for politics and international relations and hope that the 2012 scenario is an unusual blip or low point in an otherwise upward trajectory and that those choosing our disciplines continue to do so for positive reasons, including a genuine love of the subject (see Briggs and Saunders, 2013: 12–13).

Many students opt to continue studying politics at postgraduate level. They may, for example, opt to study a taught master's degree and these are many and varied. Examples include: MA in Politics, Political Theory, Globalising Justice or Women's Studies, to name a few. Others proceed to studying politics as part of a research degree, such as at MPhil or PhD level. The acquisition of research skills, such as qualitative and quantitative methodological approaches, form an integral part of postgraduate research. Study at this level enables the scholar of political studies to specialise in their chosen field of research. Studying politics will be examined in greater depth in Chapter Three.

What is politics?

Having highlighted the continued popularity of politics at both A-level and at degree level in university, it is necessary to focus in more detail upon ascertaining what politics actually means. People often have a general understanding of what politics entails but are hard-pressed to provide a concise definition. Conjuring up visions of particular politicians, political parties and the yahboo adversarial nature of Westminster politics constitutes many initial impressions of what politics encapsulates. In the mid-1980s, for example, when people were asked what politics meant to them many replied simply with two words, 'Margaret Thatcher'. Politics was personalised, to a certain extent, and for many members of the ordinary public, Margaret Thatcher came to epitomise what politics was all about. Today's politicians might equally represent politics in the minds of many; David Cameron, Nick Clegg and Ed Miliband, indeed Barack Obama, may perhaps symbolise the personification of politics – although possibly not to the same extent as Mrs Thatcher did in her heyday. Asked to proceed beyond this impressionistic approach, many respondents find it difficult to determine accurately what is meant by politics.

Bold claims have been made about the importance of politics; for example, the Ancient Greek philosopher Aristotle (384BC–322BC) dubbed it the 'master science', essentially because politics helps society to determine how other knowledge and 'sciences' should be used. Aristotle also claimed that 'man is by nature a political animal', thereby epitomising the relevance of politics to our very existence. One twentieth century, key text on the topic of politics is the American scholar Harold Lasswell's work *Politics: Who Gets What, When, How* (1936, 1958). Even today, for many commentators the title of Lasswell's text serves to epitomise what is meant by politics, i.e. that it involves the allocation of scare resources and the notion that power comes to play in terms of how those resources are shared or, as is often the case, are not shared. Lasswell, a leading American political scientist and professor at Yale University, focused upon the difficult decisions that have to be made in terms of the allocation of often scarce and, certainly finite, resources; power is seen as the ability to participate in the decision making process. Those who have more power are likely, therefore, to be able to commandeer more of those resources for themselves and politics involves the process in which that allocation takes place. Professor Bernard Crick gave a key account of what politics entails in his work entitled *In Defence of Politics* (1962). Likewise the co-authored book *What is Politics?* (1987) written with his son Tom furnished key information on the topic for the aspiring student. It examined what the discipline entails, looked at how it is taught and gave some thought to where to study politics. As they state, the '. . . activity of politics arises from the basic human problem of diversity' (Crick and Crick, 1987: 6). Professor Bernard Crick was also instrumental in the decision for citizenship to be taught in schools. He headed up an advisory group on citizenship education in schools and its 1998 Report, dubbed the Crick Report, highlighted the need for young people to be taught the basics in relation to politics and the political system. Granted, the reality of citizenship in schools was, for many young people, very different from that envisaged by Professor Crick but it did go some way towards creating a more politically knowledgeable and engaged generation. It has been claimed (see for example a 2006 report by the inspectors of Ofsted) that for many young people citizenship classes involved examining topics such as drugs-awareness, relationships and anti-bullying strategies. These are all laudable subjects but not the type of citizenship that was envisaged by Professor Crick and his colleagues when they published their Report in 1998. The 2006 Ofsted Report stated that

> there is not yet a strong consensus about the aims of citizenship education or about how to incorporate it into the curriculum. In a quarter of schools surveyed, provision is still inadequate, reflecting weak leadership and lack of specialist teaching.
>
> > (see http://www.ofsted.gov.uk/resources/towards-consensus-citizenship-secondary-schools)

By 2010, however, the situation was more positive, with Ofsted stating there had been '. . . steady progress as citizenship becomes more widely understood and acquires depth in the light of experience, but also highlights what these schools need to tackle if citizenship is to be firmly established' (see http://www.ofsted.gov.uk/resources/citizenship-established-citizenship-schools-200609). It appears that citizenship teaching is now much more in sync with that envisaged by Bernard Crick and his colleagues. It has taken a while to become embedded but that does now seem to be happening. The more that citizenship does focus upon teaching the rudiments of politics and how the political system operates, not to indoctrinate but to inform, the more likely it is that young people will wish to study politics at GCSE, A-level and even undergraduate level. If citizenship teachers can ignite that passion in young people for political study, it is highly likely that this will continue to further and higher education. Organisations such as the Association for Citizenship Teaching, set up in 2001 by Professor Sir Bernard Crick, have a key role to play in terms of continuing to promote the teaching of Citizenship. Their mission is '. . . to support the teaching of high quality Citizenship and to promote wider public understanding of the subject [and to] promote research into the participation of young people in society' (http://www.teachingcitizenship.org.uk/about-act). Chris Waller is their Professional Officer; he highlights the intrinsic value of citizenship education and states,

> Citizenship education is the only National Curriculum subject that teaches young people about their rights and responsibilities as citizens – and how they can participate effectively in society – by developing

their understanding of politics, democracy, the law and the economy. It is intellectually rigorous and can be shown to transform schools. Since its introduction as a statuary subject in secondary schools in 2002 the subject has evolved – despite the vacillation of the Coalition government during its curriculum review. Indeed, that review and the decision to maintain the subject's status has consolidated it further. Citizenship has been thoroughly surveyed by Ofsted in three major reports since 2002 and was the subject of a ten year study by NFER. All the evidence points to a growing skill in teaching this complex subject in schools, whilst at the same time pointing out that there are still challenges to be met, including the number of specialist teachers in schools. Whilst Citizenship has the badges of other subjects – a GCSE that is one of the favoured eight best subjects and an A Level, it is the mantra that Citizenship is a subject and yet more than a subject that makes it so special. The subject should be seen in three contexts; the curriculum, the culture of the school and the links with the community in empowering young people to take their learning beyond the classroom into public life.

(email correspondence with author, October 2013)

The ACT's Waller succinctly sets out the value of citizenship education, both to individuals and to the wider society. Its emergent popularity as an academic subject certainly provides grounds for optimism.

Returning to the central theme of unpicking politics, Adrian Leftwich's (2004) seminal text *What Is Politics?* provides a detailed narrative in answer to that very question of what exactly do we mean when we refer to politics? As Leftwich states, '. . . it may often appear that what is being studied as politics in one place seems very different to what is being studied elsewhere' (2004: 3). He proceeds to highlight how politics is taught differently in different countries and even at different universities. Some might focus upon institutions, some might concentrate more on political theories and others on political methods. The student of politics can, therefore, examine the subject in a number of different ways. Borrowing from Birch (2002), as Leftwich puts the question,

. . . is the study of politics a scientific endeavour which seeks to identify, on an explanatory and probabilistic basis, some *general* regularities, patterns and processes (if not laws) underlying *all* politics, as economists claim to do for economic activity, or as chemists might do

for chemical reactions and interactions? Or, is the study of politics a
more humanistic, historical, normative and hence non-scientific exercise, concerned with the qualitative understanding and evaluative analysis (and moral judgement) of *particular* processes at particular times
and in particular places? Or can it and should it be both . . .

(2004: 5)

Essentially, the student of politics may examine the discipline in a number of
different ways.

A tripartite definition is often used when thinking about what constitutes
politics. Politics is viewed, on one level, as being about institutions, about the
examination and study of institutions such as Parliament, the political parties,
the monarchy, pressure groups, local councils, etc. The interaction and operation of those institutions is what constitutes politics. This approach to what is
politics is very much focused upon key participants and how they interact
with each other. As Leftwich states, '. . . this approach holds that *institutions*
are fundamental in shaping political (and other) behaviour in societies and are
therefore vital to our understanding of the forms and features of politics'
(2004: 10). A second approach is whereby politics is regarded as involving
conflict; wherever a situation of conflict occurs then politics comes into play.
Politics involves the allocation of scare resources. Resources are finite and
difficult decisions have to be taken, therefore politics comes into play. If you
decide to spend more on healthcare then correspondingly it follows that you
will have less to spend on education or defence. As Crick and Crick state,
'Politics is the study of conflicts of interests and values that affect all of society and how they can be conciliated' (1987: 1). The decision making process
is at the heart of politics. Certainly, in politics, you cannot please everyone.
This is possibly why it takes a certain kind of mentality to go into politics
whereby you will inevitably alienate, displease and dissatisfy particular sections of society. If you possess an innate need to be loved don't go into politics! There will inevitably be winners and losers and, to a certain extent, this
depends upon ideological perspectives. Political ideology may lead politicians to decide that it is better to spend more on healthcare as opposed to
defence, and vice versa. A third definition of what is politics, an all-
encompassing approach that widens the scope of what is politics, is whereby
politics is viewed in the widest terms possible. Politics, using this definition,
is everything; it includes all aspects of human interaction, and politics here
stems from the basic human condition of difference. We are all different and
it is how we reconcile those differences and which points of divergence are

31

considered important that impact upon politics. Using this third analysis, differing 'types' of politics, such as office politics and sexual politics, enter into the equation. This is due to the existence of power. As Adrian Leftwich highlights, 'There is one overriding concern of those who study politics and that is a concern with *power*, political power – and its effects' (2004: 19). Who does the washing up at home, for example, might be regarded as political because it could relate to who holds the power. This links in with attempts to widen our understanding of politics. Politics has often been regarded as relating to the public arena. The old adage of politics being a 'man's world' comes to mind; as being primarily composed of men in suits. White, male, middle-aged and middle class is the traditional interpretation of a politician. Using an expression borrowed from James Mitchell (Professor of Public Policy at the University of Edinburgh) that he employed to describe the Scottish National Party membership, namely, '. . . male, pale and stale', Meryl Kenny and Fiona Mackay (2012) use the term to describe local politics in the run-up to the 2012 Scottish local elections. The UK Parliament, likewise, remains overwhelmingly male, with current levels of women MPs hovering around the 22 per cent mark (in 2013, 147 out of 650 MPs were female, 22.6 per cent). Women still, therefore, constitute fewer than a quarter of the total number of MPs. Would this be more of a talking point if it were the other way round and women constituted more than 75 per cent of our elected representatives at Westminster? One can surmise that it would be so and would certainly rank higher up the political agenda. Women are, however, forming a higher proportion of younger MPs, which does give grounds for optimism. As Parliament's website states, 'Of the 28 current MPs under the age of 30, half are female' (http://www.parliament.uk/education/online-resources/parliament-explained/ women-in-politics/). It appears that, for many political commentators and political scientists alike, politics is still regarded as overwhelmingly male. Many feminists have pointed out how, traditionally, the public arena has been regarded as being intrinsically male, whereas the private arena, in particular the world of the home, has been viewed as female and, correspondingly, less political (for a historical perspective see, for example, the work of Siltanen and Stanworth). As Judith Squires points out, the fact that '. . . women have conventionally been defined in terms of their relation to the domestic, this particular conception of the political has effectively marginalized women as political actors' (2004: 120). She proceeds to state that '. . . having eroded the boundaries of the political, feminists have then gone on to demand the reconfiguration of these broadly conceived sets of power relations' (*Ibid.*). Squires' analysis highlights how in answer to this question of what is politics, feminists have flagged up '... an endorsement of the ubiquity of politics' (*Ibid.*: 123) and focused upon '... exploring and advocating ways in which social relations might be ordered differently' (*Ibid.*: 123–124). For Squires, this involves endorsing '... a broad power-based conception of politics rather than a narrow institution-based conception' (*Ibid.*: 132) and '... the demand for the reform of all the institutions governing relations of power, including the old formalistic and public institutions of politics, but extending beyond these to the traditionally "non-public" and private domain' (*Ibid.*). This involves, therefore, recognising this all-encompassing nature of politics but also thinking about how we could and should organise ourselves differently, one such example being the press for greater equality in terms of childcare and domestic duties (*cf.*: Fiona Mackay's text *Love and Politics: Women Politicians and the Ethics of Care* (2001) for more information on this topic). Feminists have, therefore, challenged conventional definitions of what constitutes politics. There is some dispute as to who first coined the term but the feminist mantra is generally recognised as being 'the personal is political'. Carol Hanisch published an essay of that name in 1970 but she claims that she did not decide upon the actual title. Shulamith Firestone and Anne Koedt, the anthology editors, are thought to have come up with the captivating heading. Many feminists point out that the phrase was in use by 1970 and it is, therefore, difficult to attribute it to one person. The phrase is associated with consciousness-raising and getting women to see that they are also political beings; it is connected to moves to expand our notions of what constitutes politics. The movement away from solely being associated with mainstream politics and the world of political parties and institutions is a significant coup for the feminist movement. This recognition that what occurs behind closed doors may also be political is a step towards women being able to reclaim their place in politics. Societal ills, such as domestic violence, for example, have moved from being regarded as a personal/private issue to being a political issue related to questions of misogyny, patriarchy and power. The widening of the political arena and notions of what constitutes politics has brought such issues into the political arena and demanding of state involvement and action.

Alongside this expansion of what is politics and making the personal political too, there is also the involvement of many more women in mainstream politics. As stated, current levels of female members of Parliament are hovering just under the 150 mark. It was at the 1997 General Election in the United Kingdom that the numbers of women elected to Parliament doubled from the sixty elected in 1992, the previous general election, to 120 in the last general election of the twentieth century. Albeit most of these came from the Labour Party, 101 to be precise (some via the all-women shortlists that were subject to a legal challenge in the 1996 case of Jepson and Dyas-Elliott versus the Labour Party), it still constituted a sea-change in British politics with a visible change in the make-up of the House of Commons and questions being asked about whether more women in politics would make a difference (see Bochel and Briggs, 2000). Some felt that not only had the physical make-up of politics changed, even on a basic level with the rows of men in suits being interspersed with women in brightly coloured garb, but there was also a feeling, in certain quarters, that the actual 'style' of politics had changed. No longer quite so confrontational as it had been, the inclusion and involvement of many more women in politics was said to have resulted in a more consensual approach to politics, less adversarial and more co-operative, committed to getting the job done as opposed to postulating, pontificating and having an over-inflated sense of 'self'. More women in politics was felt by many commentators to have resulted in change for the better (*cf.* the works of Rosie Campbell, Sarah Childs, Joni Lovenduski and Philip Cowley, amongst others, for further expansion in relation to the effects of more women in politics). Politics, therefore, in terms of both the theory and the practice was moving towards greater inclusion of women, the female 'voice' and experience.

Politics does, inevitably, retain a focus upon the mainstream political institutions but the fact that what constitutes politics is wider than may at first be realised may serve to make it more interesting to many academics and scholars. It certainly widens the scope of the study and many universities now offer specific modules on women and politics, gender and the policy making process, anti-politics, to name a few. This helps with understanding the all-pervasive nature of politics and enables understanding of how it impacts upon our lives in numerous different ways. The campaign *You don't do politics, what do you do?* was part of a government strategy to get people to realise how politics impacts upon their daily lives. The cartoons with the voiceovers from actors Jim Broadbent and Timothy Spall were a government initiative, first used in the 2004 European elections and then re-run in the following year's General Election to get people to see how politics impacts on them directly. Issues such as not winning in sport, the increasing cost of purchases, and the proliferation of such anti-social concepts as litter, graffiti were all highlighted by the character who had previously claimed not to 'do politics'. As the commentary stated, 'Politics affects almost everything, so if you don't do politics, there's not much you do do.' Granted, the impetus behind the campaign was to get out the vote; politicians of all parties were becoming increasingly concerned by the low level of turnout in elections. The 2001 UK General Election, for example, had a turnout of only 59.4 per cent. This was the lowest turnout in a general election since the so-called Khaki Election of 1918 – with its specific and particular issues of economic and physical dislocation and all that entailed. The campaign was, therefore, not solely about raising awareness in terms of what constitutes politics and how pervasive it is in our everyday lives but was fuelled by a desire from politicians to avoid an 'armchair revolt' whereby apathy and disillusionment would lead to voters staying away from polling stations, and indeed possibly not even being on the electoral register, in their droves. It was, however, interesting that politicians were seeking to encourage voters to make that connection between politics and their daily lives. Indeed, the current Coalition Government is equally concerned about non-voting and about people not being on the electoral register. It has recently launched a research campaign for academics and others to focus upon ways of encouraging people to ensure that they are on the electoral register – especially with regards to young people, who are the sector of society least likely to be registered to vote and, correspondingly, least likely to exercise that right to vote. Getting people to recognise politics and its impacts on their lives remains of key importance to politicians as it is central to *their* own political survival. This battle to get the message out there is not driven by altruism!

The low turnout in UK politics across the board is of concern and interest to politicians and political scientists alike. Traditionally, turnout in general elections has been about 75 per cent. Around three quarters of those who were eligible to vote have usually turned out to do so. Local elections have usually had a much lower turnout, around the 30 to 40 per cent mark, exceptions usually being when a general election was held on the same day as a local election, as happened, for example, in 1979 and in 1997. In 1997, the election that returned the largest ever Labour majority with the landslide of 179, the turnout in the General Election was 71.5 per cent, the lowest since 1935. So even though Labour were basking in the glow of victory, turnout was starting to become an issue. The 2001 Election saw, as stated, a further drop in turnout and even though levels rose slightly in 2005 and 2010, to 61.3 and 65.1 per cent respectively, concerns still abound in relation to the apparent disengagement of the electorate from mainstream politics. Certain local elections and also the European elections have exacerbated these concerns; turnout in the 2009 European elections, for example, stood at 34.7 per cent, down from 38.5 per cent in 2004, albeit up from the nadir of 24 per cent in 1999. The European election turnout in the UK has, from the first one in 1979, remained relatively static in the low thirties.

A more recent set of elections that again sparked debate about politics and levels of political disillusionment was the election held on 15 November 2012 for the new Police Crime Commissioners. Overall, the turnout was an abysmal 15.1 per cent. As the Electoral Reform Society states, the '. . . lowest turnout of any election in British peacetime history' (http://www.electoral-reform. org.uk/police-and-crime-commissioners/). Analysts state that people did not really know what they were voting for, that many perceived the police crime commissioners to be a waste of money and that people were also put off voting in the midst of winter.

Certainly, the importance of politics seems to have been forgotten or ignored by those not bothering to turn out and cast their vote in the various elections outlined above. Some see it as constituting a crisis of democracy. The Labour politician Margaret Beckett, referring to the low turnout around the start of the new millennium, labelled it the 'politics of contentment'. Beckett was implying that people were generally happy with their lot in society and, therefore, did not feel galvanised enough to go out and cast their vote. Certainly, there is a view that states that apathy is not necessarily a negative aspect in that it could, as Beckett points out, equate with contentment, satisfaction and acceptance of the *status quo*. It is interesting to see how politicians are able to put a positive spin on the fact that many voters were refusing to engage with the political process. Having said this, it is worth highlighting the difference between positive and negative abstention. Positive abstention is where voters look at what's on offer and decide that there is nothing there that they find attractive. They make a positive decision not to vote, having weighed up the party manifestoes and other 'promises'. Negative abstention implies less of a conscious decision and may involve factors such as it is raining on polling day, there is something on television that they wish to watch at a peak time when people would normally be going to cast their vote. Indeed, there are oft cited examples of television programmes that are said to have kept voters at home, such as an episode of the old Alf Garnet programme *'Til Death Us Do Part* or even an episode of *Eastenders* featuring the shooting of the character Phil Mitchell that was said to have kept voters away from the polls. If voters are indeed so fickle then politicians have their work cut out to ensure that they get out the vote.

One remedy that has been proposed in an attempt to rectify low turnout and possibly go some way towards solving the problem of political engagement (although the two are not necessarily one and the same) is the introduction of compulsory voting. Compulsory voting, as has been pointed out by numerous scholars, is actually a misnomer as it refers to compulsory turnout. Voters are forced to attend the polls but they can always tick the box labelled 'None of the Above' to express their dissatisfaction with the whole range of political parties and candidates on offer should they so desire. Some countries already operate a system of compulsory voting, two of the more notable ones that are often cited being Belgium and Australia. Belgium has had compulsory voting since 1893, whilst Australia has forced its electorate to the polls since 1924 (1915 in the State of Queensland). There is a burgeoning literature in this area (*cf.*: Watson and Tami, 2000; Baston and Ritchie, 2004; and Briggs and Celis, 2010 for further details) that highlight the key arguments for and against compulsory voting. Various strategies are employed by differing countries that relate to the use of incentives and punishments (the 'carrot' or the 'stick') to get out the vote. Commentators often illustrate how the state compels its citizens to act in a number of different ways, for example the compulsion to undertake jury service, to pay taxes or to send one's children to school. Using this analysis, the compulsion to vote in an election is just a further extension of the state ensuring its citizens fulfil their duties. Opinion is polarised as to whether or not compulsory voting is a positive approach for a state to take. Some regard it as the state forcing the citizen to fulfil their civic duty whereas others view it in a negative light and see it as an infringement of civil liberties. The low turnout in elections has meant that, more recently, the question of compulsory voting has been placed firmly on the political agenda. Notable high profile advocates of compulsory voting have included the Labour politicians Geoff Hoon, Peter Hain and former leader Neil Kinnock, Lord Kinnock of Bedwellty. In an interview (with the author, 10 October 2006), Lord Kinnock highlighted the fact that, not only are people not voting, they are not even 'thinking' about not voting. Lord Kinnock stated that

> Democracy is a state of responsibility and voting is a responsibility of that and just as you've got a responsibility to get your child to school, you've got a responsibility not to park on double yellow lines, you've got a responsibility not to burn smoky fuel in smokeless zones, you've got a responsibility to vote.

For Lord Kinnock, the message is clear, if people are not voting then they should be forced to fulfil their civic duty.

Essentially, there is such disengagement between people and politics that they do not see it as an issue. Allied to this, one key aspect of this current malaise with politics is the fact that it is certain groups who are less likely to vote than others. One of the key groups is young people. This differential

37

turnout is of increasing concern to politicians. It is the case that all sectors of the electorate are not voting in equal measure. Particular groups are less likely to cast their vote than others, a key case in point being young people, who are less likely to vote in elections than their older counterparts. At the 2005 General Election, for example, only 37 per cent of the youngest sector of the electorate, the 18- to 24-year-olds actually turned out to cast their vote. Just over a third of the youngest voters voted. This did rise slightly in the 2010 General Election, up by 7 per cent to 44 per cent but, nonetheless, still a relatively low figure by any standard, with more not voting than doing so. If the added variable of gender is brought into the equation then it can be illustrated that young women are the sector of society least likely to vote at all. In 2005, for example, only 35 per cent of 18–24-year-old women voted in comparison with 39 per cent of 18–24-year-old young men. This rose slightly in 2010, with 39 per cent of young women voting in comparison to 50 per cent of young men but, nonetheless, the gender gap was still evident amongst young voters and had in fact risen from 4 per cent in 2005 to 11 per cent in 2010. Surely, the suffragettes would have expressed grave concern about such figures! Pragmatically speaking too, if young people are less likely to vote than older people, it perhaps makes sense for politicians and policy makers to focus their energies and policies on the older sector of society. It could be, therefore, that not only are young people not voting, their views, opinions and interests are less likely to be heard by the decision makers within our society. Their disengagement from the political process means that they can be ignored by the politicians.

This chapter has, hopefully, explained and outlined the importance of politics as an area of study. As Adrian Leftwich helpfully points out,

> . . . anyone entering the discipline of Politics for the first time should be prepared to encounter a rich and pluralistic enterprise which is, above all things, an *explanatory* enterprise, concerned with understanding the forms and features of political power, especially, and explaining its uses, abuses and both its policy and practical consequences.
>
> (2004: 20–21)

Certainly, part of the attraction of politics is the fact that it is a 'living' discipline, dealing with people, with the here and now and the day-to-day unfolding of events. Harold Wilson said, in 1964, 'A week is a long time in politics' and that remains a truism. The pace of change in politics is part of the attraction for many students. It is certainly not a static discipline as one might label other disciplines, where perhaps a new theorem may emerge every few years but which generally remains the same. With regards to politics, students need to keep abreast of contemporary affairs otherwise they will quickly fall behind in terms of studying politics. As well as the changing nature of the discipline, there are so many different aspects and angles to be studied, from political institutions to political philosophies, from political concepts to different countries and cultures. The importance of politics as a discipline should not be overlooked. As well as being a fascinating area of study, it is also valuable as a means of gaining employment. In one sense, higher education institutions might be seen as a training ground for the next generation of politicians, policy makers and policy analysts, alongside preparation for other careers that are less readily recognisable as being linked with having studied politics. Students enter a wide and varied number of career pathways. The discipline of politics certainly has relatively high levels of graduate employment according to the Destination of Leavers from Higher Education (DLHE) Survey data (See http://www.hesa.ac.uk/index.php?option=com_content&task=view&id =1899&Itemid=239) published by the Higher Education Statistics Agency (HESA). Aside from this pragmatic approach, studying politics can be a challenging and engaging topic area for its own sake and not simply because of the career opportunities it affords – although, as stated, it certainly does that too. Politics, as a discipline, requires certain intellectual skills. It is intellectually stimulating, challenging and encouraging students to think critically and ask questions that perhaps they had not considered before. Politics is central to our lives, to the way we live and to how we live. Little wonder then that Aristotle dubbed it the 'master science'. In terms of this master science, there are many areas that the discerning student of politics can investigate. It is to this fascinating topic of how politics is studied that attention now turns in the next chapter, Chapter Three.

Chapter bibliography

Baston, L. and Ritchie, K. (2004) *Turning Out or Turning Off? An Analysis of Political Disengagement and What Can be Done About It*, London, Electoral Reform Society.

Birch, A. H. (2002) *Concepts and Theories of Modern Democracy*, second edition, London, Routledge.

Bochel, C. and Briggs, J. E. (2000) 'Do women make a difference?', *Politics*, Vol. 20, No. 2, May: 63–68.

Briggs, J. E. (2013) 'A world of choice', *The New Statesman Political Studies Guide 2013*, London, *New Statesman*: 10–11.

Briggs, J. E. and Celis, K. (2010) 'For or against: compulsory voting in Britain and Belgium', *Social and Public Policy Review*, Vol. 4, No. 1: 1–33.

Briggs, J. E. and Curtis, S. (2012) 'Learned societies analyse recruitment trends', *PSA News*, Vol. 23, No. 3, September: 13–14.

Briggs, J. E. and Saunders, G. (2013) 'UCAS applications data for politics and international relations: follower of fashion or bucking the trend', *PSA News*, Vol. 24, No. 2, June: 12–13.

Burns, L. (2013) 'Do your duty', *Times Higher Education*, 7 February: 28.

Campbell, R. and Childs, S. (2010) 'Wags, wives and mothers . . . but what about women politicians?', *Parliamentary Affairs*, Vol. 63, No. 4: 760–777.

Childs, S. (2006) 'The complicated relationship between sex, gender and the substantive representation of women', *European Journal of Women's Studies*, Vol. 13: 7–21.

——(2008) *Women and British Party Politics*, London, Routledge.

Childs, S. and Cowley, P. (2011) 'The politics of local presence: is there a case for descriptive representation?', *Political Studies*, Vol. 59: 1–19.

Coward, R. (2013) 'A degree for two Es', *The Guardian*, 24 January.

Crick, B. ([1962] 2000) *In Defence of Politics*, Harmondsworth, Penguin.

——(1998) 'Education for citizenship and the teaching of democracy in schools', London, QCA.

Crick, B and Crick, T. (1987) *What Is Politics?*, London, Edward Arnold.

Hanisch, C. (1970) 'The personal is political', in Firestone, S. and Koedt, A. (eds), *Notes from the Second Year: Women's Liberation, Major Writings of the Radical Feminists*, New York, Radical Feminism: 76–78.

Kenny, M. and Mackay, F. (2012) 'More of the same? Women and the Scottish Local Government Elections 2012', http://genderpoliticsatedinburgh.wordpress.com/2012/04/18/more-of-the-same-women-and-the-scottish-local-government-elections-2012-5-2/, accessed 3 December 2012.

Lasswell, H. D. (1958) *Politics: Who Gets What, When, How*, New York, Meridian Books.

Leftwich, A. (ed.) (2004) *What Is Politics?*, Cambridge, Polity Press.

Lovenduski, J. (2005) *Feminizing Politics*, Cambridge, Polity Press.

Mackay, F. (2001) *Love and Politics: Women Politicians and the Ethics of Care*, London, Continuum.

Ofsted (2006) *Towards Consensus? Citizenship in Secondary Schools?*, ref: 2666, London, Ofsted.

——(2010) *Citizenship Established? Citizenship in Schools 2006/2009*, ref: 090159, London, Ofsted.

Siltanen, J. and Stanworth, M. (eds) (1984) *Women and the Public Sphere*, London, HarperCollins.

Squires, J. (2004) 'Politics: a feminist perspective', in Leftwich, A. (ed.), *What Is Politics?*, Cambridge, Polity Press: 119–134.

Watson, T. and Tami, M. (2000) *Votes for All*, London, The Fabian Society.

Websites

http://www.electoral-reform.org.uk/police-and-crime-commissioners/, accessed 31 August 2013.

http://www.hesa.ac.uk/index.php?option=com_content&task=view&id=1899&Itemid=239, accessed 12 September 2013.

http://www.ofsted.gov.uk/resources/citizenship-established-citizenship-schools-200609, accessed 4 June 2013.

http://www.ofsted.gov.uk/resources/towards-consensus-citizenship-secondary-schools, accessed 4 June 2013.

http://www.parliament.uk/education/online-resources/parliament-explained/women-in-politics/, accessed 30 August 2013.

http://www.teachingcitizenship.org.uk/about-act, accessed 18 August 2013.

http://www.ucas.com/about_us/media_enquiries/media_releases/2013/20130130c for press release, 'UCAS reports 3.5% increase in applications to higher education', 30 January 2013, accessed 21 February 2013.

Note

1 Parts of this chapter appeared in the *New Statesman Guide to Political Studies* 2013 and in *PSA News*, June 2013.

3

Studying politics today[1]

This chapter examines issues involved in studying politics at university. It focuses upon the question of politics and the quest for a 'right' answer. Allied to this is the thorny issue of bias. What topics can you expect to study at higher education level? The key areas of focus will be highlighted here. The benchmarking statements for politics will be highlighted. The emphasis is upon the academic study of politics, studying it as you would any other subject, history, for example. The idea is that you acknowledge and recognise the difference between fact and opinion and accept that there are occasions when we may have to 'agree to disagree' in politics. The notion of highlighting alternative viewpoints is important here; for example, some people believe X, some people believe Y, etc. We don't always need to come down on one side of the political fence or another. This chapter also investigates *how* we study politics; in particular, the use of new media in the teaching and learning of politics will be assessed.

The truth is out there . . . or is it? The search for the 'right' answer

There is undoubtedly, in education, a quest for the 'truth' and for knowledge that might be seen as incontestable. One aspect that the student of politics will inevitably encounter, relatively quickly, is that there may not necessarily be a right or wrong answer, only perhaps particular and partial versions of the truth. Sometimes a version of the truth may only be a particular picture, for example, there was once an advert for a broadsheet newspaper featuring two photographs depicting the same scene. One photograph showed an old man being pushed forward by a young guy with piercings and a Mohican haircut. Initial, possibly prejudicial, interpretations might be that the old man was being attacked or mugged by a young hooligan. The second photograph is identical to the first in every respect, except that this one pans out and reveals the full scene. This time, in the global picture, it is evident that something is falling from nearby scaffolding and the young man is, in fact, saving the older man from certain danger. These two photographs constitute a graphic and visual illustration of this notion of particular and partial versions of the truth. A Platonic version of reality may be evasive and, indeed, may be a fallacy. It may depend upon how one views the situation and what are regarded as the priorities or yardstick against which to measure various factors. For example, as will be seen in Chapter Six, depending upon which aspect is regarded as important in analysing various electoral systems, this will impact upon which electoral system is preferred. Democracy, equality, fairness, to illustrate, may be applied as the underlying guiding principle and this will dictate the chosen system.

Likewise, in many other areas of politics personal preference and, indeed, political bias, political ideology, will impact upon decision-making. A socialist ideological perspective will lead to a specific interpretation of events and this will inevitability contradict those approaching from a liberal or conservative perspective. Who is to be the final arbiter in deciding which version of the truth is the correct version? Each side will claim to have 'seen the proverbial light'. This is the problem with politics but also its manifest attraction for many scholars. With regards to issues such as abortion, divorce law reform, and the issue of gay marriage who is say what is right and what is wrong? There are not necessarily right or wrong answers only well-argued ones. Political philosophers, politicians and policy makers have argued over these questions for decades. Likewise, more central questions such as how should government be organised and who should govern over us have intrigued and vexed political thinkers for centuries, from Plato and Aristotle through to, relatively speaking, more 'contemporary' thinkers such as Schumpeter, Michels, Lasswell and Almond and Verba. How we live, govern and organise ourselves is at the heart of politics. People do not live in isolation and, therefore, in view of the social nature of humankind, politics comes into play.

The problem of bias

The issue of bias is a central theme that the student of politics will encounter. Part of the skill of the political scientist is to decipher what constitutes bias and to be able to differentiate fact from mere opinion. Statistical and quantitative data may go some way towards rectifying this situation but, even here, the old adage of 'lies, damned lies and statistics' comes into play. Statistics are not foolproof and may be interpreted differently in order to put forward a particular argument or message. Opinion polls, for example, are notoriously flagged up by political parties and politicians when they work to their own advantage and tend to be downplayed when the message is less favourable. The notion of 'spin' and conveying a positive message and image is crucial for parties and politicians alike. Being able to decipher bias and see through the hype is part of the attraction for many students of politics. Parties are guilty of not simply conveying facts but of putting their own version of events forward via the media.

Studying politics at university provides opportunities for a wide variety of options to be covered. As mentioned in Chapter Two, politics can be studied alongside a wide variety of disciplines, some of which are fairly obvious, such as politics and international relations, politics and law, politics and history, politics and journalism, and other combinations that less readily spring to mind. These include, for example, politics and drama, politics and Arabic, politics and television studies. Degrees in politics, or which include politics as a major or minor subject, usually adhere to the guidelines set out by the Quality Assurance Agency (QAA). These subject benchmarking statements for politics (http://www.qaa.ac.uk/Publications/InformationAndGuidance/Pages/Subject-benchmark-statement-Politics-and-international-relations.aspx) outline what the student of politics will cover in a politics degree. The benchmarks are relatively vague and, to a certain extent, deliberately so, to enable a wide interpretation of what can and must studied in a politics degree. As the benchmarking statement states, 'Subject benchmark statements provide a means for the academic community to describe the nature and characteristics of programmes in a specific subject or subject area. They also represent general expectations about standards for the award of qualifications . . .' (QAA, 2007: iii). In addition, the benchmark documents '. . . provide general guidance for articulating the learning outcomes associated with the programme but are not a specification of a detailed curriculum in the subject' (*Ibid.*). The politics document contains guidance in relation to subject knowledge and content, the generic intellectual skills and the personal, transferable skills. It provides a comprehensive overview of what the student 'doing politics' at university may expect to cover and the skills they are likely to acquire.

The academic study of politics

Academics who study politics often prefer to study it just as one would any other subject, history, for example. It is also the case that one can highlight particular perspectives by saying some people believe 'x', some people believe 'y', *ad infinitum*, and leave the listener or audience to make up their own minds as to which version of events they prefer to believe and/or accept. It is not necessary for a conclusion to be reached whereby 'x', 'y' or some other is paraded as the answer.

Fact versus opinion

As stated, part of what the student of politics has to do is to differentiate between established fact and mere opinion. It can be illuminating to begin to understand that much political hype and hyperbole is precisely that, possibly exaggerated by 'spin' doctors in order to attract the electorate to support their party. The student of politics needs to decipher the value judgements from irrefutable fact. This may not always be as straightforward as it seems when political parties and politicians are experts at conveying their message as established fact. Political marketing is big business and just as the retail industry sells products so those involved in politics have to sell parties and politicians (*cf.* the work of Dominic Wring, also Darren Lilleker and Jennifer Lees-Marchment for information about political marketing). The idea is that politicians have to listen to what the market wants and when they do this they will achieve success – as Lees-Marchment highlights in relation to the Labour Party and how its victory in 1997 was due to it having (eventually) taken on board what the electorate wanted.

Agreeing to disagree

Politics is certainly an academic discipline where students may find themselves 'agreeing to disagree', in that it is may be unlikely that debate will lead to a resolution and reconciliation between conflicting viewpoints. There is not necessarily an answer and, therefore, the only response might be a truce.

Alternative viewpoints

In some measure, part of the attraction of politics is the way in which alternative viewpoints are flagged up. These may be viewpoints that emanate from
a particular ideological perspective. Analysing a situation from a feminist perspective may lead to an entirely different interpretation to one where a male
centric approach is adopted. Ideology is a difficult concept to determine
accurately; one study found, for example, twenty-seven different interpretations of the term (see Naess *et al.*, 1956). As Andrew Heywood highlights,
it is '. . . one of the most controversial concepts encountered in political
analysis' (Heywood, 2007: 44) and, particularly in the past, it has '. . . had
heavily negative or pejorative connotations' (*Ibid.*). It is certainly fair to say
that ideology is often associated with being blinkered or like wearing a
metaphorical intellectual straitjacket. The term is said to have been first
used by the French philosopher Antoine Destutt de Tracy (1754–1836). In
the nineteenth century, Karl Marx was one of the leading thinkers to flesh
out a specific ideological perspective and, more recently, contemporary
writers have flagged up notions of the 'end of ideology' or of a liberal
democratic ideological dominance (*cf.*: the works of Daniel Bell, and also
Francis Fukuyama). Certainly, there are those who regard it as limiting to be
associated with a particular ideology or to be regarded as taking an
ideological stance. Margaret Thatcher, for example, deplored the notion
of ideology and did not like to be seen as ideological. Ironic perhaps, especially when one thinks of Thatcherism as being a political doctrine and the
extent to which it did have ideological underpinnings. To say the least, there
are few politicians whose name has been applied to a political philosophy or
'ism'.

How we study politics – small groups, large groups

With regards to how politics is taught and studied in higher education,
the most common way is via the traditional lecture and seminar arrangement.
Lectures usually take place in large, often tiered, lecture theatres and,
dependent upon the specific module being studied, might hold any number up
to about 100/150 students and even beyond this. Indeed, in some academic
circles, there is a move towards the greater use of MOOCs (Mass Open
Online Course) as a replacement for the traditional lecture in a physical
environment. With MOOCs, students study online and there are, in theory at
least, no limits to participation levels via the open access. The reality can

see limitations placed upon access, via closed licences and suchlike, and so the degree of openness is debatable. Returning to the traditional lecture, the skills that the student needs to acquire in a lecture are active listening and accurate note-taking – not simply trying to write down every word uttered by the lecturer. The art of being selective is a skill in itself and knowing what to note and record is just as important as knowing what not to write down.

The large lecture has its uses, although there are some academics and analysts who question its value as an aid to learning. There has been debate as to the average attention span of students in lectures. Some studies cite this to be as little as ten to fifteen minutes but other research (*cf.*: Bunce *et al.*, 2010) questions the methodological approach employed by some studies and highlights how it is notoriously difficult to accurately ascertain the average attention span of students in lectures. Having said this, it is quite likely that this figure is much lower than the duration of the average lecture. Granted the Bunce *et al.* research is not specific to politics students but it does perhaps indicate that the traditional lecture is possibly not the best way to maintain student interest and engagement. Their research found that attention lapses were lower when students were required to participate in the lecture (for example, by answering questions with their hand-held 'clicker'), an argument perhaps for moves towards more student participation. The large lecture has a place in terms of 'doing politics' but possibly more as a way of sparking interest in particular aspects of the discipline as opposed to conveying detailed information. The performance aspect of the large lecture definitely has merit. An interesting and exciting lecture given by an engaging lecturer who is passionate about their discipline can certainly help to promote the study of politics and to enthuse students.

The pedagogical topic of teaching politics to small groups may perhaps be regarded as a non-issue given the increase in applications to study politics at university. According to Professor Wyn Grant, 2,741 students took up a politics and international studies place in 2000 and by 2005 this had increased to 4,366. Grant highlights that in '. . . 2007 there were 23,000 politics undergraduates and 9,625 postgraduates, many of them from outside the UK' (2010: 164). Figures from UCAS, cited by Professor John Benyon, highlight that acceptances to study politics were up by 90 per cent in 2009 (from 2000) (2010: 18). Having said this, even though applications and actual places are up, for a variety of reasons – some say it's the Obama Effect, coalition politics and/or the conflicts in Iraq and Afghanistan (Davies, 2009: 6), others cite an increasing politicisation facilitated by a focus upon issues such as the increase in tuition fees – and politics tutors are faced with increasing numbers of students, for the majority of political scientists/politics tutors there will remain an optimum class size. As Bogaard *et al.* state, 'Teaching in small groups is a common and highly valued practice in the social sciences and humanities' (2005: 116). They proceed to highlight the general '. . . conviction that small group teaching is a particularly useful device to encourage critical learning and understanding of complex issues' (*Ibid.*).

This section concentrates upon teaching politics to small groups, as opposed to focusing, for example, upon the traditional lecture scenario. The lecture usually involves a tutor imparting information to a much larger group – some universities may have, for example, politics lectures involving a hundred plus students. Generally, the skills that the student needs to acquire are active listening skills and note-taking. The lecture is very much a tutor-led experience, often with relatively little student participation. A much smaller learning environment, the seminar places much greater emphasis upon student participation and involvement. Seminar size varies from institution to institution and from course to course. It is probably a fair assessment, however, to say that average seminar size ranges between fifteen and thirty people. Quite often, within this environment, the tutor assumes the role of facilitator or guide; the trajectory of the seminar will often be led by the students themselves with the politics lecturer taking more of a backseat/observing role. This is, nonetheless, still a pivotal role within the classroom/learning environment.

In part, the aim of this chapter is, therefore, to consider strategies and approaches that the politics lecturer may employ to facilitate teaching and learning within small groups. It is hoped that the chapter offers ideas and suggestions that may be of use within the classroom situation. First of all, it is necessary to devote some discussion to this question of size. What constitutes a small group? How small is small? Is there, in fact, an optimum size for the teaching and learning of politics? What kinds of skills will students acquire through these small groups? In addition to enhancing their political knowledge, for example, it may be that students are acquiring various transferable skills such as team-building skills, problem-solving techniques and presentational skills, all valuable skills for the politics graduate to possess and that should enable them to enhance their employability – especially in this new age of austerity, where anything the student can do to give them added leverage in the jobs market is to be applauded. Goldsmith and Goldsmith highlight the many challenges facing politics tutors today, including

... maintaining the quality of provision in the face of growing student numbers; the demand on universities to address not only the academic needs of students, but also to prepare them for the labour market; and, finally, the necessity to adapt pedagogy to new developments in information and communication technology.

(2010: S63)

In addition, one of the main points to consider is what is the purpose of a seminar? Is it to reinforce and expand upon ideas and opinions that were introduced in preceding lectures? Or, do they provide opportunities to discuss related topics that may or may not have been covered in the lectures? So, you need to think about the purpose of a particular seminar, what is it designed to achieve?

Size matters . . .

The old cliché and double entendre, that tired and ubiquitous innuendo of size matters, is actually rather apposite as we consider the teaching and learning of politics. Student feedback indicates that students enjoy being taught in smaller groups and often feel that they benefit and learn to a much greater extent than if they were part of a huge lecture audience. The lecture has its place in the higher education environment; lectures can be a place to learn the key aspects of a particular topic, especially when given by a tutor who is passionate about their discipline. Lectures can constitute a performance and be inspirational, instilling a desire in the recipient to go off and engage with the subject matter in greater depth. Some question the relevance of the lecture in twenty-first century higher education. The former head of the National Union of Students, Wes Streeting, is quoted as saying that, come the revolution, in his opinion, the '. . . lecture would be first up against the wall' (2009: 17). He continues by asking why is it '. . . in the age of mass higher education, that we keep packing lecture theatres with hundreds of students for a format designed for teaching no more than 20 in an elite system?' (*Ibid.*). Some commentators question the value of lectures, in terms of average attention span, for example, and whether students do learn if they are simply being 'talked at' for fifty minutes. For many, however, the real learning takes place within the seminar/classroom environment. It is necessary, therefore, to focus upon the teaching of politics to small groups.

Ten tips for teaching small groups: some practical suggestions

1 Breakout sessions – three to four in a group and relay responses to whole group. Provide three or four questions in advance of the session with short indicative reading lists. For example, political theory, questions relating to whether or not there is a right to disobey the law in a democracy.

According to recent research, size does matter as far as academic achievement is concerned (Attwood, 2010: 11). The results of a five-year survey conducted by the London School of Economics and University College London reveal 'robust evidence of a negative class-size effect – on average, larger classes reduce students' academic achievement' (*Ibid.*). If this advice is heeded, there could be a movement towards smaller class sizes as a way of improving student performance. With the increase in student numbers, size matters. Seminar size can be an issue. Some groups might be as large as thirty. Breaking a large group up into smaller groups to discuss a particular topic or issue and then asking them to report back is a technique that may help here. It may also encourage some of the more diffident members of the group to contribute. They may feel more confident in a smaller group.

As stated, small group teaching does militate against the trend of increasing class sizes. We still need, however, to have an armoury of coping strategies to enable us to deal with smaller groups. There are many different strategies that the tutor of politics may wish to employ when they are faced with a small group. Many of these techniques, strategies and approaches are considered in this chapter. One of the easiest approaches to take is to break the group up into smaller groups. Three to four students per group is often regarded as optimum. The groups are then given a task – for example discussion of three or four questions. The groups are asked to (s)elect a rapporteur to report the findings of the group back to the group as a whole. Alternatively, the tutor may choose the spokesperson for each group. Small group discussions ensue and then the rapporteur/spokesperson has to relay the findings of their small group back to the whole seminar. This strategy is useful for enabling the more reticent members of the group to relay their thoughts, knowledge and beliefs. They may feel more confident about expressing their viewpoints knowing that this will be relayed by a third party. It is also a useful device for facilitating group cohesion and for enabling students who may be meeting for the first time to get to know one another. This method works best with preparation. Tutors may wish to prepare a set of questions and an indicative reading list so that students prepare their response or at least have the opportunity to ponder the problems prior to the actual seminar.

> **2 Debates** – for and against the motion, possibly being coerced into arguing contrary to one's own beliefs. For example, 'This House believes that prisoners should have the right to vote.' 'This House believes that feminism is passée as a political theory.'

Another concomitant advantage of breakout groups is that they can serve to foster a team spirit. Concepts such as leadership, problem-solving techniques and consensus building all come into focus here. The real world often involves working as part of a team and so this approach again helps to nurture those transferable skills that are important in the workplace environment. Students have to learn to listen to the views of their peers but also to know when it is appropriate and necessary to take the initiative themselves. These small groups are an ideal conduit for the acquisition of these vital team-building skills.

Student-centred

The small group seminar should emphasise student participation and it should be very much student-centred, with the tutor acting more in the capacity of a facilitator or guide. This is particularly apposite as far as students of politics are concerned because it is fair to say that politics students, on the whole, are not passive learners. The nature of the discipline lends itself to conflict, debate and argument. Politics students like to debate and to argue. In part, this is probably why they chose to read politics at university. The ability to differentiate between fact and mere opinion is a key skill and debate in these small groups will probably encourage students to hone their talents in this area. Given that politics lends itself to a multitude of opinions and differing perspectives, small groupwork is usual in this respect in that it enables differing opinions and viewpoints to come to the fore.

The general idea is that students should be involved as much as possible, especially given that student-centred learning is said to be more effective. The old Chinese proverb, 'I hear and I forget, I see and I remember, I do and I understand' is relevant here. This is the very essence of student-centred learning. For those wanting to see some of the best examples of student-centred learning, observe teaching practice in a primary school. This is where some of the most innovative teaching methods are taking place with respect to pupil-centred learning. A day spent observing in a local primary school will no doubt reveal pupils actively engaged in a whole host of different tasks and projects. Higher education can learn from these approaches employed at the lower echelons of education.

> **3 Student presentations** on a particular topic – ten minutes to present, ten minutes for discussion. Students need to be well briefed and need to have plenty of preparation time. For example, a presentation on women in politics, looking at why there are relatively few women in politics and what can be done to rectify this.

Most tutors would agree that the best seminars are student-centred but, in order for them to be successful, the students need to be well-briefed. They need to have researched the topic or area under discussion beforehand. There is nothing more frustrating than when students turn up for seminars and they are obviously unprepared. But tutors need to provide adequate guidance as to the most obvious sources of reference beforehand. Extensive reading lists or even indicative reading lists ought to be provided for some, if not all, of the seminars. It can be seen then that student-centred learning is not an easy option.

'Let's have a heated debate. . .'

Debates are a useful device in the small group scenario. The tutor needs to decide what role they should adopt too. They could, for example, play Devil's Advocate. In an early text about the teaching of politics, Roberts alludes to this,

> He [*in the 1960s, the assumption is that the politics tutor is male*] must therefore be skilled at guiding discussion and eliciting the views of the less voluble, as well as being competent to put an opposition case where an entire class takes one side of a controversial political question.
>
> (Roberts, 1969: 122)

Students could choose their own stance or they may be forced to adopt a particular line of argument. This tactic means that rather than giving the group carte blanche to pursue whatever perspective appeals, the tutor prescribes the approach to be taken. This means that they may have to pursue a line of argument that is countervailing to their own particular perspective or opinion. This results in a situation where they have to really think about the counter-arguments. This can work particularly well if the seminar takes the form of a debate. Students need to be given time to prepare their case so they can clearly research and rehearse the arguments to be pursued. It is fair to say that students can sometimes be reluctant to argue counter to their own thoughts and beliefs so tutors may encounter opposition initially but it is an effective way of getting someone to at least recognise an alternative viewpoint even if they do not espouse the counter-arguments. Political theory classes often work very well in this respect. Debates centring on topics such as the arguments for and against abortion, the existence of capital punishment, and whether there is a right to disobey the law in a democracy have ensured that students of political theory engage with the subject matter. The debate needs to be properly organised with plenty of preparation time and opportunity for the students to research their perspective beforehand. Each side needs to be allocated a set amount of time for them to present their case to the group and then time needs to be allowed for the whole group to discuss and debate the merits and demerits of each particular perspective.

Problem solving

The essence of small group teaching is to encourage students to become critical thinkers. It is not, therefore, just about imparting knowledge and factual information to our tutees, it is about encouraging them to think for themselves. The acquisition of problem-solving techniques is invaluable for students both in the classroom and in the workplace environment. One way to facilitate the development of these skills is to use a case-based approach. Such case studies might be centred upon real events or fictional scenarios. The University of York and also the University of Huddersfield have both been involved in projects to devise case studies intended to help the teaching and learning of politics. Topics are wide-ranging but include, amongst other aspects, cases to encourage understanding of theoretical concepts such as democracy or toleration and also contain investigations into contemporary issues such as press freedom. Students are provided with suggestions for background reading and it is certainly the case that the more the students put into their research the more they will get out of these case studies.

> **4** Create a '**Democracy Wall**' – give small groups different coloured Post-it™ pads and they have to put their comments, sometimes one word responses on the wall. For example, highlighting the basic tenets of conservatism, highlighting legislative changes that have impacted positively upon gay rights.

New(ish) technology – new media in teaching and learning politics – podcasts, social media, VLEs, etc.

Obviously, a great deal of lecturer/student interaction takes place in seminars. New technology can be used to enhance that interaction. At the University of Lincoln (my own institution), for example, we are currently being shown the merits/possibilities offered by a system such as Optivote™, whereby an audience response system à la *Who Wants to Be a Millionaire?*, can be used to ascertain student opinion/understanding (Gormley-Heenan and McCartan (2009) have undertaken research in this area). This enables tutors to take a quick straw poll. It can also be used to ascertain whether opinion has changed throughout the course of a class. For example, on a topic such as whether voting should be made compulsory or whether the voting age should be lowered to 16, it has been used to gauge opinion on these matters. It can also be used to ascertain the level of knowledge on any given topic. Its value should not be overestimated but it does have its uses and can, for example, enhance a debate by providing a snapshot of opinion. The system is probably more beneficial when applied to a large lecture situation but it can equally be used in seminars.

> **5 Speed discussions** (à la speed dating) – two lines, each moving in opposite directions after five minutes, have the chance to share ideas and discover alternative viewpoints. For example, students are asked to research the life and work (theoretical perspectives) of one specific political philosopher each, to ascertain the key details as they pass along the line – just a 'warm up' exercise but it does get students thinking critically.

One way of enhancing the small group situation is by making use of the wide range of audio-visual resources that are available. Those new to politics teaching have an expansive variety of resources at their disposal. Older colleagues will remember using VHS clips to supplement their teaching. It is much easier to access relevant information nowadays. The internet is an invaluable source of material – although obviously some websites are more reliable/rigorous than others. Political parties, Parliament, learned societies (such as the Political Studies Association, and the British International Studies Association), organisations such as C-SAP (the Higher Education Academy's Subject Network for the teaching and learning of Sociology, Anthropology and Politics), the University of Southampton's Citizenship project (POLIS)

55

are all invaluable sources of information. A short visual or audio clip can enhance a small group situation by illustrating or clarifying.

The micro-blogging site Twitter™ has potential for use in the teaching and learning of politics. Essentially, a tweet consists of a maximum of 140 characters. These might be in the form of a question to elicit a response or simply a point to be made. As well as being used within the classroom environment, this can also mean that discussion, on any given topic, may carry on beyond the confines of the seminar room. Some critics may argue that tweets constitute dumbing down or they may question how much one can actually say with such a limitation. It does, however, concentrate the mind and can serve to initiate a debate on any given topic area. There is talk of a digital divide between tutors who are familiar with web 2.0 technology and those who are less so. The *Times Higher Education* recognises that 'Twitter divides opinion but some scholars view it as a tool that could benefit their work' (2009: 20). In addition, many students are helping their tutors to understand and get to grips with the opportunities offered by this new technology.

> **6 Runaround** – five large cards, numbered separately one to five, are placed on the floor. Number one equals 'agree strongly', the numbers continue through to number five, which means 'disagree strongly' (two is agree, three is neither agree nor disagree, four is disagree). On any given question, students are asked to move around the room and stand by the number equating to their viewpoint or their perception of others' views. For example, 'AIDS tests should be compulsory', 'The Monarchy should be abolished' and other such controversial assertions. Students have to literally vote with their bodies/stand up and be counted.

Acting it out

Tutors may wish to use innovative techniques such as simulations and role play. For example, cabinet committee simulations are whereby students are given a particular departmental portfolio and they have to argue the case for their particular department. Again students need to be well-prepared beforehand. Students seem to really enjoy doing this. Another role-play exercise is where students are asked to negotiate a constitution at the start of setting up a new state. Professor Richard Rose of Aberdeen University (email correspondence with author, 25 November 2009) has a useful suggestion for a seminar. Rose himself was invited to put forward suggestions to George W. Bush about ideas for policy. He was given time to prepare beforehand but was told he would only have three and a half minutes to present his case (*cf.*: Rose, 2008). Rose sees this as a good seminar exercise, to get students to do a role-play exercise where they have three and a half minutes to present their policy ideas to, say, an incoming Prime Minister. He said it is also interesting to get students to prepare a policy brief when they hold opposing political opinions to the person they are told to brief!

7 **Twitter**™ – micro-blogging sites such as Twitter can be used to expand the discussion. For example, it can be used to carry on the debate beyond the classroom scenario or it can be used actually within the seminar room itself. Students can send their questions or points to be raised in the form of tweets. This often suits the more diffident members of the group or it enables points to be raised without disrupting the flow of the session. For example, to enable students to ask questions, for points of clarification, and to air their views. The 140-character tweets mean that they have to be concise and succinct in their approach.

Keeping it real

Politics is a living subject. It is necessary to ensure that the tutor keeps abreast of contemporary affairs otherwise one's perception and awareness quickly become out of date and lacking in basic knowledge. Keep up-to-date and well-informed. Make sure that handouts are revised on a regular basis. Anecdotal evidence recalls one university lecturer using handouts dated 1969 and this was the early 1980s! On the issue of handouts, it is a good idea to produce handouts either before the seminar for research purposes or after so that students have something to take away with them for future reference. Continuing this theme of updating, when one institution was assessed by the Quality Assurance Agency, the observer's fair comment was that the example of the poll tax protest was quite an old one to use and should be supplemented with more contemporary examples. Sad to learn that whilst the poll tax debacle was still fresh in the tutor's mind, it was ancient history as far as the students of the new millennium were concerned. Thompson refers to this aspect in Heater's aforementioned text, *The Teaching of Politics*,

> The whole study should involve the use of contemporary examples
> where appropriate, and these should be provided by the pupil as well

as the teacher. Illustrations should not be fossilized, as they can easily become, but draw on contemporary situations.

(Thompson in Heater, 1969: 67).

As Harold Wilson said, circa 1964, a week is a long time in politics. That still holds true today. This is, for many, part of the appeal of politics. The pace of change can sometimes be quite breath-taking. For many, that makes it exciting. Of course, giving a lecture on say, electoral systems does not necessarily involve a great deal of change but, without updating (knowledge of the May 2011 referendum on the question of electoral reform, for example), you will soon find yourself behind the times.

Preparation

One of the first points that tutors of small groups need to note is be prepared. Robert Louis Stevenson (1850–1894) wrote, 'Politics is perhaps the only profession for which no preparation is thought necessary'. In terms of teaching politics, however, it is paramount that you are prepared . . . like the good girl guide – even to the event of having a 'Plan B' should a seminar not go as you would have wished. Obviously, you need to ensure that you know your subject matter – content is important – although it is not everything; you may be an expert in your field but unable to convey that expertise. Enthusiasm for the subject, displaying your love of politics, is important. Be passionate about politics – it's contagious. It is necessary to ensure that seminars have a clear set of aims and objectives. Academics are readily familiar with the notion of specific learning outcomes. These help with the planning of seminars. Tutors should ensure that seminars are well structured, that they have a clear beginning, middle and end. This will enable students to follow the 'flow' of thought and argument.

8 **News review** – a five minute or so review of contemporary events at the beginning of each session can be useful for getting students to engage with the discipline. The tutor needs to know when to rein in the debate and also to focus upon the more relevant aspects of the news. This ensures students get into the habit of keeping abreast of contemporary affairs.

Variety

There is a case to be made for using a variety of teaching methods and styles. Variety is the spice of life. However, don't change just for the sake of change but likewise don't stick rigidly to one method. If every week, a tutor uses the 'breakout into small groups' approach, this may become a little tedious for the students. Likewise, using Twitter every week or showing an audio or video clip may lead to typecasting!

> **9 Role play and simulation exercises** – with the possibility of filming these. For example, cabinet committee simulations, model UN sessions (*cf.*: Obendorf and Randerson, 2013), local council meetings (setting the budget). Students need to prepare their policy positions beforehand and to be able to debate these and to defend their positions.

Maturity

Make use of the experience of any mature students in the group. They often provide a valuable source of information (albeit somewhat anecdotal in a subject like politics). Mature students initially may feel intimidated when faced with a class of undergraduates who have come straight from school or college, especially if they themselves are returning to study after years in a non-academic job or rearing a family. Confidence-building is crucial here and valuing their experiences in the real world. Once anxieties on both sides have been allayed, the combination of mature and mainstream undergraduates can lead to highly rewarding seminars for both parties in the equation.

> **10 Mini-tests** – on any given topic, to ascertain the level of knowledge or to discover differences of opinion. New technology, such as audience response systems, could be used to enhance this process. For example, these can range from the more mundane/basic (such as: How many members of the UK Parliament are there? In what year did Margaret Thatcher become leader of the Conservative Party?) through to more complicated questions requiring a more in-depth response (such as: Define the following terms: mandate, citizenship, socialism, democracy).

Bias

What about the issue of bias too? Should you adopt a particular political standpoint? Given that this is politics, bias cannot be ignored. The tutor needs to decide whether to approach any given topic by highlighting the range of views in existence (often preferring to say, 'Some people believe X, some people believe Y, etc.' and not coming down in support of any given stance) or whether to adopt a particular standpoint – whether or not that accords with the tutor's own personal point of view.

Presentations

Student presentations are a useful device for the teaching and learning of politics and also useful as an assessment method. They can be either individual or group presentations. It's a good idea for students to be able to practise their presentational skills and it is useful practice for many job interviews. The 'I'm happy to be here. I'm happy you're here' approach usually makes them laugh! This is where students are encouraged to make eye contact with their audience and to produce such an enthralling presentation that their audience would not rather be anywhere else at that particular moment in time – no mean feat. It might, at first, appear difficult to assess a presentation given the apparent subjectivity involved – just think of one's favourite actor and differences of opinion come to the fore. Having said this, a checklist of criteria can be devised to ensure that students can be taught the mechanics of what constitutes a good presentation. Content, delivery – including confidence, eye contact, volume of voice, engaging one's audience, appropriate speed of delivery, use of audio-visual resources – and time-management are all factors that come into play here.

Every tutor of politics will need, at some stage, to teach small groups. As Goldsmith and Goldsmith point out, 'The goal is to produce students who are "independent, enterprising problem solvers" rather than passive consumers of knowledge' (*Op. cit*: S65). It is, in part, helpful that as well as using tried and tested methods, tutors look for new and exciting ways of teaching and learning politics. The Goldsmiths are correct to say that 'there is a continuing need for innovation in teaching methods and for the cross-national dissemination of good teaching practice' (*Ibid.*: S66). The old methods are invaluable but, at the same time, there is a desire of not wanting to limit tomorrow's academics with a model of the past. It is also worth highlighting that techniques and strategies may work with one cohort of students and then, for no apparent reason, fail to work quite so effectively with another group. There may be a reason behind this, such as timing – what works effectively at 2p.m. on a Thursday afternoon in April might fail to deliver the same enthusiastic response at 9a.m. on a Monday morning in January. In this sense, always have a Plan B at your disposal. The reality here is that we are dealing with real people with all their moods, foibles and beliefs. We are dealing with people not machines. This is, in part, what makes the teaching of politics to small groups such a challenging and rewarding endeavour to pursue. Hopefully, this chapter has provided some models and approaches for consideration.

Conclusion

To summarise, this chapter has examined how politics is taught and studied at university. This vibrant, topical and exciting discipline is conveyed in a number of different ways. In part, politics can be studied in the same way as any other substantive academic discipline. The added difficulty for the student of politics is to differentiate between fact and mere opinion and to cope with the thorny problem of bias. Guidance for the study of politics is provided by the Quality Assurance Agency (QAA) and its subject benchmarking statement for politics. In terms of how politics is taught, the tendency is for it to be taught using the traditional lecture/seminar arrangement. More recently, there has been greater emphasis upon the skills acquired as part of a politics degree. In particular emphasis has been placed upon numeracy skills and quantitative data analysis as part of a politics degree (see http://www.nuffieldfoundation.org/q-step for details of a 2013 initiative in the field of quantitative methods), ensuring that politics graduates are numerate as well as literate. There has also been a push towards greater employability for politics graduates, with organisations such as the former C-SAP (the Centre for Learning and Teaching – Sociology, Anthropology and Politics) and the Higher Education Academy (HEA) placing greater emphasis upon the career paths of politics graduates. The Destinations of Leavers from Higher Education (DLHE) data, a statutory national survey of graduates, and information supplied by the Campaign for Social Science (which seeks to promote social science to the UK government and to the public at large – see http://campaignforsocialscience.org.uk/graduates-main/ which contains case studies of graduate destinations) all point to the value of a degree in politics and the many and varied career trajectories that can be pursued. It is an exciting subject to study in higher education leading on to a wide variety of interesting and challenging employment opportunities!

Chapter bibliography

Almond, G. and Verba, S. (1963) *The Civic Culture: Political Attitudes and Democracy in Five Nations*, Princeton, New Jersey, Princeton University Press.

Aristotle (1948) *Politics*, Oxford, Clarendon Press, edited by Baker, E.

Attwood, R. (2010) 'Size matters to students' grades', *Times Higher Education*, 16 December 2010: 11.

Bell, D. (1960) *The End of Ideology?: On the Exhaustion of Political Ideas in the 1950s*, New York, Free Press.

Benyon, J. (2010) 'Looking forward to a bright future', *PSA News*, June, Vol. 21, No. 2: 18–20.

Bogaard, A., Carey, S. C., Dodd, G, Redpath, I. D. and Whitaker, R. (2005) 'Small group teaching: perceptions and problems', *Politics*, Vol. 25, No. 2: 116–125.

Bradwell, P. (2009) *The Edgeless University: Why Higher Education Must Embrace Technology*, London, Demos.

Briggs, J. E. (2012) 'Teaching politics to small groups', chapter five in Lightfoot, S. and Gormley-Heenan, C. (eds), *Teaching Politics*, Basingstoke, Palgrave: 65–77.

Bunce, D. M., Flens, E. A. and Neiles, K. Y. (2010) 'How long can students pay attention in class? A study of student attention decline using clickers', *Journal of Chemical Education*, Vol. 87: 1438–1443.

Davies, C. (2009) 'Obama weaves his magic spell', *The Independent*, Education section, 9 April: 6.

Fukuyama, F. (1992) *The End of History and the Last Man*, Harmondsworth, Penguin.

Goldsmith, M. and Goldsmith, C. (2010) 'Teaching political science in Europe', *European Political Science*, Vol. 9: S61–S71.

Gormley-Heenan, C. and McCartan, K. (2009) 'Making it matter: teaching and learning in political science using an audience response system', *European Political Science*, Vol. 8, No. 3: 379–391.

Grant, W. (2010) *The Development of a Discipline: The History of the Political Studies Association*, Oxford, Wiley-Blackwell.

Heywood, A. (2007) *Politics*, third edition, Basingstoke, Palgrave Macmillan.

Jacques, D. (1991) *Learning in Groups*, London, Kogan Paul.

Lasswell, H. (1958) *Politics: Who Gets What, When, How*, New York, Meridian Books, first published 1936.

Lees-Marchment, J. (2001) *Political Marketing and British Political Parties: The Party's Just Begun*, Manchester, Manchester University Press.

Lilleker, D. G. and Lees-Marchment, J. (eds) (2005) *Political Marketing: A Comparative Perspective*, Manchester, Manchester University Press.

Michels, R. (1966 [1915]) with introduction by Seymour Martin Lipset, *Political Parties: A Sociological Study of the Oligarchical Tendencies of Modern Democracy*, New York, Free Press.

Naess, A., Christophersen, J. A. and Kvalø, K. (1956) *Democracy, Ideology and Objectivity: Studies in the Semantics and Cognitive Analysis of Ideological Controversy*, Oslo, Oslo University Press/Oxford, Basil Blackwell.

Obendorf, S. and Randerson, C. (2013) 'Evaluating the model United Nations: diplomatic simulation as assessed undergraduate coursework', *European Political Science*, Vol. 12: 350–364.

Plato (1955) *The Republic*, Harmondsworth, Penguin, translated by Lee, H. D.

Quality Assurance Agency (QAA) (2007) *Politics and International Relations: Subject Benchmark Statement*, Gloucester, Quality Assurance Agency.

Roberts, J. (1969) 'The teaching of politics in practice', in Heater, D. B. (ed.), *The Teaching of Politics*, London, Methuen: 116–125.

Rose, R. (2008) 'What would you tell the president in three minutes about Iraq?', *European Political Science*, Vol. 7: 78–83.

Salmon, G. and Edirisingha, P. (2008) *Podcasting for Learning in Universities*, Maidenhead, Open University Press.

Schumpeter, J. (1942) *Capitalism, Socialism and Democracy*, London, Allen and Unwin.

Streeting, W. (2009) 'Lectures: first target of the teaching revolution', *Policy Review*, June: 17.

Thompson, D. (1969) 'The teaching of civics and British constitution', in Heater, D. B. (ed.), *The Teaching of Politics*, London, Methuen: 50–70.

Times Higher Education (2009) 'Twitterati in the academy', 30 April: 20.

Wood, B. and Moran, M. (1994) 'The engine room of instruction: small group teaching', *Politics*, Vol. 14, No. 2: 83–90.

Wring, D. J. (2004) *The Politics of Marketing the Labour Party*, Basingstoke, Palgrave Macmillan.

Wring, D. J., Mortimore, R. and Atkinson, S. (eds) (2011) *Political Communication in Britain: The Leader Debates, the Campaign and the Media in the 2010 General Election*, Basingstoke, Palgrave.

Useful sites re. Twitter

http://chronicle.com/wiredcampus/index.php?id=3705&utm_source=wc&utm_m, accessed July 2011.

http://elearningstuff.wordpress.com/2009/04/08/using-twitter/, accessed July 2011.

http://www.blogscholar.com, accessed July 2011.

Websites

http://campaignforsocialscience.org.uk/graduates-main/ which contains case studies of graduate destinations, accessed November 2013.

http://www.nuffieldfoundation.org/q-step for details of a 2013 initiative in the field of quantitative methods, accessed July 2013.

http://www.psa.ac.uk/, accessed August 2013.

http://www.qaa.ac.uk/Publications/InformationAndGuidance/Pages/Subject-benchmark-statement-Polictics-and-international-relations.aspx for the politics subject benchmarking statement, accessed July 2013.

http://www.soton.ac.uk/citizened/, accessed July 2011.

http://www.c-sap.bham.ac.uk/, accessed October 2010.

Note

1 Sections of this chapter appeared in Briggs, J. E. (2012) 'Teaching politics to small groups', chapter five in Lightfoot, S. and Gormley-Heenan, C. (eds), *Teaching Politics*, Basingstoke Palgrave: 65–77.

4

Don't like politics

The previous chapter examined studying politics at university. This chapter looks at the negativity that is often directed at politics. As a starting point, it is useful to think of why politics is often perceived in such a negative light: *Why politics does get a bad press?* [Do we hate politics?] In part, this involves analysis of Colin Hay's work and Gerry Stoker's work. This chapter examines the negativity associated with politics and politicians. Clearly, the recent expenses scandal has impacted upon the general public perception of politicians. There is a great deal of criticism levied at politicians, some deserved, some less so. Yet, this is not only a recent phenomenon. Samuel Johnson the eighteenth century writer and poet, for example, talked of politics as being nothing more than a 'means of rising in the world'; likewise, Shakespeare referred to the 'scurvy politician'. It seems that politicians have always needed to be able to cope with criticism. This chapter analyses why politics and politicians are sometimes viewed in such a negative light.

Why negativity?

Given that politics is so central to our lives why should it receive such negativity? Occasionally when discussion takes place on the topic of politics, the layperson will make negative references to politicians and their ilk as being scheming, out for personal gain and to serve their own ends. Politics is sometimes regarded as a dirty word with pejorative connotations. Politicians have such power over our lives; perhaps this is why they are often regarded with such contempt given the power, influence and coercion that they are able to wield. There is perhaps also a perception that many politicians are in it for what they can gain personally, not just in terms of mere financial rewards – although as will be shown these can be quite substantial, especially when compared with the mass of the population, but also in terms of the kudos, power and status that is associated with the role. It is worthwhile examining a number of recent events to ascertain whether the situation has worsened in recent years.

Expenses scandal

Certainly, the expenses scandal that broke in 2009 did politicians no favours. The fact that many politicians were seen as having feathered their own nest at the expense of the ordinary taxpayer was regarded as sufficient justification for the castigation of the whole cohort of Members of Parliament. The expenses scandal, which first broke due to an investigation by the journalist and keen advocate of freedom of information Heather Brooke, highlighted the fact that there was widespread abuse of the system for claiming parliamentary expenses. The parliamentary expenses system was seen as lacking both in transparency and accountability. *The Daily Telegraph* began publishing information from early May 2009. One issue to note was the way in which the *Telegraph* published this information, in a piecemeal fashion, drip-feeding more details to a waiting public. One of the effects of this was to maintain the issue in the public eye for a significant amount of time. Leaked documentation revealed actual and alleged abuse of the expenses system. It was the Freedom of Information Act that meant that this data became accessible by journalists and, subsequently, the public at large. Granted not all of this was deliberate but certainly many Members of Parliament were claiming significant expenses at a time when the country was suffering during a time of austerity. Even in times of relative prosperity, the expenses debacle would have caused controversy but to occur during a period when a substantial sector of the ordinary population was enduring significant economic hardship in the aftermath of the credit crunch, rising levels of inflation and the soaring cost of living exacerbated the situation. People were struggling to pay their heating and food bills and yet here were politicians, perceived as receiving a high salary anyway, who appeared to be fiddling their expenses on a hitherto unknown large scale. The ensuing public outcry was vocal and intense. The mass media were keen to highlight stories such as the politician who claimed for a house for his ducks, others who submitted claims for house flipping

– this is whereby they changed their nominated second home and then were able to claim more expenses, such as stamp duty or money for renovations. MPs were nominating as their second home the one that would allow them to claim the most in expenses, claiming back interest on mortgages that had already been repaid, and even the Home Secretary, Jacqui Smith, although she asserted not to have known about them, had submitted a claim for repayment of two pornographic films that had been watched by her husband. Receipts were not required for expenses below £250 and also they could claim up to £400 a month on food. Essentially, the system was allowing them to claim a significant amount of taxpayers' money, which, to many observers, was blatantly unfair. Repayments averaged around £3,000 but Barbara Follett paid over £40,000 back into the treasury's coffers. A number of parliamentarians were subject to criminal charges, some of which resulted in subsequent imprisonment. The debacle also led to a vote of no confidence in and the resignation of the Speaker of the House of Commons, Michael Martin. This was the first time the Speaker had been ousted from office by a motion of no confidence since 1695. This showed that MPs, in particular, should not be seen as being 'above the law' but did impact upon public perceptions of politicians, leading to anger and a lack of trust and loss of confidence in politicians. As Colin Hay points out,

> If politics depends ultimately on our capacity to trust one another, if such trust in contemporary societies is increasingly conditional, increasingly fragile and in increasingly short supply, and if that is due in part to the increasing influence of a conception of human nature as narrowly instrumental and self-interested, then there can be no more important questions for political analysts than these.
>
> (2007: 162)

Likewise, Gerry Stoker cites the fact that '. . . fewer people trust both politics and politicians than in the past' (2006: 51). He goes on to postulate, however, 'Might the explanation for the change of perception be something that has happened to *citizens* to make them less trusting, rather than a shift in behaviour pattern of politicians?' (*Ibid.*). Is it the case that people have become more questioning and challenging, less willing to accept a situation at face value? Are we, as Stoker posits, '. . . all becoming critical, post-materialist citizens' (*Ibid.*: 53)? It is difficult to be able to determine the answer to this question. Having said this, the ramifications and subsequent fallout from the 2009 expenses scandal have been long and far-reaching. Some felt that it would impact upon the 2010 General Election result and especially in terms of turnout. In the event, turnout in the 2010 General Election was up slightly on the previous one, with a turnout of 65.1 per cent, although the vote did result in a hung Parliament and the subsequent Coalition Government. One of the outcomes of the expenses scandal was the setting up of the Independent Parliamentary Standards Association (IPSA). This body would examine MPs' expenses and provide more checks and balances in relation to the process.

Members of Parliament received a salary of £66,396 as of 1 April 2013. They also receive expenses, including travel, stationery and postal expenses, and the costs of running their office(s). The sum of £66,396 is certainly much higher than the average UK salary, which, according to the Office for National Statistics (ONS), was £26,500 in April 2012. It can be seen, therefore, that the expenses scandal would cause a certain level of public outrage. Having said this, the sum of £66,396, whilst significantly higher than the UK average, is not so great when compared with, for example, the pay of university vice chancellors or that of the leaders of big business. It is often argued that politicians could potentially earn more in the private sector and that if Parliament is to attract politicians of a high calibre who will be the leaders of the next generation then there needs to be adequate financial recompense. In addition, the life of an MP can be a lonely business. The hours are long and can be arduous for the conscientious and ambitious politico. Added to this, the geographical remoteness of some constituencies means that many hours are spent travelling to and from the area that they represent. It might be the case that, in the light of the expenses scandal and the resultant lower levels of respect and trust that the general public feels towards politicians, fewer people are aspiring to become a Member of Parliament. The loss of kudos and respect is quite significant and must surely impact negatively upon numbers wishing to enter the legislature. It used to be the case that the letters MP after one's name added a certain gravitas and level of social standing within one's community at least. The extent to which those levels have diminished is certainly a subject of debate.

Physical layout of the debating chamber

Another aspect that is said to impact upon public perceptions of politicians and their ilk is the yah-boo adversarial style of politics that epitomises political debate within the Houses of Parliament. This is particularly the case in the House of Commons but also, to a lesser extent, occurs in the House of Lords (even with the existence of the cross-benchers). The fact that the chambers are, for the most part, presented as two opposing sides facing each other in direct competition is said to perpetuate this notion of confrontation. This adversarial layout is said to encourage competition as opposed to co-operation, coalition and compromise. The Commons Chamber was deliberately designed to be too small so that, with all Members of Parliament in attendance, it would have the atmosphere of a crowded and exciting debating arena with participants jostling for space. This would encourage observers to regard it as the locus of the great debate. Designed to be two sword-lengths apart (see the red lines on the floor of the Commons), the prevailing philosophy was that Members of Parliament would resolve their differences or disputes through debate and discussion, as opposed to via physical force and fighting. Indeed, the very term Parliament comes from the French verb 'parler', meaning to talk or to speak. Disputes would, therefore, be reconciled in this civilised manner as opposed to the physically strongest having the upper hand by virtue of their strength and the armoury at their disposal. It is precisely this physical layout of the debating chamber, however, which for many people perpetuates their belief that politics is a bear-pit. This unedifying spectacle of Members of Parliament heckling each other, failing to listen to the opposing point of view and acting in a hostile and (as many commentators have highlighted since the increase in the number of female parliamentarians at the turn of the millennium) an increasingly sexist manner, has led many people to regard politics as an unsavoury business. The confrontational nature of politics is, for many people, a significant turn-off. The ordinary person in the street, generally, does not wish to witness this constant adversarial approach to policy making. Some see it as setting a bad example to society at large. If our politicians are unable to discuss in a seemly manner and argue the merits and demerits of particular policies without resorting to shouting and insulting one another (albeit it in an erudite and learned manner), what hope is there for the rest of us? The advent of televising the House of Commons, which began on 21 November 1989 (with the State Opening of Parliament), partly spurred on by a successful trial of televising the House of Lords, which began in 1985, and which became permanent from July 1990, has added to the perception that politics is an unsavoury affair with a noisy rabble who constitute a distinct lack of role models for society at large. A select committee had analysed the issue of whether Parliament should be televised as far back as Harold Wilson's Governments in the 1960s but MPs believed it would change the Commons and voted against its introduction at that time. In addition, there is sometimes the perception that issues become political footballs, kicked from one side to the other, not necessarily because this is in the nation's best interests but primarily because ideological divisions mean that politicians focus upon what they feel they 'should' decide as opposed to what they 'ought' to decide. This blinkered approach or ideological straitjacket alienates voters, who view decisions as being taking for political gain or capital instead of because it is the right choice to make. Clearly, this is a subjective judgement but certainly public perceptions of the political clashes impact negatively upon their view of politicians and the political world.

Televising Parliament

The decision to televise Parliament was preceded by a number of long and protracted debates. Claims were put forward on both sides of the divide. Key points included the notion that it would trivialise and sensationalise politics, that politicians would play up to the cameras, that more power would be placed into the hands of television editors and programme producers as opposed to politicians themselves, that media types would be making policy as opposed to politicians themselves. Counter-arguments included the central premise that it is democratic for the population at large to see their politicians at work and to focus upon debates as they happen and that access should not be denied to the millions who would wish to see democracy in action. It is interesting to note too that, once the decision was taken to televise Parliament, television also inevitably extended to the scrutinising committees and, rightly so, given the extent of Parliament's work that is now undertaken via the committee system. The televising of Parliament is generally regarded as a successful venture but it could be argued that the way that politicians are portrayed and, indeed, the way that they behave does inevitably impact negatively upon public perceptions of politicians and politics *per se*. The depiction of an unruly rabble, shouting, gesticulating and generally behaving badly, undoubtedly jars with the general public. Cheap political point-scoring, likewise, portrays politicians in a negative light and may contribute to the perception of politicians being an unworthy bunch.

Political trust

There is a perception that levels of trust in politics and politicians have dwindled over recent years. One study that certainly buttresses this viewpoint is the Hansard Society's *Audit of Political Engagement*. Now in its tenth year, the most recent audit, the *Audit of Political Engagement 10*, published on 15 May 2013, highlights that the general public has, indeed, become less enamoured with its politicians. In the 1950s and 1960s, there were surprisingly high levels of deference towards our politicians – indeed to most people, those exercising positions of power and authority were regarded with higher social esteem by the ordinary person in the street. The theory of deference, for example, was in part used to explain why certain members of the working class voted Conservative. They were said to look up to the Conservatives as the 'natural' leaders in society, as being those who were born to govern. Declining levels of deferential attitudes have been well documented by political scientists and psephologists alike over the past few decades. It is claimed that voters no longer regard the Conservatives as the born leader or those most fitted to the role of governing. Instead, voters have become more discerning and challenging, more willing to question and to switch their voting habits. It appears, however, that not only have voters become less deferential, they have also become less trusting overall of their elected representatives.

The *Audit of Political Engagement* provides a picture of how people view politics and the state of democracy in Britain today. One key aspect of the 2013 Report is that there is an increase in the numbers of people who are less likely to vote. Indeed, 20 per cent say they are certain *not* to vote and when the Audit's findings are broken down by age, a shocking statistic is that only 12 per cent of young people say they would vote in the next general election. It is noteworthy that this is down by 30 per cent on the 2011 *Audit of Political Engagement*. If this absence of young people from the ballot box happens in reality, this would raise significant questions about whether the voice and interests of youth were being excluded from politics. It would also reignite the simmering debate about whether or not voting should be made compulsory (an issue that was touched upon in Chapter Two). In addition to these low levels of voters expressing an inclination to vote at the next general election, there is also an increase in levels of political literacy, knowledge and awareness of how the political system operates. For example, a significant minority of respondents seem to think that the voting age is 16 (29 per cent hold this view) and a third of the public think that members of the House of Lords are elected. With regards to the European level of governance, only 43 per cent of respondents know that British Members of the European Parliament are subject to direct election. To be fair, the recent publicity surrounding the issue of lowering the voting age, alongside the fact that Alex Salmond pledged that this would happen in the September 2014 referendum for Independence in Scotland, may have led some to think that this is already in place for elections to the Westminster Parliament. On the other hand, given the level of political coverage given to this debate, how could so many respondents have got this wrong? Nonetheless, this level of incorrect information is surprising and indicates that a significant sector of the population have a lack of understanding as to how the political system operates. Issues in relation to the political system, such as lowering the voting age and reform of the House of Lords, have been debated at length in the British press and on television and online media and so these low levels of understanding may illustrate a number of factors. Firstly, people are failing to engage with these public debates. It could be the case that people do not read the newspapers every day – or at least they skip the political content and perhaps focus upon the popular press for their daily updates – buying the newspaper for the celebrity gossip, titillation and human interest stories as opposed to the political content. Secondly, is it the case that politicians themselves are not getting the message(s) across in a succinct and easily understandable manner? If information is couched in arcane, esoteric and jargonistic language, this will inevitably lead to people failing to engage and understand. The onus has to rest on the politicians, to a certain extent, to explain and clarify the 'system' whilst using language that is direct and easily accessible. Thirdly, this scenario could be related to the aforementioned lack of trust with respect to politicians and the political system. People may have switched off from the messages being conveyed by politicians. If the general perception is that politicians are simply there to have their own ends served and to feather their own nests then it is highly likely that the general population will disengage and will, therefore, not be receptive to any messages. Fourthly, the 'cult of celebrity' that appears to permeate British culture has superseded any desire to become familiar with politics and the political system. Ask people about the latest contestant on the *X Factor* or who has been voted off on *Strictly Come Dancing* and they are more likely to express a viewpoint and possess some knowledge of what is taking place. They are simply not interested in politics and that is and ought to be of utmost concern to politicians and policy makers alike. They need to ensure that people are able to see the relevance of politics to their lives. As mentioned in Chapter Two, the *You don't do politics; what do you do?* Campaign went some way towards getting people to make that connection between political decision-making and their daily lives. Politicians have, however, an uphill struggle on their hands to get people to make these connections. Perhaps citizenship teaching in schools will make some difference to these levels of awareness and understanding but there is still a long way to go and this does not address the issue of older members of society being in possession of incorrect and incomplete information. How is this group to be reached if not through the mainstream media and related outlets? On one level, factual inaccuracies are easily corrected but if people genuinely are part of the 'Am I bothered?' generation, it is extremely difficult to make them interested and have a genuine thirst for knowledge. These levels are, however, extremely worrying and, if they continue to escalate, raise serious questions about the future of politics and the future of British democracy *per se*. This disengaged, disillusioned and, what's more, don't care sector of society does lead to a focus upon what politicians can do to reach out to the voting and non-voting public.

Further analysis of the Hansard Society's *Audit of Political Engagement 10 Report* reveals that levels of satisfaction felt towards politicians are in freefall. The 2013 survey shows that public satisfaction levels with MPs are at their lowest levels since the Audit started in 2004. There are, however, some grounds for optimism in that there is a 9 per cent increase in the number of those saying that Parliament holds the government to account, up from 38 per cent in 2012 to 47 per cent in 2013. Coupled with this, there is also a slight increase in the numbers saying that Parliament debates matters that are important to people, up from 49 per cent in 2012 to 54 per cent in 2013. The 2013 Audit identified

... decreasing levels of identification of and satisfaction with MPs, beyond the levels witnessed even in the aftermath of the parliamentary expenses scandal, and yet an increase in the perceived efficacy of Parliament collectively in holding government to account and debating topical issues that matter to the public.

(Hansard Society, 2010: 51)

In addition,

Only 23% say they are satisfied 'with the way MPs in general are doing their job', the lowest level ever recorded in the Audit series. Worryingly for MPs, satisfaction levels are now six percentage points lower than they were three years ago following the parliamentary expenses scandal.

(*Ibid.*: 53)

It is clearly of concern that satisfaction levels have declined even further than they had done in the immediate aftermath of the expenses scandal. What is also clear, however, is that there is an increase in the number of people who are neither satisfied nor dissatisfied. As the Report points out, '... a rising tide of simple lack of interest appears to be driving public attitudes'

(*Ibid.*). This notion of disinterest and being 'not bothered' appears to be behind many of the responses outlined in the Audit. Again, this appears to be symptomatic of society at large and it will be difficult for politicians to reverse this trend. In terms of wanting to get involved politically at both the local and national level, as the Report illuminates, this year's audit reveals '... a considerable improvement in the desire to get involved but no real change in the degree to which the public believe this involvement will be effective' (*Ibid.*: 59). For example, 47 per cent would like to get fairly or very involved in their local area and this is up from 38 per cent in the previous Audit. At the national level, this figure is 42 per cent but, again, this is up on the previous Audit, which stood at 33 per cent. In terms of feeling they have influence at local level, only 26 per cent believe they have some influence; correspondingly at national level this figure is 16 per cent. Again, these figures are up slightly on the previous year's Audit but still remain relatively low. The respondents questioned for the Hansard Society's *Audit of Political Engagement 10* recognise that people ought to get involved; for example,

> Three-fifths of the public (60%) agree that every citizen should get involved in politics if democracy is to work properly, and a similar proportion (63%) think that if a person is dissatisfied with a political decision they should do something about it.
>
> (*Ibid.*: 64)

But when it comes down to actually doing so, it appears that relatively few actually follow these sentiments. This is summed up succinctly as the gap between the '... rhetoric and the action of good citizenship' (*Ibid.*: 68) – what they believe and what they do are two different concepts. In terms of political participation, it appears to be the case that

> ... although the public is increasingly disgruntled, disillusioned and disengaged, they appear to see the political system as neither sufficiently good nor sufficiently bad to, as yet, justify a significant increase in their focus on it. The tipping point – in either a positive or negative direction – has perhaps not yet been reached.
>
> (*Ibid.*: 82)

It will be interesting to keep an eye on subsequent Audit Reports to ascertain whether this 'tipping point' is looming on the political horizon.

Allied to the *Audit of Political Engagement*, there is also research that was carried out for the Economic and Social Research Council by Stoker *et al.* This work, *Anti-Politics: Characterising and Accounting for Political Disaffection*, examined notions of so-called 'anti-politics' and looked at what people think about politics, in particular focusing upon whether there are high levels of political disengagement and, if so, why this should be the case. Based upon focus groups and survey work, and using interesting devices such as cartoons to stimulate discussion of what is meant by politics, for example, the Report found that although there were plenty of negative attitudes towards politics, there was also '. . . a positive commitment especially to the role that representative institutions and processes could play in making collective decisions' (Stoker *et al.*, 2012: 2). Overall, the Stoker *et al.* research gives grounds for optimism in that they felt that people were putting forward interesting and thought-provoking suggestions as to how the situation could be improved. The negativity related to the fact that their suggestions were often not taken seriously enough or adhered to. Gerry Stoker highlights four factors that may be said to have contributed to the current malaise in relation to politics and why people are less engaged than they used to be. These are

> . . . the rise of a more intense individualization, the increasing special-ization that is being brought to many functions in our societies includ-ing politics, the increased complexity of the challenges faced, and a rising tide of cynicism fueled in part by the practices of the mass media.
> (2009?: 132)

These four factors may all be said to play a part in contributing to high levels of political disengagement. Stoker also highlights the fact that '. . . it is important to recognize that for most people politics is not their first choice of activity. There are trade-offs between time spent on politics and the joys of private life' (2009?: 142). This is clearly important to political scientists and those studying politics; it can assume a central place in their lives, but for the majority of the population, its positioning is less central and has to be placed in perspective alongside all the other aspects of twenty-first century living.

Further analysis of negative attitudes towards politics and politicians includes the fact that, in the twenty-first century, people might be said to have increasingly stressful lives. The pace of modern living, the relative decline in living standards in the aftermath of the credit crunch/financial meltdown means that people focus more and more upon basic economic survival, upon keeping their heads above the water (in terms of finances) and remaining in employment. They are, therefore, less inclined to focus upon other areas such as wanting to become involved and expressing a concern for politics. Feeding the children takes precedence over focusing upon the political arena; ironic perhaps, especially given the sway that politicians hold over our lives. It is about making that connection between what politicians do and how those decisions impact upon our daily lives – again we are back to the '*You don't do politics; what do you do?*' message. Conveying that central message is the key to getting people to re-engage with politics and with politicians.

Campaigning groups

Other arguments postulated as to why people dislike politics relate to the perception, rightly or wrongly, that politics is 'boring'. This must surely be a matter of how politics is conveyed to the public at large. Political scientists and their ilk will claim that there is no subject matter more interesting and captivating than politics. Rather like marketing a product, perhaps it is the case that politics needs to be repackaged so that people perceive its relevance to their lives. It is precisely this relevance to their lives that needs to be illuminated. People will often get involved in politics, especially at the local level, when it is an issue that directly affects them. Subject to accusations of being so-called NIMBYs (the Not In My Backyard Brigade), people will campaign if, for example, a new road or housing or other development is going to be built in close proximity to where they live. On the other hand, where it does not directly affect them or their family then they may choose to ignore any proposals and seek to get on with living their life. The recent (2013) issues in relation to fracking (whereby engineers drill into the earth applying high pressure water mixture to the rock to release the gas inside – see http://www.bbc.co.uk/news/uk-14432401 for more information about fracking) or with respect to the culling of badgers in certain counties (Gloucestershire and Somerset are two zones that constitute a pilot cull whereby they aim to cull around 5,000 badgers in an attempt to halt the spread of tuberculosis in cattle) illustrate how people will get involved in their immediate vicinity. Having said this, particularly where issues in relation to environmental concerns or regarding animal rights come to the forefront, activists from a much wider area are likely to also become involved. This notion of proximity or immediate impact is likely to affect whether or not people get involved in politics and, as stated, they are therefore less likely to regard politics as boring under these circumstances. They will more readily make that connection between politics and their lives.

There might also be an aspect where people feel that their concerns do not matter and that people do not really take any notice of them and of issues that relate to them. This is rather a sad state of affairs if people believe that their views and concerns count for nothing, or at least relatively little. As one interviewee said, '. . . it doesn't matter who you vote for, they are not bothered about us. My taxes won't come down' (interview with author, 4 August 2013). This is akin to that old joke of regardless who one votes for the government always wins, i.e. *plus ça change, plus c'est la même chose.* People have to be encouraged to make the connection and see that politics is for everyone and not just applicable to certain sectors of society. Having said this, and as was highlighted in Chapter Two, politics is about making difficult decisions. Hard choices have to be made and there will inevitably be winners and losers. If politicians decide to spend more in an attempt to capture older voters, the so-called 'grey vote', it may mean that they become less attractive to young people or to certain sectors of the youth vote, say, for example, NEETS, those Not in Education, Employment or Training. The recent economic cuts that have been pursued with relative vigour by the Conservative–Liberal Democratic Coalition Government have involved difficult decisions. There are winners and losers and this impacts upon public perceptions of politics. As stated previously, the nature of politics means that if you are a politician you will not be universally admired. Inevitably, you are in a no-win situation due to the fact that decisions will impact negatively on some people more than others. Difficult choices have to be made over the aforementioned allocation of scarce or finite resources. If the decision is taken to spend more on, say, fertility treatment then this may mean that there is a correspondingly lower amount to be spent on cancer services, by way of example. Likewise, if more is spent on children's services, it may mean that a local council has a correspondingly lower amount to spend on adult services. This epitomises the conflict that lies at the very core of politics. Essentially, it involves the management of that conflict, managing conflicts of interests and dealing with those with vested interests too who seek to ensure that their own ends are served (possibly at the expense of others).

Certain sectors of society have lobby groups or pressure groups that act in their interest in order to try to ensure that they either gain something that they do not already possess or to block or negate something from happening. Pressure group activity and pressure politics are examined in more detail in Chapter Seven (*cf.* the work of Wyn Grant for further information) but suffice to say at this juncture that pressure politics may serve to turn some people away from politics if they perceive that certain groups wield excessive power.

It may be, for example, that groups constitute articulate minorities and are not, in fact, representative of wider society or even of the issue under the spotlight. If groups are in possession of particular resources, be that financial resources, expertise or numbers (i.e. in terms of people within their ranks), it could be that they are able to wield a substantial amount of political power. The power of such groups and of vested interests may serve to alienate others in society who feel that they are lacking in political clout and cannot compete with the power of these groups. The extent to which such groups are representative is worthy of further investigation. Articulate and well-organised groups may be better able to achieve their aims. The gay rights lobby group *Stonewall*, for example, has been particularly successful at achieving its aims. Over the past ten to fifteen years, they have been incredibly prolific and have achieved virtually everything that they set out to. Policy has certainly worked in their favour. The national mood, led by the incoming Blair Government from 1997 onwards, shifted towards an acceptance of gay equality. Perhaps it was simply a matter of the time being right but, undoubtedly, the continued campaigning by *Stonewall* meant that gay rights remained on the political agenda and in the public eye. From the lifting of the ban on gays in the armed forces, to the removal of Section 28 of the 1988 Local Government Act through to gay adoption and, more recently, gay marriage, the gay rights movement has achieved success in a number of importance areas of policy. Having said this, homophobia has not been eradicated, indeed some areas have reported increases in homophobic attacks, and so the quest to change attitudes continues apace. Perhaps there will always be a need for such groups and never a time when they are able to disband having achieved all their aims?

Political representation – are they like us?

The concept of political representation has been examined and assessed on many occasions by politicians and political scientists alike. One early commentator on the notion was the eighteenth century Irish statesman, politician, philosopher and writer, Edmund Burke. In a speech to the electors of Bristol on 3 November 1774, Burke highlighted the difference between a representative and a delegate. Essentially, Burke argued that although the voters may choose their representative, in the sense that they are able to vote for them at election time, they cannot then dictate how and in what capacity their representative acts. Burke's beliefs underpinned modern conservatism and also classical liberalism. As he stated in his speech to the electors of Bristol, when referring to an elected representative,

... his unbiased opinion, his mature judgment, his enlightened conscience, he ought not to sacrifice to you, to any man, or to any set of
men living ... Your representative owes you, not his industry only, but
his judgment; and he betrays, instead of serving you, if he sacrifices it
to your opinion.

(Burke, 1854–6: 446–48)

The notion here is that, once elected, they are free to act upon their own
judgement and should not be beholden to the electors who put them there.
Many contemporary politicians have referred to Burke's speech when highlighting their independence and the fact that they are not delegates of their
constituents.

Another writer who has focused upon defining the concept of representation is Hanna Pitkin. Pitkin highlighted the difference between descriptive
and substantive representation, a concept that is often referred to by contemporary writers on women and politics (*cf.* the work of Sarah Childs, 2006, for
further information). Pitkin illustrates how it may not be necessary for our
elected representatives to be a precise mirror image of ourselves but rather
that they represent our opinions and interests. Alongside various other cat-
egories, she clearly differentiates between 'descriptive' and 'substantive'
representation, descriptive being where the representatives resemble those
whom they represent and substantive being where the representatives act on
behalf of the represented. Applied to the contemporary political scenario, the
argument here is that it is not necessary for our representatives to be a precise
mirror-image or microcosm of society at large in order for them to represent
their constituents. Taking this to extremes, if society is composed of approximately 15 per cent left-handed people, for example, it would not be necessary
for the representative institutions to comprise 15 per cent left-handers! It
would be unfair, however, if the interests of left-handed people were continu-
ally ignored or sidelined. It is, therefore, necessary to ensure that the interests
of certain groups are not ignored by a potentially dominant elite.

The argument in relation to political representation is essentially that
people dislike politics and politicians because they perceive them as 'other'.
This is to say that they do not believe they are like themselves. Examination
of the socio-economic backgrounds of Members of Parliament appears to perpetuate this viewpoint. Members of Parliament continue to be predominantly
'white, male, middle aged and middle class' and are, therefore, unrepresentative of society at large. There is a tendency, particularly at the higher echelons,
for them to be Oxbridge-educated and for there to be relatively few women

and members of the British Minority Ethnic classification. As Hackett and Hunter's research into the socio-economic backgrounds of Members of Parliament elected in 2010 reveals,

> Parliament today better reflects the gender balance and is more ethnically diverse, but in terms of educational and vocational background the new political elite look remarkably like the old establishment. It is surprising how many of our MPs were privately educated, went to Oxbridge and worked in the professions, particularly Conservatives and Lib Dems. It seems that our Parliament is becoming less representative in terms of education and occupation, and continues to attract similar types of people from a rather narrow professional base.

(2010: 2)

In terms of educational background, for example,

> A remarkable 34% of MPs went to fee paying private schools (compared with a national average of around 7%). Around 54% of Conservative MPs; 41% Lib Dems; and 12% Labour MPs went to fee paying schools. 20 MPs (19 Conservative and 1 Lib Dem) went to Eton (6% of all Conservative MPs).

(2010: 3)

The Conservative MP Nadine Dorries famously labelled David Cameron and George Osborne '. . . arrogant posh boys' (see http://www.bbc.co.uk/news/uk-politics-17815769) and it appears that her analysis of her contemporaries in the Conservative Party, certainly in terms of the second descriptor if not the first, is not too far out! The average age of a Member of Parliament remains relatively static at 50 years of age – it might be worthwhile contemplating whether 50-year-olds can truly represent the views and wishes of an 18-year-old, for example. Likewise, although the number of female members of Parliament has risen to its largest ever figure of 22.6 per cent, this begs the question of whether women's views and opinions are being overlooked. The same observation could be levied at the fact that only 4.1 per cent of MPs come from non-white backgrounds. In terms of occupation, only 4 per cent of MPs had a manual occupation, compared to 19 per cent with a background in business and 24 per cent whose background is categorised as 'politics'. The rise of the career politician might also be a factor that alienates the general population. Having no experience of life outside of politics, there may be a perception that such politicos are 'cocooned' from the real world.

Fame is everything

The rise of the concept of celebrity, as mentioned earlier, may also have perpetuated the notion that politics is boring. As mentioned earlier, there is a focus within society upon fame and being in the public eye. Think of politicians from previous eras, Jo Grimond, Enoch Powell and George Brown, for example, and there was not the same emphasis upon looks and how they were conveyed in the media. Nobody, least of all the politicians themselves, really bothered about how they were portrayed in the media. The emphasis was upon what they had to say and their policy proposals. Fuelled by the omnipresent and all-enveloping media coverage, politicians have to look the part as well as being able to convey their message. Michael Foot was castigated in certain sectors of the press because of his so-called 'Worzel Gummidge' appearance and politicians have learnt that to be successful, they must project a particular image. Neil Kinnock was captured on camera falling over on the beach, subjected to ridicule and possibly ruined a photo-opportunity. Boris Johnson is a good example of a contemporary politician who cultivates a particular image and has been able to use the media to his advantage.

E-petitions – eroding the power of Parliament?

One more recent innovation which *may* impact negatively upon perceptions of traditional politics is the e-petition. People can now submit an e-petition and, provided that it receives enough signatures (100,000), it may gain Parliamentary time and, thereby, possibly achieve its aims. Some see this example of direct democracy (albeit with a gatekeeper dimension, i.e. the minimum number of signatures and Parliament still being able to veto a debate) as returning power to the people, others see it as circumnavigating or short-circuiting the power of Parliament. They permit the public to participate in politics in a way that does not require a great deal of effort on behalf of the individual citizen. A halfway house is to view this as a tandem approach whereby the role of the Member of Parliament is still crucial in representing the views of their constituents but e-petitions provide a useful device for the ordinary person to engage with politics. Petitions have a long history in relation to Parliamentary politics (*cf.* those in relation to the abolition of slavery or votes for women) but it is still early days in respect of e-petitions. The

epetitions.direct.gov.uk site was launched in August 2011. Will they reinvig-
orate politics or are they frivolous and easily ignored? It remains to be seen.
As the Hansard Society states, '. . . the public is generally more likely to sign
a petition than they are to engage in most other forms of democratic activity
apart from voting' (2012: 5). If they capture the 'mood' of the people they
may be a powerful tool (such as one in relation to the 1989 Hillsborough
Disaster) but, as with the one arguing that left-handers are a persecuted minority, which only gained forty-four signatures (see http://news.bbc.co.uk/1/hi/
magazine/6943871.stm), they may reveal that apathy continues to rule!

Conclusion

There may be many reasons why people dislike politics. A few of these have
been highlighted within this chapter. It could be that a more extensive and
wide-reaching programme of political education, such as through citizenship
education, especially of the type envisaged by the late Professor Bernard
Crick, might rectify this situation. It could also be the case that strategies such
as making voting compulsory might encourage people to take more of an
interest in politics. It is the law that people have to ensure they are on the
electoral register and perhaps now it is timely for the law to be amended so
that compulsory voting is introduced. Coercion is not to be used lightly but
relatively low levels of turnout mean that questions continue to be asked as to
how low is too low. Extreme measures might be used; one suggestion mooted
is that if young people are not voting, for example, perhaps they should be
debarred from being able to take a driving test. Rather draconian perhaps but
illustrating a clear linkage between rights and responsibilities and illustrating
that people need to participate in societal norms, in structures, in order to be
able to reap the benefits, thereby linking voting to benefits and rewards. This
chapter has focused primarily upon the national level, upon Westminster
politics, but it is fair to say that similar arguments apply at other levels of
governance, local, devolved and European levels. The perceptions of politics
outlined above emerge in relation to differing tiers of governance too; examination of levels of turnout, for example, in these elections would support this
thesis. Elected representatives at all levels struggle to gain support.

This negativity and apathy is almost like a contagion. Colin Hay captures
the negativity associated with politics when he states,

'Politics' is a dirty word, a term that has come to acquire a whole array
of almost entirely negative associations and connotations in contem-

porary discourse. Politics is synonymous with sleaze, corruption and duplicity, greed, self-interest and self-importance, interference, inefficiency and intransigence.

(2007: 153)

As Gerry Stoker emphasises,

Politics matters because it, too, is an ingredient in what is needed for a good life. It is about recognizing that those affected by a decision have a right to a say about it and that in a complex world where our lives overlap and intersect with so many others we need to find ways to communicate, to agree to disagree and to cooperate.

(2006: 206)

People would do well to remember this fact. The centrality and importance of politics to people's lives can sometimes be lost. Politics is often seen as unexciting, unrepresentative and populated by self-serving politicians who are in it for the money, kudos and power. Turning our attention to the next chapter, Chapter Five, it is pertinent to examine this concept of power in greater depth. Those of us who are enamoured by politics will hopefully have our faith restored!

Chapter bibliography

Almond, G., and Verba, S. (1963) *The Civic Culture*, Princeton, Princeton University Press.

Burke, E. (1854) *The Works of the Right Honourable Edmund Burke*, 6 vols, London, Henry G. Bohn, 1854–56, Works 1: 446–448.

Childs, S. (2006) 'The complicated relationship between sex, gender and the substantive representative of women', *European Journal of Women's Studies*, Vol. 13, No. 1: 7–21.

Grant, W. (2004) 'Pressure politics: the changing world of pressure groups', *Parliamentary Affairs*, Vol. 57, No. 2: 408–419.

——(2005) 'Pressure politics: a politics of collective consumption?', *Parliamentary Affairs*, Vol. 58, No. 2: 366–379.

Hackett, P. and Hunter, P. (2010) *Who Governs Britain? A Profile of MPs in the New Parliament*, London, The Smith Institute.

Hansard Society (2012) *What Next for E-petitions?* London, Hansard Society.

——(2013) *Audit of Political Engagement 10*, London, Hansard Society.

Hay, C. (2007) *Why We Hate Politics*, Cambridge, Polity Press.

Pattie, C., Seyd, P. and Whiteley, P. (2004) *Citizenship in Britain,* Cambridge, Cambridge University Press.

Pitkin, H. F. (1967) *The Concept of Representation*, Los Angeles, California, University of California Press.

Stoker, G. (2006) *Why Politics Matters: Making Democracy Work*, Basingstoke, Palgrave Macmillan.

——(2009?) *Antipolitics in Britain: Dimensions, Causes, and Responses*, at http://www.idi.org.il/media/1429259/ByThePeople_STOKER.pdf, accessed 12 May 2013.

——(2011) 'Anti-politics in Britain', in Heffernan, R., Cowley, P. and Hay, C. (eds), *Developments in British Politics Nine*, Basingstoke, Palgrave Macmillan: 152–173.

Stoker, G., Hay, C., Fox, R. and Williamson, A. (2012) 'Anti-politics: characterising and accounting for political disaffection', *ESRC End of Award Report*, RES-000-22-4441, Swindon, Economic and Social Research Council.

Websites

http://news.bbc.co.uk/1/hi/magazine/6943871.stm, accessed 10 May 2013.

http://www.bbc.co.uk/news/uk-14432401 for more information about fracking, accessed 10 July 2013.

http://www.bbc.co.uk/news/uk-politics-17815769, accessed 10 May 2013.

5

Policy makers and power brokers

This chapter investigates the contested concept of power and analyses where power lies in the policy making process. The policy making process is highlighted and explained. Differing models of policy making are depicted before analysing varying types of power – economic, financial, bureaucratic, etc. Students of politics need to know about how policies are made and debates centring on the locus of power. Differing ideological perspectives, concepts of left and right, will also be highlighted in this chapter.

What is policy?

It is necessary to determine what is meant by policy. Policy, as with most political concepts, can be interpreted in differing ways. To simplify matters, Andrew Heywood states that in '. . . crude terms, policy consists of the "outputs" of the political process' (2007: 425). Primarily, however, policy can be seen as rules and regulations or it can be seen as financial resources and how they are spent. As Michael Hill (2005: 7) illustrates, there are many differing interpretations of the term 'policy'. He cites a former top civil servant, Cunningham, who rather tellingly stated that policy is '. . . rather like the elephant – you recognise it when you see it but cannot easily define it' (Cunningham, 1963: 229 cited in Hill, 2005: 7). This may explain the difficulties involved in trying to define policy but it does not advance the quest a great deal. Hill quotes other attempts to narrow down the term but he himself is probably closer to a definition when he states that policy '. . . may sometimes be identifiable in terms of a decision, but very often it involves either groups of decisions or what may be seen as little more than an orientation' (Hill, 2005: 7). He proceeds to state, that given the multitude of differing definitions of policy this might '. . . imply that it is hard to identify particular occasions when policy is made' (*Ibid.*). Hill highlights how the various interpretations make reference to a 'web of decisions' (Easton, 1953: 130 cited in *Ibid.*) and 'interrelated decisions' (Jenkins, 1978: 15 cited in *Ibid.*). Implicit in all of these analyses is the notion that policy is a complex process of links and connections. A great deal of policy is concerned with policy succession or policy termination (*cf.*: Hogwood and Peters, 1983, and Hogwood and Gunn, 1984), with determining how to end a policy or, at least, how to adapt it. Policy can also involve non-decision-making. This might be, for example, ensuring that issues are kept off the political agenda completely or that, where they are raised, they are quickly sidelined (*cf.* Heclo, 1972). It is worthwhile assessing what contributes to the complexity of this process. One concept that most certainly does complicate the situation is the concept of power, to which attention now turns.

Power – what is it? Where does it lie?

Politics inevitably involves the contested concept of power. It is interesting to think about how much power and control the ordinary person ought to have over the policy making process. The concept of power is difficult to determine accurately. This is particularly evident when examination is made of the policy making process and looking at how policies are made, who has most success in getting their policy areas on to the political agenda and which policies are more likely to be successful. It is worthwhile assessing exactly what is meant by the concept of power. This is a key concept as far as politics is concerned. Essentially, power entails the ability to do something or to get someone to do something that they might otherwise not do. As Jones states about power, in '. . . essence this means the ability to get someone else to do what they otherwise would not have done' (Jones, 2014: 7). Power needs to be differentiated from related concepts such as authority and influence. Authority involves the power or the right to control or to judge or to prohibit the actions of others; the implication here is that those who have this power have the right to do something. Often it can be a particular position or role that permits someone to have authority over others, for example the holder of a particular political office or particular role such a being a member of the police force. Authority is, according to Jones and Norton (2014: 8), '. . .

power with the crucial added ingredient of legitimacy'. Influence is the effect of one person or thing on another; this influence or ability to have power or sway might emanate from inherent abilities or characteristics that a person possesses, it might be due to their personal wealth or their position. Influence occurs without the use of overt or tacit threats (*cf.*: Cairney, 2012b: 49). At this juncture, therefore, it is necessary to highlight that there are different types of power such as economic power, political power and bureaucratic power. Economic power is relatively straightforward, the notion that money or financial clout equates with power. Someone such as, say, Richard Branson may have relatively little political power but may have significant economic power due to the huge personal fortune that he has amassed. It is debatable the extent to which that personal fortune might be used to garner political power, although, in some instances, the two are synonymous. History is populated with wealthy individuals who have also had a significant amount of political power. Having said this, would winning the lottery tomorrow mean that you would necessarily be more powerful than you are today? It may make life and personal circumstances more comfortable and mean that you have the ability to make more decisions *vis-à-vis* personal choices but does it necessarily mean you are more powerful?

Political power, as stated, is not necessarily the same as economic power. The policy makers in society are able to make decisions, to reiterate Lasswell's definition of politics, in terms of 'who gets what when and how' (see Chapter Two). They are the ones able to make the difficult decisions concerning the allocation of scare resources and, as such, are in a powerful position. Often, by virtue of having won an election, they are placed in a powerful political position. Others have to appeal to these power-brokers if they are to have their needs met. There are all sorts of factors that impact upon the extent of that political power. Victory in an election may not count for a great deal if the result is a minority government or a government with a small majority. A huge majority, such as the 179 that Tony Blair enjoyed when the Labour Party was re-elected to office after eighteen years in opposition, meant that the Labour Party was in a strong position, being able to railroad through virtually any policies that they desired. The power of the ballot box should not be underestimated but even here there are limits and constraints upon the power of politicians. The checks and balances of the political system serve to rein in unbridled power. Public opinion, expressed through channels such as the media and via pressure groups, can also serve to limit governmental power or the power of the political classes *per se*.

Bureaucratic power is often associated with the administration or the civil service. These people are permanent and amass a significant amount of expertise. As will be analysed in Chapter Six, their permanency and expertise mean they can often outwit and, possibly, manipulate an inexperienced minister. They are in possession of the 'facts', as they see them, and have a wealth of information at their fingertips. The power of the bureaucrat is often associated with so-called 'red tape' and the focus upon a rule-driven approach. Often inflexible, bureaucratic power can come up against direct opposition from political power. Ministers are the elected politicos and, therefore, are the final decision-makers but the power of the permanent civil servants should not be underestimated. It can be seen how the theoretical power of ministers might be usurped in practice by the actual power of the bureaucrats.

The old adage 'knowledge is power' is also true. Those in possession of certain knowledge or information are able to use that knowledge to their own ends. They can also withhold that knowledge and that, likewise, can be an important weapon to wield. It is often said, for example, that the National Health Service could not have been set up without the support of doctors and the nursing profession. They possessed the medical knowledge and, therefore, were in a powerful position. Pressure groups, similarly, have a certain amount of power when they are the experts in a particular field or area. Governments often look to pressure groups to supply them with answers to particular questions or to provide detailed statistical data analysis as to the likely outcome should a particular policy change be enacted. Environmental groups, for example, might supply information in relation to the possible consequences if 'fracking' is to be pursued in earnest. Medical pressure groups might highlight the dangers of the growing levels of obesity in society and provide quantitative data to buttress their arguments. Granted, there are 'lies, damned lies and statistics' but facts and figures, although open to interpretation, do lend weight to political arguments.

Charismatic power is another concept worthy of investigation. There are certain individuals who are said to possess power and authority as a result of particular personal qualities or attributes that they possess. If asked to name charismatic leaders, for example, key names are often cited such as Margaret Thatcher, Arthur Scargill and Boris Johnson, to name but a few. Strange bedfellows indeed but what they have/had in common is the ability to sway or lead people. Popular culture might lead us to dub them 'Marmite' characters in that they tend to be people who are either loved or hated in equal measure. They are certainly not mediocre people. The concept of charisma has been analysed by many political scientists. What is it that makes an individual exude charisma? It is difficult to pinpoint and to define accurately. A rousing speech and great oratory skills, delivered with a passion and a sense of conviction and self-belief, play a part in the ability to mobilise and garner support. In addition, a sense of confidence that one's direction and approach are the correct route also aids the charismatic leader. Margaret Thatcher, for example, was dubbed a 'conviction politician', full of self-belief. 'The Lady's not for turning. You turn if you want to' was a famous jibe in the direction of her predecessor, Edward Heath, for performing his infamous policy u-turns but it also illustrates her determination to pursue a particular path. It is worth noting that many people who did not share Margaret Thatcher's political beliefs often admired her for her strength of conviction. On the opposite side of the political divide, Arthur Scargill was equally convinced that he was correct and was able to rouse his followers in an almost evangelical fashion. The Mayor of London, Boris Johnson, although possibly less overtly charismatic in the same manner as Thatcher and Scargill, also has a huge personal following and can certainly be credited with being in possession of particular personal skills and attributes. Critics sometimes bemoan the lack of charismatic leaders at the moment. The leaders of the three main political parties, David Cameron, Nick Clegg and Ed Miliband, have all been criticised for being relatively lacklustre as far as charisma is concerned. It is difficult to pinpoint accurately exactly what constitutes charisma. Difficult to define, it is possibly summed up by that old adage you recognise it when you see it. As the French might say, the possessor exudes a certain '*je ne sais quoi*'. This hardly helps to define charismatic leadership. Oratory skills are presumably part of the package. Certainly, charismatic leaders of the past have been able to deliver a powerful and rousing speech, to encourage the masses to support and follow them and their cause. David Lloyd George was a master of the art of public speaking, for example. The ability to talk to the masses is a relatively rare skill. Speaking in public is a popular phobia. The art of talking in public and being able to garner support and followers through doing so is a relatively elusive talent. More contemporary politicians need to be adept at media manipulation. They have to be able to reach out to people in their own homes via the television and radio and, more recently, possibly also to connect with people through social media such as Facebook™ and Twitter™. Talking directly to people in their homes was a skill that the inter-war prime minister, Stanley Baldwin, honed to perfection so it is not a new phenomenon. It is said that people felt that he was talking directly to them on a one-to-one basis so he was able to connect with the electorate through his so-called 'fireside chats'. Nowadays, politicians often try to do this via appearing on television programmes such as ITV's *This Morning* or the BBC's *The One Show*. These are not overtly political programmes and, therefore, it could be that it makes politicians appear less remote and more like the ordinary person in the street. Some politicians find this approach of talking directly to people a hard skill to master, perhaps coming across as insincere or smarmy. Talking directly to the electorate via a camera is a talent in itself. Other qualities that constitute charismatic leadership might be more ethereal, more intangible and difficult to quantify, almost an inner quality that the person exudes, making others listen to what they have to say and want to remain within their ambit.

In terms of where power lies in the policy making process, it is generally held that power tends to be concentrated in the hands of a relative few. The ability to effect change is an important tool. Granted, we live in a democracy but in terms of who has the ability to change policy, this is a talent afforded to the relative few. Representatives are elected to act on behalf of the people, the essence of representative democracy. The mass of the population, therefore, watches from the sidelines. Within the ranks of the elected representatives, those in possession of real power are in the minority. Compared with the total number of Members of Parliament, those in the government are in the minority. Furthermore, within the government, the cabinet concentrates the power base even more, with the prime minister seen as *primus inter pares* or first among equals. Debate continues to rage over questions of cabinet versus prime ministerial government and opinion is divided. New technology may serve to expand the possibilities for political participation amongst the population at large but whether this will translate into genuine power remains to be seen. The e-petition system, for example, whilst facilitating public participation in the form of an electronic plebiscite remains subject to oversight by gatekeepers, first of all in terms of ensuring that the 100,000 signature threshold is surpassed and then secondly in determining whether the topic is worthy of Parliamentary debate.

Given that power is often regarded as residing in the hands of a small minority, it is worth questioning whether or not elitism is an accurate reflection of where power lies in society today. Jeremy Paxman alluded to the notion of *Friends in High Places* (1991), as stated in his eponymous text, in that due to kinship networks and inter-marriage, etc., he claims that a relatively small number of people are in possession of real power. Is it the case, therefore, that there might be social mobility to an extent but, generally speaking, it would be difficult for most people to rise up from the lower echelons and possess power? The idea of a meritocracy is perhaps something that politicians highlight but the reality is probably far removed from this nirvana. The expansion of higher education is one factor that has led to a degree of social mobility over the past forty or fifty years but is this just a veneer that belies the fact that for most people their position in life is fixed at birth?

Policy making process – what is it, how are policies made?

The policy making process is complex and subject to differing interpretations. The policy making process is epitomised by a multiplicity of political actors. There are many differing models that are used to explain how policy making takes place. These include pluralism, corporatism, the Whitehall model, the ruling class model, the incremental model and the rational model of policy making (*cf.* Jones, 2014: 466–467). Pluralism, primarily based around the work of Robert Dahl, argues that policy emerges as a result of interaction between a multiplicity of groups. The ruling class model believes policy emanates from an elite group, a dominant social class who rule in their own interests. Corporatism sees policy as emerging from the government, big business and the trade union movement; under this model interest groups become enmeshed in the machinery of government. The Whitehall model emphasises the power of bureaucrats in the policy making process; essentially the argument here is not just that civil servants are on tap but that they are often on top. The incremental model of policy making is based upon the work of Charles E. Lindblom, whose seminal thesis was published in an article entitled 'The Science of "Muddling Through"' in 1959. Lindblom puts forward the hypothesis that policy making takes place on a step-by-step or incremental basis. The crux of Lindblom's hypothesis is that policy making evolves over time, in a series of (comparatively) small changes or increments (in the same way as people paid a salary often receive an annual increment, or increase, on their salary). In this way, change does occur but it may be less perceptible and, therefore, possibly more likely to be accepted by those affected by the policy. Contrast this model with the rational model of policy making. The rational model of policy making is largely associated with the work of the American political scientist, Herbert Simon. His model of rational decision making sees policy making as involving selection of the perceived best policy from a range of options. This is where the process occurs almost in one fell swoop, where change is, to a certain extent, imposed from above and can be very different from what has gone before. It is a fair assessment to say that most policy making occurs in an incremental manner. The step-by-step approach is how most policies come into being. In one sense, this is a safety net or mechanism for ensuring that relatively few policy errors come to fruition. Small, incremental changes are easier to rectify should a problem come to light. It might be easier to amend a small change as opposed to trying to turn back the tide when huge sweeping changes look likely to prove disastrous. As Peter Dorey highlights, incrementalism involves '. . . piecemeal and reactive adjustments to existing policy, with an emphasis on minimal change and maximum continuity' (2005: 44).

Having stated that incrementalism is the norm, this is not to say that there has not been huge sweeping change on occasions. A classic example of a policy that is said to embody a huge change, very different from previous policies, is the poll tax or, to use its 'proper' name, the community charge. The poll tax was introduced by Margaret Thatcher's Conservative Government. It was introduced in Scotland on 1 April 1989 and then a year later it was introduced into England and Wales. It was intended to replace the former system of local government finance called the rates. The rates, a form of property tax, was a system of local taxation that had existed for more than four hundred years in various forms. The poll tax was essentially a tax on heads, i.e. the basic premise was that everyone over the age of 18 years of age would pay a set flat-rate tax that would be used to pay for local authority services. Many Conservatives, in particular, felt that this would be a fairer system of taxation in that more people would pay the community charge or poll tax and also there was a feeling that it would increase levels of local accountability. This is to say that with more people paying local taxation, more people would, in theory at least, want to know what their local councillors were doing. In part, this was a political decision too, with many Conservatives feeling that this would act as a brake upon the activities of many Labour-controlled local authorities. Certain sections of the press had dubbed Labour councils the 'loony left', an image that stuck in the minds of many people. It was felt that people-power would curb these left-wing councils. The reality, however, was slightly different. The roll-call for paying the poll tax was taken from the electoral register. A significant minority of people decided not to put their name down on the electoral register, thereby disappearing for poll tax purposes and effectively disenfranchising themselves in the process. The upshot was that significant numbers of people did not pay the poll tax. The tax suffered from numerous problems. These were many and varied but, just to highlight a few, married couples and cohabitees were jointly liable for paying each other's poll tax if the other one defaulted. Critics felt that the so-called 'party of the family', the Conservative Party, was essentially condoning a policy that might lead to marital and domestic disputes if one person was made to pay for the other's poll tax. The tax was costly to collect and administer. It cost twice as much to collect the poll tax as it did to collect the old rates. One of the key problems with the poll tax, however, was that many people felt that the reality was different to their initial understanding of the tax. Many felt that there were some grounds for praise if everyone would be paying the same amount; the phrase 'a duke would pay the same as a dustman' was often quoted. The reality, however, was that the actual amount payable varied from local authority to local authority and there were often huge differences in the amount paid. High spending councils, providing many services, tended to have high poll tax rates, whereas other councils, especially those not providing quite so many services, could charge a lower rate. Anomalies included one particular street where the two sides straddled local authority boundaries in London. Here existed a bizarre situation where people living in virtually identical houses were paying vastly different sums in poll tax.

Given all the problems and the fact that many within the Conservative Party's own ranks were vehemently opposed to the policies (culminating in resignations by local councillors, for example) it was only a matter of time before the policy was scrapped. In 1993, after a change of Party Leader, with John Major replacing Margaret Thatcher, the community charge was replaced by the council tax. Still in existence today, the council tax represents a return to a form of local taxation based upon property. The poll tax was, therefore, a relatively short-lived form of local taxation, its numerous problems and the amount of political opposition that it encountered meant that its days were numbered from the outset. In terms of the policy making process, however, and sparking the interest of policy analysts, the poll tax is, as stated, a classic example of a policy failure. Its introduction represented a rational approach to policy making in that it was imposed from above and represented a policy that was very different from what had gone before. This is not to say that rational policy making is always doomed to failure but certainly, in this case, the decision makers got it wrong. They underestimated the amount of political opposition that would be encountered and they lost the moral high ground. Many people were galvanised into political protest as a result of this policy, quite often people, such as members of the clergy, for example, who had never before been involved in political protest. The fact that it was relatively short-lived indicates the strength of opposition. It can be argued that there is no such notion as a popular tax and the rates would fit into this category too. There had been many critics of the old rating system. In Scotland, for example, there had been lots of vocal opposition and criticism of the rating system in the 1980s whereby they had often witnessed huge increases in rates. Hence, this in part explains the decision for the community charge to be introduced in

Scotland a year earlier than in England and Wales. With the benefit of hindsight measures to offset the negative aspects of the rates might have been a better policy approach as opposed to bringing in an entirely new, and as some saw it unfair, system, very different from what had gone before. It can be seen that politicians who wish to bring in swift change do so at their peril.

Rationalism is, as outlined above, '. . . whereby policy makers consider more carefully and explicitly their policy goals, and various ways in which these might be best achieved' (Dorey, 2005: 44). Herbert Simon (1957), as stated, is generally regarded as having founded the rational model of policy making. Dorey highlights this move towards greater emphasis upon evidence-based policy making. Rational approaches to decision making involve an assessment of the problem, weighing up all the information and analysing the pros and cons. Different solutions to the policy problem are ranked in order of preference. A conscious choice is then made as to which is the best route to take, i.e. after weighing up all the evidence that is likely to achieve the desired outcome. Rationalism has been criticised for being better able to describe a theoretical process as opposed to how policies are actually made in reality. In addition, ideology often plays a key role in the policy making process and the rational approach to decision making does not fully account for this. As Bill Jones states, 'This approach assumes that decision makers behave in a logical, sequential fashion [that] they will identify their objectives, formulate possible strategies, think through their implications and finally choose the course of action that on balance best achieves their objectives' (Jones, 2014: 467). Alternatives to incrementalism and to rationalism have also been expounded (cf. the work of Dror, 1964, and Etzioni, 1967). Mixed-scanning, for example, is a middle route associated with the work of Etzioni. Under this interpretation, there are big or fundamental decisions and then smaller or less important decisions. The approach taken depends upon the categorisation. As Cairney highlights, Etzioni's mixed-scanning approach '. . . draws on the analogy of weather satellites to recommend a combination of broad scanning of the overall terrain and "zeroing in" on particular areas worthy of more research' (Cairney, 2012b: 102). The essential point to note in terms of analysing how policy is made, therefore, is that there are many models used to explain the process and also that theory and practice are often very different.

Models of policy making

Andrew Heywood states that '. . . during the 1960s and 1970s a distinctive area of study, policy analysis, was developed. This set out to examine how policy was initiated, formulated and implemented, and how the policy process could be improved' (*Op. cit*: 425). As Heywood so rightly points out, policy is said to occur in three main stages. These are the policy *initiation* stage, the policy *formulation* stage and the policy *implementation* stage. The policy initiation stage is where there is the germ of an idea and actors in the process are beginning to think about getting the issue on to the political agenda. Policies are clearly the result of many different interested groups and people but they primarily emanate from the political parties. The key players involved in the policy making process primarily are the politicians. A function of political parties is to devise policies. They are in the business of wanting to bring about change (in their view for the better). Party manifestoes are clearly one way in which they present their policy proposals and ideas to the public at large. As well as emanating from the parties, policies might also emerge from the media. Newspapers and television programmes are able to spotlight an issue and get publicity for a particular topic or cause. Even documentary and drama programmes have the potential to highlight an issue. The 1960s television programme entitled *Cathy Come Home*, for example, highlighted the plight of homelessness and helped to ensure that the topic made it on to the political agenda. Newspapers have campaigned on particular issues, such as, for example, the *Sun* and the *News of the World* newspapers campaigning for the public to be made aware when known paedophiles were living in their immediate vicinity, leading to the introduction, in 2011, of the so-called Sarah's Law (named after eight year old Sarah Payne, murdered by a convicted paedophile in 2000). A further example of a newspaper campaigning on a specific issue and impacting upon policy is *The Daily Telegraph* pursuing the issue of MPs' expenses in 2009 and illuminating the blatant abuse of the system. Outcomes included an independent audit being set up in 2009 chaired by former civil servant Sir Thomas Legg, which published its findings in October of that year. There was also the setting up of the Independent Parliamentary Standards Authority (IPSA), created by the Parliamentary Standards Act 2009. In 2010, it was given responsibility for setting MPs' salaries under the provisions of the Constitutional Reform and Governance Act 2010. A third example of a newspaper helping to shape policy is *The Guardian* newspaper and the 2011 phone hacking scandal. This is where the phones of public figures were hacked. The subsequent outcry led to the Leveson Inquiry, a public inquiry headed by Lord Justice Leveson. One of the key outcomes here impacting on policy was the fact that the Leveson Report, published in November 2012, recommended an independent press regulatory body, thereby replacing the existing Press Complaints Commission. Likewise, pressure groups that often focus upon a specific cause or sector of society are able to galvanise support for their campaigns and issues. Motoring organisations, for example, are able to concentrate their efforts on policies aimed at ameliorating the lives of motorists. Environmental groups self-evidently favour policies that protect our natural surroundings. The public at large, provided they are able to galvanise enough supporters, are also potentially able to initiate policies. Petitions have long been a way for the public to try to initiate policy change, albeit rather difficult to bring to fruition without the support of power brokers in the long term. The petition to extend the franchise to women, presented to Parliament by the Liberal politician John Stuart Mill in the 1860s, being a case in point. A more contemporary manifestation of the petition, the e-petition, as mentioned in Chapter Four, has the potential to initiate policy provided that it attracts at least 100,000 supporters. Passing this numerical threshold hold means that it may then gain time to be debated in Parliament – although this is not guaranteed. Petitions and e-petitions alike at least let politicians know that there is strong public feeling and sentiment on any given issue.

Policy formulation is the next key stage in the policy making process. This is clearly after the germination stage and is where the details of the policy are thrashed out before the policy is put into practice. This is a crucial stage in the process as it is vital that all possible consequences and outcomes are considered. Some outcomes are more obvious than others. It is important to try to avoid any unintended consequences. Policies have to be practicable, they have to be workable. All interested parties and experts in the field need to be able to present their case to the policy makers and to put their side of the argument/divide. Civil servants tease out the finer points of the policy and work out the practical implications.

The final stage in this tripartite approach to policy making is the policy implementation stage. Evidently, this is where the policy idea becomes a reality and is put into practice. Real change occurs at this stage. This is where politicians, in particular, can see the fruits of their labour. The Conservative Party policy regarding the sale of council houses, for example, enacted under the provisions of the 1980 Housing Act, effected real change in terms of home ownership. This was a flagship Conservative policy but it was to prove particularly attractive to many previous Labour supporters. These were people who were enticed by the prospect of being able to buy their own council house, homes that had previously only been available to rent. The added bonus was that often this was at a price that was greatly reduced due to the government subsidy. Advocates of the policy pointed out that many of these council house purchasers could rightly claim that they had already bought their properties if the rent was taken into consideration, i.e. arguing that morally the property was already theirs. Critics of the policy were vehemently opposed to selling off the nation's assets, especially when the dwindling housing stock was not being replaced by affordable homes to rent. For these people, the policy permitted politicians to benefit from people's self-interest.

Policy implementation is a vital stage in the process and it is often said that this is where problems occur. This is where so-called 'street-level bureaucrats' (*cf.* Lipsky, 1980) can have an effect too. These people are at the sharp end of policy making and probably recognise more than most that there is a finite amount of resources available and so difficult choices have to be made. Lipsky emphasises the discretionary powers at their disposal (*Ibid.*: 161). They are at the sharp end of policy and have to use their personal judgement – despite the existence of rules and 'red tape'. 'Stickiness' often occurs at the policy implementation stage. An ill-thought-out policy, possibly rushed through for political gain, can fail at this point. This is where it directly impacts upon people's lives. People feel the effects of the policy. For example, the policy to extend the licensing hours, leading, some say, to a 24-hour drinking culture, especially at weekends, impacted on people at the implementation stage. Critics say that it led to higher levels of alcohol abuse, binge drinking and the closure of many public houses, which struggled to compete in an increasingly competitive market. It can sometimes be difficult to establish a direct causal link but, nonetheless, there will be those who will make a case that 'x' happens as a direct result of 'y' policy.

Policy transfer

Another phenomenon in relation to the policy making process is the notion of policy transfer. This is usually where policies, for want of a better term, 'border hop'. States look to others, learn lessons that may lead to blatant copying. It is said, for example, that many policies in relation to maternity benefits and maternity provision result from states looking at and learning from their neighbours. Policies have crossed the Atlantic. Blair's 'welfare to work' approach was said to have been directly poached from the United States. Perhaps policy transfer is a positive in that politicians ought to look to where a policy has been trialled and where it appears to be working well. Copying might mean that fewer mistakes or policy failures occur if other governments have acted in the role of guinea pigs. Having said this, surely to be a trail-blazer with a policy that works is the goal of every policy maker. Plagiarised policies, although tried and tested, mean that others got there before you.

Michael Hill (2005: 246) cites many examples of policy transfer, including privatisation policies, new public management techniques being applied to the public sector, anti-money laundering policies, national environmental strategies, adoption of central banks, tobacco control, electoral systems (*cf.*: Hill, 2005, chapter twelve for more detail on policy transfer). Hill writes on the topic of policy transfer stating,

> Not only do national policy makers look around at what is occurring elsewhere when they design their own policy, but it is also the case that there are a number of international organisations that are explicitly in the business of offering policy prescriptions – notably the various United Nations agencies, the World Bank and the Organisation for Economic Co-operation and Development.
>
> (Hill, 2005: 88)

Part of the issue is, as Hill points out, to ascertain '. . . how decisions are made to accept or reject ideas from elsewhere . . . [and] circumstances in which policy transfer is or is not facilitated' (*Ibid.*: 89). Likewise, Paul Cairney writes, '. . . the study of transfer gives us the ability to explain not only why policy changes, but also the extent to which that change is common throughout the world' (Cairney, 2012b: 16). He continues,

> In some cases, transfer follows learning, when the knowledge of one system is used to inform policy in another. However, the transfer of ideas or policy programmes is also about power and the ability of some countries to oblige or encourage others to follow their lead.
>
> (*Ibid.*: 20)

This is an interesting point that Cairney makes as to whether the policy transfer has occurred voluntarily or whether the country taking on board the policy feels obliged or coerced into doing so. According to Peter Dorey, the '. . . actual phenomenon of looking abroad for policy ideas is not in itself new or novel, although the practice does seem to have become more extensive and explicit since the late 1980s' (2005: 40). Dorey examines three specific areas of policy transfer, namely, the setting up of the Child Support Agency (CSA), the introduction of welfare to work policies and the use of so-called Zero

Tolerance in response to inner-city crime and youth offending (*Ibid.*). All three policy areas were imported from examples overseas. An interesting point to note, however, is that policy makers do not necessarily need to visit their overseas counterparts to gain an insight into their policy areas given the extent to which interns, advisors and officials often work overseas. Dorey highlights how, during Tony Blair's second term of office, '. . . the Strategy Unit included officials from governments in Australia, Canada, France, Germany and the USA' (*Ibid.*: 44). Clearly, the twenty-first century world is shrinking in size!

Policy networks

A more recent phenomenon, as far as analysis of the policy making process is concerned, is a focus upon the concept of policy networks (*cf.*: the work of Rod Rhodes). This is where there are groups of people with related interests who are all involved in the creation of a specific policy. As Paul Cairney states, policy networks are where policy makers in government '. . . come together with other public and private sector actors to negotiate and make shared decisions' (2012b: 157). According to Cairney, '. . . much public policy is conducted primarily through policy networks which process "technical" issues at a level of government not particularly visible to the public, often with minimal policymaker or senior civil service involvement' (2012b: 12). He proceeds to state that participants '. . . tend to be specialists and we find in many fields that relationships develop between those who deliver policy and those who seek to influence it' (*Ibid.*). Cairney posits that there has been a shift from these policy networks taking place out of the spotlight to '. . . a more competitive and complex political system, containing a much larger number of groups, experts and other policy participants, which makes it much more difficult for policy issues to be insulated from attention and for groups to restrict debate' (*Ibid.*). Add to this the impact of the European Union on policy and also the fact that devolution has taken place and the scenario is even more complicated. Peter Dorey states that the

> . . . policy networks approach suggested a continuum which drew attention to the existence of two sharply contrasting types of relationship between organized interests and policymakers in a particular policy subsystem, ranging from policy communities at one end, and issue networks at the other.

> (2005: 132)

Policy communities have limited membership and are usually centred around a government department and its close contacts; as Dorey states, '. . . based on close and closed relations and interactions between policy makers and organized interests' (*Ibid.*: 149). An example of a policy community is the health policy community (*Ibid.*: 138). Issue networks, on the other hand, are the exact opposite. These usually have '. . . a relatively large and diverse membership, with a plethora of organized (sometimes loosely organized) interests and several government departments, reflecting the diverse or multifaceted nature of the policy issue involved' (*Ibid.*). Dorey (*Ibid.*: 153) cites the 'poverty lobby' with its multiplicity of players as an example of an issue network. These networks might include the political parties outside of Parliament and also specific organisations such as think tanks, such as the Institute for Fiscal Studies or Demos, who provide the power brokers with information and detailed analysis of possible policy consequences. On specific issues, these think tanks can hold considerable sway. They contain the expertise and have often conducted detailed research projects that help the politicians in the decision making process. The notion of a network is the central theme here. The fact that policy emanates from a process involving many different groups who each have a stake in the procedure is an important one. Partnerships, bargaining and trade-offs also feature in this approach.

Ideological perspectives – left and right

Political ideology plays a central part in the policy making process. There are differing interpretations of what is meant by ideology. It can be seen that ideology is often central to whether a policy comes to fruition or, indeed, even whether it gets on to the policy making agenda in the first instance. There is the power to include and be able to get issues on to the agenda but, correspondingly, there is also the power to exclude and keep issues off the political agenda and even from being debated at all. Ideology is a contested concept, subject to a myriad of differing interpretations. As mentioned in Chapter Three, one study cited twenty-seven different meanings of the concept. Politicians have often shied away from being associated with ideology. Margaret Thatcher did not like to be associated with ideology and yet who would deny the ideological underpinnings of Thatcherism. Bizarre that a politician so ill disposed to ideology would be one of the few politicians whose name is eponymous with a specific ideological approach. Some regard ideology as extremely limiting, a sort of ideological straitjacket limiting free will and critical thinking. Instead of assessing a potential policy on its merits, it is as if the ideology sets the parameters of the debate and the scope of the discussion. Ideology is important with respect to the policy making process as it has the potential to impact upon which policies are pursued and how they bring about social and political change. Different ideological perspectives are often regarded as being located on a left/right political continuum. The terminology of left and right is said to date from the time of the French Revolution. It refers to the physical location of the king's (Louis XVI) supporters within the National Assembly, with those loyal to him sitting to the right and his opponents, or those who favoured revolution, sitting to the left. The left–right dichotomy is often associated with social class cleavages, although nowadays some regard this as an outmoded analysis. Ideology can, however, help to provide us with a framework in relation to understanding differing policy perspectives, with, for example, those on the right of the political spectrum being more likely to favour free market, laissez-faire responses to policy problems and those on the left of that continuum being more predisposed to state intervention and welfare state-type solutions. Ideology, therefore, helps with categorising and generalising. It can provide us with a framework for analysis that helps with understanding the policy making process. As with most generalisations, however, there may be exceptions that prove the rule. There may be occasions when those regarded as being on the right of the political spectrum, for example, introduce a policy that might be considered more in tune with the views and beliefs of a left-wing political party and vice versa. The Blair Government, for example, was said to have become increasingly right-wing and moved away from Labour's traditional heartland by introducing policies designed to appeal beyond its core vote. Prior to coming to power in 1997, the decision to revise Clause Four of the Labour Party's Constitution in 1995 was part of that bid to capture and retain the support of voters who had previously not voted for the Labour Party. Likewise, although constrained by being part of the Coalition Government, the Liberal Democrats under Nick Clegg's leadership were widely criticised for supporting the increase in higher education tuition fees once they came to power. Ideology can provide guidance as to which policies will be pursued but it is not a guarantee. Policies are followed for numerous reasons, ideology being one factor amongst many. It appears that politics has moved from a focus upon ideology to a move towards populist policies. Critics might regard this as selling one's principles; others may see it in a more pragmatic light. Policy purity is no use perhaps if one remains in the political wilderness – as the Labour Party, in particular, knew only too well between 1979 and 1997. Likewise, the Conservative Party were forced to adapt, regroup and reassess during their time in opposition between 1997 and 2010.

Conclusion

It can be seen that the policy making process is complex and contains a multiplicity of political actors. Key participants in the process include the political parties and the politicians. The power brokers include the government, cabinet and prime minister and the parties in Parliament. Beyond this, there are many other actors involved, to a greater or lesser degree, in the policy making process. These include pressure groups, the media and the public at large. Differing models are used by policy analysts in an attempt to describe and explain this process. These models include the differing stages in the process, namely policy initiation, policy formulation and policy implementation. Starting with the germ of an idea, moving on to working out the intricacies of the policy, through to enacting the policy and making it a reality, there are key stages in the process. Policy makers have hurdles to traverse at every stage and even reaching the policy implementation stage is no guarantee of success – as the numerous policy failures enacted by governments of all political colours testify. Models of policy making range from the pluralist model, the corporatist model and the Whitehall models. It is interesting to examine these models from the perspective of where power lies. Debates surrounding what constitutes power also engage the student of politics. The phenomenon of policy networks helps to explain the myriad of groups involved in the process and the interactions that take place. Policy transfer also illustrates the way in which policies 'travel' between states, with governments hoping to learn from their overseas and neighbouring counterparts. As a concept, political ideology is open to a multitude of differing interpretations. It can be useful, however, in furnishing a way of helping us to interpret and analyse the policy making process. In summary, therefore, the policy making process is complex but it provides a fascinating area of study for the student 'doing' politics. Politicians want to bring about change and nowhere is this illustrated more clearly than through the policy making process.

Chapter bibliography

Benson, D. and Jordan, A. (2011) 'What have we learned from policy transfer research? Dolowitz and Marsh revisited', *Political Studies Review*, Vol. 9: 361–378.

——(2012) 'Policy transfer research: still evolving, not yet through?', *Political Studies Review*, Vol. 10: 333–338.

Blanco, I., Lowndes, V. and Pratchett, L. (2011) 'Policy networks and governance networks: towards greater conceptual clarity', *Political Studies Review*, Vol. 9: 297–308.

Cairney, P. (2012a) 'Complexity theory in political science and public policy', *Political Studies Review*, Vol. 10: 346–358.

——(2012b) *Understanding Public Policy: Theories and Issues*, Basingstoke, Macmillan.

Cunningham, G. (1963) 'Policy and practice', *Public Administration*, Vol. 41: 229–238.

Dahl, R. A. (1961) *Who Governs?: Democracy and Power in an American City*, New Haven, Connecticut: Yale University Press.

Dolowitz, D. and Marsh, D. (2000) 'Learning from abroad: the role of policy transfer in contemporary policy-making', *Governance*, Vol. 13, No. 1: 5–24.

——(2012) 'The future of policy transfer research', *Political Studies Review*, Vol. 10: 339–345.

Dorey, P. (2005) *Policy Making in Britain: An Introduction*, London, Sage.

Dror, Y. (1964) 'Muddling through: "science" or inertia?', *Public Administration Review*, Vol. 24: 153–157.

Dussauge-Laguna, M. I. (2012) 'On the past and future of policy transfer research: Benson and Jordan revisited', *Political Studies Review*, Vol. 10: 313–324.

Easton, D. (1953) *The Political System*, New York, Knopf.

Etzioni, A. (1967) 'Mixed-scanning: a "third" approach to decision-making', *Public Administration Review*, Vol. 27: 385–392.

——(1993) *The Spirit of Community*, New York, Touchstone Books.

Fawcett, P. and Daugbjerg, C. (2012) 'Explaining governance outcomes: epistemology, network governance and policy network analysis', *Political Studies Review*, Vol. 10: 195–207.

Griffin, L. (2012) 'Where is power in governance? Why geography matters in the theory of governance', *Political Studies Review*, Vol. 10: 208–220.

Heclo, H. (1972) 'Review article: policy analysis', *British Journal of Political Science*, Vol. 2: 83–108.

Heywood, A. (2007) *Politics*, third edition, Basingstoke, Palgrave Macmillan.

Hill, M. (2005) *The Public Policy Process*, fourth edition, Harlow, Pearson Education.

Hogwood, B. W. and Gunn, L. (1984) *Policy Analysis for the Real World*, Oxford, Oxford University Press.

Hogwood, B. W. and Peters, B. G. (1983) *Policy Dynamics*, Brighton, Harvester.

Jenkins, W. I. (1978) *Policy Analysis*, London, Martin Robertson.

Jones, B. (2014) 'The policy-making process', chapter 22 in Jones, B. and Norton, P. (eds) (2014), *Politics UK*, eighth edition, Abingdon, Routledge: 464–483.

Jones, B. and Norton, P. (2014) *Politics UK*, eighth edition, Abingdon, Routledge.

Jordan, A. G. and Richardson, J. J. (1987) *British Politics and the Policy Process*, London, Unwin Hyman.

Lindblom, C. E. (1959) 'The science of "muddling through"', *Public Administration Review*, Vol. 19: 79–88.

——(1979) 'Still muddling, not yet through', *Public Administration Review*, Vol. 39: 517–526.

Lipsky, M. (1980) *Street-Level Bureaucracy*, New York, Russell Sage.

McCann, E. and Ward, K. (2012) 'Policy assemblages, mobilities and mutations: toward a multidisciplinary conversation', *Political Studies Review*, Vol. 10: 325–332.

Parsons, W. (1995) *Public Policy: Introduction to the Theory and Practice of Policy Analysis*, Aldershot, Edward Elgar.

Paxman, J. (1991) *Friends in High Places*, London, Penguin.

Rhodes, R. A. W. (1997) *Understanding Governance*, Milton Keynes, Open University Press.

——(2006) 'Policy network analysis', in Moran, M., Rein, M. and Goodin, R. (eds), *The Oxford Handbook of Public Policy*, Oxford, Oxford University Press: 425–447.

Rhodes, R. A. W. and Marsh, D. (1992) 'Policy networks in British politics', in Marsh, D. and Rhodes, R. A. W. (eds), *Policy Networks in British Government*, Oxford, Clarendon Press: 1–26.

Richardson, J. J. and Jordan, A. G. (1979) *Governing Under Pressure*, Oxford, Martin Robertson.

Simon, H. A. (1947) *Administrative Behaviour*, New York, Free Press.

——(1957) *Administrative Behaviour*, second edition, New York, Macmillan.

Street, J. (2011) *Mass Media, Politics and Democracy*, second edition, Basingstoke, Palgrave.

Wilkinson, K. (2011) 'Organised chaos: an interpretive approach to evidence-based policy making in Defra', *Political Studies*, Vol. 59: 959–977.

6

The key actors[1]

Turning now to an examination of the key institutions and actors encountered in the world of politics, it is necessary to focus upon these key players. This chapter assesses the key institutions involved in the study of politics and also the key players in the process too. Analysis is made of whether these actors change over time and how much power the ordinary person in the street has in the political process. Political participation levels are highlighted here and assessment is made as to whether people have real power or whether they are being placated, whether others, higher up the political process, are paying lip-service to their views without necessarily taking any of their thoughts and observations on board. When *Doing Politics* the key actors and institutions and areas of focus that one encounters are: government, cabinet and prime minister, Parliament, politicians, political parties, media, judiciary, pressure groups, electoral systems. It is worthwhile briefly examining each of these key actors and institutions in turn.

The executive

One of the key areas of investigation is the role fulfilled by the government, the cabinet and the prime minister. Collectively known as the executive, in theory they 'execute' or carry out the law that has been made by the legislature (Parliament). The government is drawn from the two Houses of Parliament (the House of Commons and the House of Lords) and usually consists of around 100 people. Most of the members of the government emanate from the

House of Commons but some members are drawn from the House of Lords. Indeed, certain key positions such as that of the Leader of the House of Lords will inevitably come from the Lords as this is where the office resides. Some observers confuse the government with the governing party but not all members of the governing party will be members of the government. Indeed, it may be that there is a situation, as with the contemporary scenario since the 2010 General Election, whereby no party has an overall majority, thus resulting in a coalition government. The cabinet comprises between, on average, nineteen to twenty-three people who are taken from the government. It includes all the departmental heads, including the Chancellor of the Exchequer who heads up the Treasury, who is effectively responsible for holding the purse strings of the government. One of the powers of the prime minister is the power of appointment and dismissal, the power to 'hire and fire', and this power extends to selecting and, occasionally, dismissing members of the cabinet. The cabinet is the body that, headed up by the prime minister, runs the country. The cabinet has its origins in the eighteenth century and is said to have emerged during the reign of King George I (who reigned from 1714 to 1727). The king spoke relatively little English so it was left to leading ministers to preside over decisions. Robert Walpole (1676–1745) came to the forefront and is generally viewed as the first British prime minister with his term being viewed as 1721–42. The office of prime minister, therefore, is said to have emerged in the modern sense in the eighteenth century. The position of prime minister was dubbed by the constitutional writer and journalist Walter Bagehot (1826–1877) *primus inter pares* or First Amongst Equals (hence it can be seen where Jeffrey Archer sought inspiration for the title of his book). Writing in 1867 in his famous text *The English Constitution*, Bagehot espouses the idea that the prime minister possesses more power than the others in the cabinet given the powers that the office entails but that, ultimately, it is the cabinet that dominates the decision making process. Bagehot also infamously described the cabinet as '. . . a hyphen which joins, a buckle which fastens the legislative arm of the state to executive arm of the state' (1867: 14). The prime minister is the leader of the country, the leader of the cabinet and the leader of their party. It is interesting to analyse the extent to which the prime minister is powerful and to assess the limitations on those powers. Particularly over the course of the twentieth century increasing powers were invested in the office of prime minister – as Richard Crossman pointed out in the introduction to a second edition of Walter Bagehot's *The English Constitution* published in 1963, cabinet government had been superseded by prime ministerial government. He later amended his opinion slightly (in 1970) to say that it is also the case that how the role is defined depends upon the personality of the individual incumbent. The notion being that, if an individual is a strong domineering person, the likelihood is that they will also be a strong, domineering prime minister. Likewise, if someone is more of a conciliatory, consensual character then these are qualities that are likely to be reflected in the way in which they approach being prime minister. The assessment is that the office of prime minister does have a significant number of powers and these powers have grown and developed exponentially over the past one hundred years or so but how these powers are manifested depends upon the individual concerned. Clearly, Margaret Thatcher can be flagged up as fitting into the former camp. She was dubbed the Iron Lady and her comments such as 'The Lady's not for turning. You turn if you want to', a direct gibe at her predecessor Edward Heath and his infamous policy u-turns, clearly mark her out as a strong, prime minister. James Callaghan, on the other hand, is characterised by a more consensual approach. Undoubtedly, there are external factors that impact upon how much power a particular prime minister is able to wield. The existence of a Parliamentary majority, or not, as the case may be, affects the power of the prime minister. Tony Blair entered office in May 1997 with a majority of 179 – meaning that, even if all the other parties grouped together, the Labour Party would still have 179 more Members of Parliament, or we might wish to think of them in terms of votes, than the others. Clearly, anyone in this position would be able to virtually railroad through Parliament any policies that they desired. Contrast this with a prime minister heading up a government with a small majority or even heading up a minority government. They are much more beholden to their Members of Parliament in a situation where every vote counts.

In relation to the cabinet, there are two key principles or constitutional conventions (so called because these principles are not enshrined in law but the conventions are so strong that it is virtually the same thing) that carry weight. One is the notion of individual ministerial responsibility and the other is that of collective cabinet responsibility. Individual ministerial responsibility relates to the idea that each individual minister or departmental head is responsible for the decisions taken within his or her department; it also relates to personal misconduct. In the final instance, they may have to resign for any wrong or poor decisions taken under their leadership. Essentially, it is a kind of the 'buck stops here' ruling. One classic example that is often cited is Lord Peter Carrington resigning as Foreign Secretary in April 1982 over his department's failure to foresee the invasion of the Falkland Islands. Other examples include Edwina Currie, in 1988, over the salmonella in eggs case and Norman Lamont, in 1993, in part over the Exchange Rate Mechanism (ERM), and Estelle Morris, in 2002, in part due to criticism of her performance as Secretary of State for Education. More recently, David Laws resigned (2010) as Chief Secretary to the Treasury, Liam Fox resigned (2011) as Defence Secretary and Chris Huhne resigned (2012) as Secretary of State for Energy and Climate Change – all three in relation to their personal conduct/misconduct. As a departmental head they have to be fully aware of what is happening within their sphere of influence. Ignorance is no excuse and, even though it is a virtual impossibility to be aware of everything occurring within a specific department, they have to try to retain control at all times.

Collective cabinet responsibility is the phrase used to describe the fact that members of the cabinet have to essentially all be in agreement – and indeed, it permeates down beyond the cabinet. They have to present a united front in respect of policy and ideas emanating from the cabinet. If they cannot agree, they have to either remain silent or, in the final instance, they may be forced to resign. The convention was suspended, temporarily, in 1975 to allow members of the divided Labour Cabinet to campaign either for or against membership of the European Economic Community (EEC), as the forerunner of the European Union was called at that time. It is also suspended when there are 'free votes' in Parliament on issues that are a matter of individual conscience, divorce and abortion law reform being two such issues. Again a classic, oft-cited example of collective cabinet responsibility leading to a resignation is Michael Heseltine, who resigned as Minister of Defence in January 1986 because he did not agree with the rescue bid being pursued for the troubled Westland Helicopters organisation. He felt so strongly about this issue that he was unable to remain silent and thereby hide his dissent. Other resignations due to collective responsibility include Peter Kilfoyle, in 2000, who as Under-Secretary of State for Defence opposed the policy direction of the Blair Government and, in particular, felt that Labour had forgotten its heartlands, in particular its grass-roots in the northern industrial areas; Robin Cook, in 2003, likewise Clare Short in the same year, who were both unhappy with the government's stance *vis-à-vis* Iraq. The doctrine of collective cabinet responsibility can essentially be used by a prime minister to silence their potential dissenters. As the old adage goes, better to be inside the tent . . . you know the rest!

The legislature

The legislature makes the laws. With regards to the legislature, this is composed of the two houses, the Commons and the Lords, and the third component is the sovereign. Nowadays, power effectively resides with the House of Commons, having transferred during the early part of the twentieth century from the House of Lords. The role of the sovereign is predominantly symbolic. The monarch reads out the Queen's Speech at the beginning of each Parliamentary session but this is not actually written by the Queen, it is written by the prime minister. In addition, the sovereign gives Royal Assent to Acts of Parliament, legislation emanating from Parliament. This is purely symbolic in that not since the reign of Queen Anne (1702–1714) has Royal Assent been refused and there would be a constitutional crisis were this to happen. The House of Commons is made up of 650 Members of Parliament; legislation has been passed to reduce the number of MPs to 600. These are elected to represent a geographical area (or constituency) covering the whole of the United Kingdom. Members of Parliament are elected for a five-year term. This used to be changeable as one of the powers of the prime minister was the power to call a general election. This has changed relatively recently to fixed-term Parliaments of five years' duration so the date of the next general election is already known. Previously, prime ministers could choose to call a general election at a time that they thought was more favourable to their chances of winning. Fixed term Parliaments take that power away from the prime minister and possibly provide a greater degree of stability and certainty. Members of Parliament are involved in making laws and in scrutinising the work of the government. Nowadays, much of this work takes place in committees. Members of Parliament have a number of differing, and sometimes competing, roles to fulfil. For example, they represent their constituents (so they represent a specific geographical area), they (usually, as there are very few independent MPs) represent a political party so they have to adhere to their party's policies and have to obey the party whip, they represent the national interest – especially if part of an overseas delegation, for example – and they also represent their own personal interests and beliefs; for example, a Member of Parliament might be a Catholic and this might impact upon their views regarding topics such as abortion. The physical layout of the House of Commons with its two sides facing each other, quite literally two sword lengths apart, is said to perpetuate an adversarial approach to politics that, unlike an arc or horseshoe shaped chamber, is less inclined towards cooperation and consensus. As stated in Chapter Four, politicians have come in for a great deal of criticism relatively recently. The expenses scandal certainly did them no favours. As a profession, the role of a politician is regarded in rather a poor light by many. The 2013 *Audit of Political Engagement 10*, for example, highlights that although public perceptions of Parliament as a whole have improved, with 47 per cent (Hansard Society, 2013: 56) believing that Parliament is able to hold the government to account (an increase of 9 per cent on the previous year's audit), only 23 per cent are satisfied that MPs do a good job (*Ibid.*: 53). As the Audit reports, 'Public attitudes towards MPs continue to decline; fewer people can name their own MP and are satisfied with the work of MPs generally than was the case even in the aftermath of the parliamentary expenses scandal' (2013: 17). There is a significant amount of work to be undertaken if attaching the suffix MP to one's name is to regain the kudos that it once possessed.

With its roots in the fourteenth century, the House of Lords is the second chamber or upper house in our bicameral legislature. Currently composed of around 825 members, the House of Lords has undergone a number of changes in recent years. Twenty-six members of the House of Lords are senior Church of England bishops and only ninety-two hereditary peers remain in the Lords. There has been an attempt made to modernise the House of Lords and to bring it more in line with perceptions of what a twenty-first century legislative body ought to look like. The Coalition Government had wanted an elected House of Lords, believing the existing composition of the Lords to be unrepresentative and undemocratic. This, however, has not been forthcoming. Opponents believed that an elected Lords would jeopardise the position of the elected House of Commons by undermining its supremacy. Traditionally, membership of the House of Lords has been based upon the hereditary principle. Indeed, it was only in 1958 that life peers were allowed; these peerages are not passed on when the holder dies. Recent changes have involved reducing the number of members of the House of Lords and allowing more 'ordinary' people to be elevated to its ranks. These include, for example, the campaigner Baroness Helen Newlove, whose husband, Garry Newlove, was killed by a gang of youths who were harassing their neighbourhood. Baroness Newlove, who was given a peerage in May 2010, has worked tirelessly to get the issue of anti-social behaviour on to the political agenda and focus upon working with young people to enable them to help their local communities and to steer clear of trouble. In December 2012, she was appointed the Victims' Commissioner. The House of Lords fulfils a scrutinising role and provides a check upon the work of the government. They have the power to delay legislation and although this time has been reduced in the final year of a parliament it can act as a virtual veto. They can make the government think again about possibly rushed or ill-thought-out policy proposals. There is a belief that some of the more interesting, and possibly esoterical, debates take place within the

House of Lords. Certainly, they have more time to engage in general debates than the House of Commons, which is pressured to ensure that all of the government's business gains Parliamentary time.

Political parties

Another key institution that epitomises politics today is the political party. The political party existed prior to the twentieth century but really grew and developed during that time. The Whigs and the Tories were the two predominant encampments prior to the turn of the last century but, especially over recent years, there has been the growth and development of modern mass parties. Alongside the metamorphosis of the Whigs into the Liberal Party and the Tories into the Conservative Party during the nineteenth century, a key twentieth century development was the emergence and expansion of the Labour Party, which initially at least aimed to represent the newly enfranchised working classes. Much later in the twentieth century there was the breakaway so-called 'Gang of Four' (David Owen, Roy Jenkins, William Rodgers and Shirley Williams) from the Labour Party who formed the centrist Social Democratic Party. This fought the 1983 and the 1987 General Elections alongside the Liberal Party as the SDP–Liberal Alliance. In 1988, the two parties merged to become the Social and Liberal Democrats, eventually becoming the Liberal Democrats. The Liberal Democrats finally took a share of political power after the 2010 General Election when, under the leadership of Nick Clegg, they formed part of the Coalition Government alongside David Cameron's Conservatives.

There are a whole host of political parties that contest elections, many of which stand relatively little chance of being elected and, indeed, some of which are frivolous or publicity-seeking parties, for example the Citizens for Undead Rights and Equality Party, which stood in the 2010 General Election, the Death, Dungeons and Taxes Party that had candidates in the 2005 General Election and, going even further back in time, the I Want to Drop a Blancmange Down Terry Wogan's Y-Fronts Party, whereby Pamela Stephenson contested the Windsor and Maidenhead constituency under this party banner in 1987. Political parties are symptomatic of modern politics. Generally, in order to be electorally successful candidates need to belong to a political party. As stated, relatively few independent candidates win elections. There are rare exceptions, such as Martin Bell, who became the Independent MP for Tatton from 1997 to 2001, and also Richard Taylor, who became the Independent MP for Wyre Forest from 2001 to 2010. Taylor's campaign was based on the single issue of support for the reinstatement of Accident and Emergency services at Kidderminster Hospital.

The main political parties in the United Kingdom, however, are the Conservative, Labour and Liberal Democratic Parties at Westminster and the Scottish National Party and the Welsh Plaid Cymru in their respective nations. Other political parties include the UK Independence Party, led by the inimitable Nigel Farage, and also the Green Party – whose first ever MP was Caroline Lucas, elected in 2010 for the constituency of Brighton Pavilion. In Northern Ireland, the key political parties include the Democratic Unionist Party, the Progressive Unionist Party, the Ulster Unionist Party, the Social Democratic and Labour Party, Sinn Féin, the Alliance Party of Northern Ireland. One interesting point to note, in the aftermath of the 2010 General Election, as Philip Cowley states, is that 'After the 1997 general election the UK was governed by one political party. After the 2010 general election it was governed by ten' (Cowley, 2011: 91). He highlights how after

> . . . the Scottish and Welsh elections in 2007, both the Scottish National Party and Plaid became parties of government, and in Northern Ireland the executive comprised five separate parties: the Democratic Unionists, Sinn Féin, the Ulster Unionists, the Social Democratic and Labour Party and the Alliance.
>
> (*Ibid.*)

The process of devolution has certainly, therefore, changed the political landscape. In order to be electorally successful, political parties generally need to represent a broad church of interests and their support needs to be geographically concentrated – especially for elections to Westminster whereby the first past the post electoral system (also known as single plurality or simple majority) is still in existence. This is a winner-takes-all electoral system. Candidates gain nothing for coming second and, therefore, it helps if support is heavily concentrated in specific areas. The referendum or plebiscite held in May 2011 gave people the opportunity to vote to change the electoral system but, for various reasons, the vote went in favour of the first past the post system being retained. Political parties want to occupy the positions of political power. They organise elections and mobilise supporters. They provide the key players in the political system and perform an invaluable function in the contemporary political system. They furnish the personnel who will stand as candidates and also those who work behind the scenes to focus upon issues such as preparing the policy proposals for inclusion in manifestoes and running the constituencies on a day-to-day basis. Political parties are a familiar feature of the contemporary political landscape and perform a key function.

The media

The mass media is another key institution that the student of politics needs to analyse. Sometimes dubbed the Fourth Estate of the realm, the mass media has changed significantly over recent years. Traditionally composed of newspapers, radio and television, the media now encompasses new forms of political communication such as the internet, mobile phone technology and social media. News and political information have become much more instantaneous. There is twenty-four hour availability and the proliferation of citizen journalism, with ordinary people able to posts blogs, videos tweets and updates, meaning that individual citizens are often relaying the news as it happens. This contrasts with previous eras whereby people were told the news by professional news agencies. The Arab Spring of 2011 is said to have been triggered and facilitated by this new empowerment of those at the grassroots, people who, aided by relatively cheap and accessible technological advancements, were able to disseminate their interpretation of the truth. These were often versions that directly contrasted and were juxtaposed with official or governmental accounts.

In the United Kingdom, the media, in particular the press, have come in for considerable criticism due to the phone hacking scandal. The investigation headed by Lord Justice Leveson into press standards and ethics reported that the press should have an independent self-regulatory body that would be underpinned by legislation. The Liberal Democrats and the Labour Party supported this recommendation but the Conservatives did not like the notion of statutory underpinning. The issue of press freedom and standards remains a key concern.

Judiciary

A central feature of British politics is the judiciary. Alongside the legislature and the executive, it forms the three branches of government. England and Wales, Northern Ireland and Scotland each have their own judicial systems. The legislature makes the law, the executive 'executes' or carries out the law and the judiciary interprets the law. The head of the judiciary is now the Lord Chief Justice but it used to be the Lord Chancellor – who was in the

113

interesting position of being a member of all three branches – and somewhat refuted the idea that there is a separation of powers. The Lord Chancellor used to be the Lords' equivalent of the Speaker of the House of Commons; after the 2005 Constitutional Reform Act this role was performed by the Lord Speaker. An independent judiciary is a central feature of the British system of government and part of the reason why the British system of governance has generally been held in such high esteem by many other countries. The idea that everyone is subject to the rule of law and not subject to the arbitrary whim of a dictator or elite group is a crucial aspect. The judiciary has undergone a number of significant reforms over recent years. Notably, the creation of a Supreme Court constitutes a key change. This was set up in October 2009 and was a result of the 2005 Constitutional Reform Act. The Supreme Court has a President and Deputy President; in 2014 these were Lord Neuberger of Abbotsbury and Lady Hale of Richmond, respectively, and ten other Supreme Court Justices. It is the Supreme Court and also the highest appellate court, having taken over the judicial functions from the House of Lords. It meets in Middlesex Guildhall in Parliament Square, Westminster. One of the key factors behind its creation was a much clearer separation of powers. It does not have the same powers as the United States' Supreme Court; as Philip Norton states, it '. . . has a physical similarity to, though not the powers of, its US namesake' (Norton, 2014: 437). In addition, whilst it has changed slightly in recent years, the socio-economic background of the judiciary as a whole remains predominantly white, male and upper-class. In 2011, there were only 22.3 per cent female and 5.1 per cent black, Asian and minority ethnic judges (Ministry of Justice, Consultation Paper cited in Norton, 2014: 445).

The civil service

The permanent civil service provides the personnel who carry out the day-to-day functions of and running of government. In theory at least, civil servants are available to provide help and advice to ministers. Ministers are the decision makers leading the direction that a particular department of state should take and ensuring that their policy priorities are given prominence. The reality can often be slightly different. Given that average ministerial tenure is relatively short (usually only about 1.3 years) permanent civil servants can effectively run rings around an incoming, inexperienced minister, who may take a while to 'find their feet' in their new role. Drawing parallels with Alex Ferguson's and Bill Gates' relative lack of achievement 1.3 years into their respective roles at Manchester United and with Microsoft™, Cleary and Reeves state, '. . .1.3 years is generally not long enough for even the most talented of individuals to achieve their potential' (2009: 2). Senior civil servants (mandarins), on the other hand, have the expertise, knowledge and power. It is suggested that, often, rather than simply presenting a minister with a set of policy proposals or possible alternative strategies, they can, in fact, be leading and steering the direction in which policy heads. Instead of options A, B and C being set out with equal weighting, they may in fact highlight the benefits of route A over and above routes B and C, thereby making policy as opposed to simply administering policy – being 'on top' as opposed to simply 'on tap'. In addition, the socio-economic background of senior civil servants in particular has received a great deal of criticism. With a continuing Oxbridge bias and recruits who tend to have degrees in the classics, ancient history and such like, critics question the relevance of the senior civil service to contemporary society. Previous investigations into the civil service, such as the 1854 Northcote-Trevelyan Report and the 1968 Fulton Report, highlight the lack of change within the civil service. There was a belief that there was too much of an emphasis upon nepotism and Buggins' Turn in relation to recruitment and promotion. In addition, there was a perception that there was a lot of waste within the civil service. Margaret Thatcher dubbed it a 'bloated bureaucracy' and pledged to tackle such issues. Since Mrs Thatcher's time as prime minister, in particular, the administration has been slimmed down, many of its functions have been 'hived off' to quasi independent bodies and it

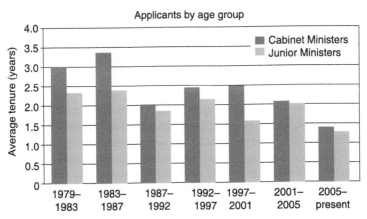

Figure 6.1 Average Ministerial Tenure (*Source:* Cleary and Reeves, 2009: 3).

is now on the whole considerably more streamlined. Nonetheless, key questions for political scientists centre around these issues outlined above as to whether the senior civil service still hold too much political sway and whether or not they are unrepresentative of society at large.

Pressure groups

One important aspect of the political process is pressure groups. These are groups of people whose aim is to influence those in positions of political power without actually wanting to occupy those positions themselves, the important word here being 'influence'. This definition, therefore, enables us to differentiate pressure groups from political parties – where the aim of parties is to at least try and gain power via the electoral process. Pressure groups are classified in a number of different ways. One classification divides them into promotional (or cause) groups and protective (or sectional) groups. Promotional groups are those which seek to 'promote' a particular cause; they try to get a particular issue onto the political agenda by focusing the media spotlight upon it. Examples of promotional groups include: ASH – Action on Smoking and Health, which is an anti-smoking group that, as they say, 'works to eliminate the harm caused by tobacco'; CAMRA – the Campaign for Real Ale, in their words campaigning for 'real ale, community pubs and consumer rights'; PETA – People for the Ethical Treatment of Animals, with their tag line that 'animals are *not* ours to eat, wear, experiment on, use for entertainment or abuse in any way'. Many such groups are international in nature, PETA being a case in point, but also many cause groups are local, single-issue groups that might be set up to oppose a particular planning application or against a new road building or rail extension project. Some see this as a rather negative or blocking form of participation. Success effectively means maintenance of the *status quo* and, in that sense, may be relatively difficult to measure because the outcome is that nothing changes. These types of groups are often criticised for being spearheaded by NIMBYs, the Not In My Backyard Brigade, who are only participating in pressure group activity because this is an issue that directly affects them. Nimbyism is often, therefore, portrayed in a negative light but perhaps this is rather unfair given that people will inevitably be more likely to be galvanised into action when their lives, families and neighbourhoods are threatened. The other key type of pressure group, the protective genre, strives to protect the interests of its membership. Trades unions are the classic example of this type of pressure group. Their *raison d'être* is to work towards gaining better pay, working conditions and other benefits for their membership. The National Farmers' Union (NFU) or the National Union of Teachers (NUT) are examples of such protective groups. It is worth highlighting that the divisions between pressure groups are not always as straightforward as they may, at first, appear. There is some overlap and there may be occasions when, for example, a protective pressure group acts in a promotional way, for example when a trade union seeks to highlight a specific issue – for example the University and College Union (UCU) promoting the cause of higher education *per se*.

One criticism that is often levied at pressure groups is that they are simply articulate minorities who are good at making their case and getting their point across. The point being made is that they may, in fact, be unrepresentative of wider society. Certainly, the more literate and educated members of society may be better able to convey their message but this is not to say that others do not have a valuable contribution to make even if, for various reasons, they are less skilled at making their point. Allied to this, many of the skills required by pressure group activists require a certain amount of confidence and level of articulation. Speaking in public, for example, is often rated as one of the most prevalent phobias, with many people, from all walks of life, ranking it alongside arachnophobia and other such fears. Who is to say that those with the best speakers are those with the 'best' or most laudable cause and aims?

A key and prolific writer in the field of pressure groups is Wyn Grant. Grant refers to pressure groups as 'insider' and 'outsider' pressure groups. The insider groups have a substantial amount of power and legitimacy, so much so that they often become enmeshed in the political system themselves and almost become an extra arm of government. They may be on governmental committees and provide politicians with information and statistical data. For example, when the government was considering making the wearing of seatbelts compulsory in cars in the early 1980s, they relied on motoring organisations to furnish statistics as to the estimated number of lives that might be saved by the introduction of just such a policy. A number of pressure groups, related to the licensing trade or to the health professions, for example, were able to provide the government with data in relation to the impact of the extension of the licensing laws prior to both the Thatcher Government and the Blair Governments introducing such policies. 'Outsider' pressure groups, as the name implies, are outside of the locus of power and the machinery of government. They do not have the ear of the government and have to use other methods to get their message across. Such methods might include trying to gain publicity for their cause or organisation using gimmicks, demonstrations, boycotts, 'buycotts' and petitions, for example. Indeed, some outsider groups might be so far away from the usual democratic structures of power that they may be extremist or terrorist organisations. The tactics that they are prepared to use are outwith legitimate means of protest; some animal rights organisations have used such extreme measures in the past to try to achieve their aims or to gain publicity for their protest.

In terms of specific factors that pressure groups require, in varying degrees, in order to achieve their aims, it is generally held that they need numbers (people or supporters) – some pressure groups contain huge numbers of supporters within their ranks and they are able to mobilise them at relatively short notice. Richard Heffernan highlights how

> ... the Countryside Alliance mobilised 400,000 people to protest attempts to ban foxhunting in September 2002 and some 1.5 million people marched in London against the imminent intervention in Iraq in February 2003. In 2007 the high-profile Make Poverty History campaign brought together some 540 British member organisations ...
>
> (2011: 174)

Another commodity that pressure groups require is finance. They need a certain amount of cash at their disposal in order to campaign, produce leaflets, pay for coaches to London or other areas, etc. Pressure groups possess cash in varying degrees. The wealthier pressure groups may find it much easier to get the government to listen to their arguments. A third aspect is expertise. Pressure groups contain experts within their ranks. They have the ability to utilise this knowledge to either provide information to those in positions of political power or, equally, to withhold that information. As mentioned above, statistical data and information might be used to influence the policy making process and elicit policy change. Power is often regarded as being in a series of concentric circles and there is a generally held belief that there is a qualitative difference as to where particular groups are able to exert their pressure. If you are able to wield power near the centre of those concentric circles, say towards the prime minister and cabinet, it is more likely that a group will achieve its aims. The importance of having the ear of the government should not be underestimated. On the other hand, public opinion, which is often regarded as being at the outer edge of those concentric circles, might appear to be relatively ineffectual but significant pressure from public opinion *per se* may have the effect of leapfrogging other aspects of power and getting the prime minister and cabinet to take note.

Electoral systems

A key aspect of any political system is the electoral system. Electoral systems vary but they impact upon the outcome of an election. Elections to the Westminster Parliament, as stated, continue to use the first past the post electoral system. This majoritarian system means the winner takes the seat and a winning candidate might win by one vote over their nearest rival. There may be, and are quite likely to be, more people who do not want the winning candidate than who do. In addition, support needs to be geographically concentrated in order for seats to be won. The recent devolution measures that were instigated in 1999 with the setting up of the Scottish Parliament and the Welsh Assembly saw the introduction of proportional representation for these elections. Proportional Representation (PR) is a blanket term that is used to describe a number of different electoral systems. The common feature is that, under these systems, seats are allocated in proportion to the number of votes cast. One of the most often cited systems is the Single Transferable Vote (STV). This is used in the Republic of Ireland and uses large multi-member constituencies. In order to be elected, candidates need to attain a quota of the total votes cast. It is known as the Droop Quota, and any candidate reaching this figure is automatically elected.

There are advantages and disadvantages with all electoral systems and no system is perfect. Under first-past-the-post for example, in a three-cornered race the winning candidate may have secured little more than a third of the total votes cast. Likewise, under the Single Transferable Vote, with its large multi-member constituencies, the traditional MP–Constituent link may be lost. The method chosen depends on which principle ranks uppermost. It might be fairness, democracy, equality or some other. Given that the referendum held in May 2011 over whether to use the Alternative Vote electoral system for Westminster Parliamentary elections resulted in a resounding 'no' vote, this issue has moved off the political agenda for the foreseeable future.

Key actors and do they change over time?

It is interesting to assess whether these key actors and institutions involved in politics are a constant or whether they change over time. The socio-economic background of the power brokers within society remains remarkably static. There is relatively little room for manoeuvre and for social mobility. Analysis of the socio-economic backgrounds of MPs, for example, reveals that they remain predominantly 'white, male, middle-aged and middle class' and remarkably resistant to change. Granted there are more female MPs than ever before; in 2013 there are 147 out of 650 (22.6 per cent). Likewise, the number of MPs from a Black and Minority Ethnic background increased to 27 at the 2010 General Election and included Shabana Mahmood as Britain's first female Muslim MP, representing Birmingham Ladywood, and Helen Grant, in Maidstone and the Weald, as the Conservative Party's first black female MP. The most noteworthy feature generally, however, is the lack of change. Within the civil service too, at the higher echelons, there remains a preponderance of people from Oxbridge with degrees in classics and suchlike. It appears to be the case that those recruiting the next generation of senior civil servants or mandarins continue to recruit in their own image so it is a self-perpetuating phenomenon. In addition, as the broadcaster Jeremy Paxman captured in his book *Friends in High Places* (1991), through kinship and marital ties what is interesting is how those in positions of power form a relatively small network.

People power

It is debatable how much power the ordinary person has when pitted against these key institutions. It is interesting to analyse whether they have real power or whether they are simply being placated, with a metaphorical pat on the head. It is also worthwhile assessing whether those at the higher echelons are taking on board their wishes and concerns or whether mere lip-service is being paid. There are opportunities for people to be involved in politics; usually this is through having a say in the operation of their community. It enables them to be able to participate politically in the decision-making processes in relation to their local area. Having said this, theoretical perspectives on decision-making highlight the fact that there are varying degrees of participation. One of the key writers in this area, Sherry Arnstein, made a seminal contribution to the debate with her 'ladder of participation'. Although writing as far back as 1969, her analysis of varying degrees of participation being akin to a ladder remains pertinent today. Indeed, it was adapted slightly by Hart in 1992 to refer specifically to children's political participation. Essentially, Arnstein argues that participation occurs at differing levels, rungs, and there is a qualitative difference as to where you participate. Indeed, some participation is not real participation in that it constitutes therapy, placation or lip-service. This occurs when, for example, people believe that they are participating but in actual fact their views are simply ignored or at least sidelined. The higher up the ladder the more real participation occurs. As Hart states in relation to children's participation,

Tokenism might be a way to describe how children are sometimes used on conference panels. Articulate, charming children are selected by adults to sit on a panel with little or no substantive preparation on the subject and no consultation with their peers who, it is implied, they represent. If no explanation is given to the audience or to the children of how they were selected, and which children's perspectives they represent, this is usually sufficient indication that a project is not truly an example of participation.

(Hart, 1992: 10)

It is necessary, therefore, to consider the extent to which any participation is in fact real participation or is mere lip-service or tokenism. John Stuart Mill wrote of the value of participation *per se* and related it to what the Ancient Greeks termed the 'good life'. Participants often refer to this aspect of their role. They are often surprised by the unintended consequences that their participation brings. In addition to working towards achieving their stated aims, there are often other benefits such as the camaraderie that volunteering brings, the ability to learn new skills or to recognise and appreciate skills that they already possessed but which perhaps had lain dormant or which they had not been able to bring to the forefront. Whilst recognising that this notion of participation being an end in itself does have value, there must be a point at which participants, if they have an end-goal towards which they strive, must become disillusioned and feel that they are wasting their time and energies. There has to be a point at which enough is enough. If significant amounts of time and energy are invested but to no avail, questions will eventually be asked as to whether there is a point to the participation.

Participation is essential for democracy to exist. Paul Whiteley highlights how political participation is '. . . at the heart of democratic government and civil society, and without it there can be no effective democracy' (2012: 34). He proceeds to highlight how '. . . social capital refers to co-operative relationships between individuals based on mutual trust and norms of reciprocation' and proceeds to emphasise the value and importance of volunteering to this social capital. Whiteley states, '. . . unpaid voluntary activities make a very important contribution to social capital, which, in turn, has all kinds of benign effects on society and politics, and therefore, trends in volunteering take on a particular significance for supporting civil society' (2012: 76). Participation takes many and varied forms. As Young points out,

Among these new forms of participation, political consumption –

which I define as a consumer's decision either to punish (i.e. boycott) or reward (i.e. buycott) private companies by making selective choices of products or brands, based on social, political or ethical considerations – is often highlighted as an alternative mode of political/civic engagement.

(2010: 1066)

It can be seen, therefore, how the notion of participation covers a wide range of activities and extends to non-participation, especially where there is conscious decision-making taking place, for example, as in the case of a boycott.

Post-affluence thesis

Participation is often regarded as a luxury that is more likely to take place in times of relative affluence as opposed to times of austerity. Ronald Inglehart's post-affluence thesis (*cf.*: 1977a and 1977b) epitomises this notion. The idea is that if people are worried about feeding their children, paying their bills and generally dealing with the problems of basic survival then they are less likely to turn their attention away from their own immediate concerns and become interested in issues such as the environment or animal rights. Using this analysis, the current period of financial downturn and austerity might lead to lower levels of volunteering and involvement as people focus upon basic economic survival. Whilst there is a great deal of merit in Inglehart's thesis, critics point out participatory actions that are associated with austerity and not affluence, the Jarrow March which took place in October 1936 being a case in point or, more recently, the protests against the increase in higher education tuition fees. Chapter Seven analyses Inglehart's work more specifically in relation to new social movements. What is interesting, therefore, as revealed by this research, is the extent to which people like to participate in their local communities. People who are not necessarily affluent but who feel a deep commitment and bond to their local area continue to volunteer and act on behalf of their local community. It does appear to be the case that these people are motivated into action and helping others for more altruistic reasons than the post-affluence thesis permits.

Political engagement and social capital

Using data from the Hansard Society's *Audit of Political Engagement* – which has taken place every year since 2004 – Gerry Stoker highlights how the numbers of those stating that they have undertaken voluntary work ranged from 23 per cent in 2003 to 25 per cent in 2010, with the high point being 29 per cent in 2009, the lowest points being 22 per cent in 2005 and 2008 (Stoker, 2011: 25). Essentially, approximately a quarter of respondents claim to have participated in voluntary work. This is relatively high when compared with those who claim to be politically active, for example. Ekman and Amna (2012) refer to latent or 'standby' participation – as opposed to actual or conventional participation, this is to say participation potential as opposed to actual participation or, as the *Audit of Political Engagement 10: The 2013 Report* cites, '. . . episodic forms of participation when the circumstances warrant it' (2013: 72). Accordingly, 39 per cent of the Audit's respondents fall into the latent or standby category (*Ibid.*: 74). As the Report states, 'On the right issue, and with a suitable political stimulus, around four in 10 standby citizens could potentially be converted from latent to manifest participation in the future' (*Ibid.*: 82). The Audit refers primarily to political participation.

Paul Whiteley examines political participation through the role of voluntary organisations and volunteering in encouraging civic engagement. As stated (p. 121), he highlights the notion of social capital as referring to '. . . cooperative relationships between individuals based on mutual trust and norms of reciprocation' (2012: 76). He proceeds to state, '. . . unpaid voluntary activities make a very important contribution to social capital, which, in turn, has all kinds of benign effects on society and politics, and therefore, trends in volunteering take on a particular significance for supporting civil society' (*Ibid.*). Social capital has been linked with '. . . improved health, better educational standards, lower crime rates, enhanced political participation, and improved economic performance' (*Ibid.*). Given the link between volunteering and social capital, it is easy to see the value of volunteering to society *per se*.

Volunteering and active citizenship provide people with the opportunity to become involved in their locality/neighbourhood. In addition to the local community potentially benefitting from their involvement and actions, it is clear that individuals themselves may also benefit from this participation. The opportunity to be able to 'give back' to their community, even if this is only a few hours per week, potentially manifests itself in a feeling of being valued and having a purpose in life. Too often, life in twenty-first century western society involves an emphasis upon materialistic aspects and monetary gains. It is clear, however, that volunteering provides the opportunity to 'give back' to the local environment in a way that goes beyond mere financial reward. This emphasis upon altruism and selflessness for the greater good of the community should not be underestimated. In addition to this aspect, however, it is clear that the volunteers themselves also stand to gain through participation. It is evident that volunteering helps the acquisition and honing of a number of transferable skills – even though the volunteers acquiring these skills may not necessarily be aware of or able to articulate the precise nature of these skills. Confidence-building, group working, negotiating and problem-solving techniques, amongst others, often accompany volunteering activities. The participants themselves may not always appreciate and recognise that they are using these techniques and acquiring these skills but it is certainly the case that this is *precisely* what is inadvertently happening to many volunteers. If, as Whiteley highlights above, social capital involves '. . . mutual trust and norms of reciprocation' (*Ibid.*: 76) then this reciprocation is clearly evident when examining the benefits accrued by the participants in volunteering activities. They too stand to gain from the experience, alongside the community that they seek to serve. Those benefits may not necessarily be tangible but they certainly exist!

As stated in Chapter Two, e-petitions constitute a contemporary device that enables people to participate politically and to have their voices heard. Provided sufficient numbers are attained, 100,000, then there is the likelihood (not a guarantee, however) that the topic will be debated in Parliament. Petitions have a long history but the e-petition is a relatively recent phenomenon. Petitions do, however, permit the ordinary person to participate in politics.

Conclusion

This chapter highlights the key aspects, institutions and actors one encounters when *Doing Politics*. It can be seen that power resides in a number of different organisations, institutions and people. The executive body is key to this concentration of power but, even here, it is not without its limitations. The person at the pinnacle of power, the prime minister, has a tremendous amount of power and authority that goes with the office but is still subject to checks, balances and limitations. The office-holder cannot simply ride roughshod over the views and wishes of their cabinet. Likewise, they are constrained by Parliament, by their party and by the public at large. Significant reforms have taken place relatively recently in relation to various institutional bodies, the judiciary and the House of Lords being two key examples. Similarly, the media, especially the broadcast media, are undergoing a number of key changes in this first quarter of the twenty-first century. These changes are in part in response to new technology and the implications for citizen journalism and the immediacy of coverage. The recent Leveson Report into press stand-ards and ethics illustrates that there are still questions to be raised over the media industry, in particular in relation to a number of ethical considerations – the phone hacking scandal being a case in point.

The student of politics can expect to study all of these institutions in a sig-nificant amount of depth. The key institutions encountered by the student of politics are many and varied. It is now necessary to turn our attention to another locus of power, people power – especially when that is channelled through the medium of new social movements.

Chapter bibliography

Arnstein, S. R. (1969) 'A ladder of citizen participation', *Journal of the American Institute of Planners*, Vol. 35, No. 4, July: 216–224.

Briggs, J. E., Parks, L. and Mendiwelso-Bendek, Z. (2013) '"Many hands make light work": the contribution of volunteering to community cohesion', *Taking Part?*, ESRC Research Cluster, ESRC Report.

Carman, C. (2010) 'The process is the reality: perceptions of procedural fairness and participatory democracy', *Political Studies*, Vol. 58: 731–751.

Cleary, H. and Reeves, R. (2009) *The 'Culture of Churn' for UK Ministers and the Price We All Pay*, Research Briefing, London, Demos.

Cowley, P. (2011) 'Political parties and the British party system', in Heffernan, R., Cowley, P. and Hay, C. (eds), *Developments in British Politics Nine*, Basingstoke, Palgrave Macmillan: 91–112.

Ekman, J. and Amna, E. (2012) 'Political participation and civic engagement: towards a new typology', *Human Affairs*, Vol. 22, No. 3, July: 283–300.

Grant, W. (2000) *Pressure Groups and British Politics*, Basingstoke, Palgrave Macmillan.

——(2005) 'Pressure politics: a politics of collective consumption?', *Parliamentary Affairs*, Vol. 58, No. 2: 366–379.

——(2008) 'The changing patterns of group politics in Britain', *British Politics*, Vol. 3, No. 2: 204–222.

Hansard Society (2013) *Audit of Political Engagement 10*, London, the Hansard Society.

Hart, R. A. (1992) 'Children's participation from tokenism to citizenship', *United Nations Children's Fund*, Innocenti Essays Number 4, Florence, UNICEF: 1–41.

Heffernan, R. (2011) 'Pressure group politics' in Heffernan, R., Cowley, P. and Hay, C. (eds), *Developments in British Politics Nine*, Basingstoke, Palgrave Macmillan: 174–195.

Helliwell, J., Layard, R. and Sachs, J. (2012) *World Happiness Report*, New York, The Earth Institute, Columbia University.

Inglehart, R. (1977a) *The Silent Revolution*, Princeton, NJ, Princeton University Press.
——(1977b) *Modernization and Post-Modernization: Cultural, Economic and Political Change in 43 Countries*, Princeton, NJ, Princeton University Press.
John, P., Fieldhouse, E. and Liu, H. (2011) 'How civic is civic culture? Explaining community participation using the 2005 English citizenship survey', *Political Studies*, Vol. 59: 230–252.
Milbrath, L. W. (1965) *Political Participation: How and Why Do People Get Involved in Politics?*, Chicago, Rand McNally.
Mill, J. S. (2005) *On Liberty*, New York, Cosimo, first published in 1859.
Norton, P. (2014) 'The judiciary', chapter 21 of Jones, B. And Norton, P. (eds), *Politics UK*, eighth edition: 436–459.
Parry, G., Moyser, G. and Day, N. (1992) *Political Participation in Britain*, Cambridge, Cambridge University Press.
Pateman, C. (1970) *Participation and Democratic Theory*, Cambridge, Cambridge University Press.
Paxman, J. (1991)[1987] *Friends in High Places: Who Runs Britain?*, London, Penguin.
Power Inquiry (2006) *Executive Summary and Recommendations of the Report of Power: An Independent Inquiry into Britain's Democracy*, York, Joseph Rowntree Trust.
Putnam, R. (2000) *Bowling Alone: The Collapse and Revival of American Community*, New York, Touchstone Books.
Pykett, J., Saward, M. and Schaefer, A. (2010) 'Framing the good citizen', *British Journal of Political and International Relations*, Vol. 12: 523–538.
Stoker, G. (2011) *Building a New Politics?*, London, British Academy.
Theakston, K. (1999) *Leadership in Whitehall*, Basingstoke, Macmillan.
Whiteley, P. (2012) *Political Participation in Britain: The Decline and Revival of Civic Culture*, Basingstoke, Palgrave Macmillan.
Young, M. B. (2010) 'To buy or not to buy: who are political consumers? What do they think and how do they participate?', *Political Studies*, Vol. 58: 1065–1086.

Note

1 Part of this chapter, on participation, appeared in Briggs, J. E., Parks, L. and Mendiwelso-Bendek, Z. (2013) '"Many hands make light work": the contribution of volunteering to community cohesion', *Taking Part?*, ESRC Research Cluster, ESRC Report.

7

New social movers and shakers

The aim of Chapter Seven is to focus upon the politics that takes place in civil society, that is to say beyond the realm of the political arena, beyond what we would usually consider as mainstream politics. Attention now turns to less formal methods of political activity and political participation. There has been a significant amount written about involvement in formal politics and analysis made of the formal political arena as the locus of political power. This chapter seeks to redress the balance somewhat by focusing upon 'other' modes of political involvement and political participation. New social movement activity and involvement via what has been termed 'global civil society' are examined in detail in this chapter. In addition, investigation is made as to whether these 'newer' forms of political activity and involvement appeal to differing sectors of society to a much greater extent than hitherto. For example, is new social movement activity more likely to appeal to younger people and those who have never had any political involvement in mainstream politics before? Contemporary protest groups such as *Fathers 4 Justice (F4J)* and the *Plane Stupid* campaign will be highlighted here as examples of contemporary protest movements.

What are new social movements?

New social movements do, in the words of the infamous advert, what it 'says on the tin'. They are (relatively speaking) new, they are concerned with people so they are inherently social and they concern action or activity so they may realistically be labelled as a movement. One key factor that marks out new social movements is that they are to be found located in civil society as opposed to in the political arena. Claus Offe's (1980) oft quoted phrase is that they 'bypass the state'. They are primarily concerned with people as opposed to politics. It is this very location that, in part, helps us to determine whether or not a group can be classified as a new social movement. New social movements *may* act in a political capacity and, indeed, many of them do, such as for example when the women's movement has campaigned for abortion rights for women, but it is this primary aspect of being situated in civil society that helps to define them. They relate to people power in that they are composed of people organising themselves as opposed to people being coerced or coaxed into action by the government or by the political parties. The action begins in society as opposed to the political arena. As Mario Diani states, 'A social movement is a network of informal interactions between a plurality of individuals, groups and/or organizations, engaged in a political or cultural conflict, on the basis of a shared collective identity' (1992: 13). Diani clearly encapsulates the key elements embodied by new social movements with the emphasis upon networks, informality and a sense of a collective identity.

A second way of helping us to classify a group as a new social movement is to examine how they organise themselves. A key factor here is the way in which new social movements tend towards being non-hierarchical in that they shy away from traditional power structures and have loose and informal ties (*cf.*: Scott, 1990: 33). As Della Porta and Diani state, 'Many of them emphasize participation and direct democracy, oppose delegation of power and privilege consensual decision making' (2006: 141). The notion of a top-down approach to organisational structure and power is anathema to them. In fact, they espouse the opposite approach, from the grass-roots upwards, with ideas in relation to the movement's aims and objectives and *vis-à-vis* how they organise themselves emanating from the grassroots membership and being governed by essentially a bottom-up approach. Traditional power structures, if one were to draw a diagrammatic representation, would often be like a pyramid. New social movements have shied away from this approach and have tended not to prefer power being vested in the hands of a leader or a leadership group. The whole essence of a new social movement is that power resides with the membership as a whole, as opposed to in the hands of an elite few. Power to the people and a democratic approach lie at the heart of how new social movements operate. This is direct democracy in action, as opposed to elitism or even representative democracy. Elitist theory is associated with a number of key intellectuals, one of whom is the German writer and sociologist Robert Michels. In his text *Political Parties* (first published in German in 1911 and then in English in 1915), Michels sets out the so-called 'iron law of oligarchy'. The oft-quoted famous phrase from Michels work '. . . who says organisation says oligarchy' aptly captures this notion that, wherever you get a group of people, you will always find a smaller segment of that same group who will wish to retain power and form the leadership role. This group, possibly due to their talents, qualities and abilities, might be more suited to governing than others. It may be that they are able to assume this leadership role through being born into it or it could be that they are in possession of particular skills and abilities that make them more suited to fulfilling the role of leader(s). Either way, they are more fitted to assuming the mantle of leader than the rest of the group. It is appropriate, therefore, that they should constitute the oligarchy leading and directing the rest of the larger group. Michels was essentially writing about political parties but it is interesting to ascertain whether this phenomenon can be equally applied to new social movements. Is it the case that it is natural that a leader or leadership group will 'emerge' from within these new social movements? Is it, therefore, futile for them to shy away from traditional concepts of leadership as the reality is that these will emerge naturally? That aside, even if it is natural for an oligarchy to emerge, surely new social movements are to be commended for at least trying to focus their attentions upon the grass-roots level and upon a wider dispersal of power than is traditional in organisational structures? One issue that may result from this approach though is that the lack of a leader or leadership figurehead might be regarded in a negative light in relation to links with the media. Given that new social movements will need the oxygen of publicity, not to have a leader might be debilitating. The media need a spokesperson or key figure to approach whenever there is a story associated with a particular group or organisation. Not having such a central person may lead to a lack of publicity and a loss of 'voice'. The environmental movement has traditionally shied away from having a central figure but, relatively recently, the move towards the use of spokespeople has certainly helped them to get their message across. The art of media manipulation is a skill that all new social movements need to master if they are to move towards achieving their aims. Given the all-pervasive role of the media and the way in which they constantly impact upon our daily lives almost to the level of saturation point, new social movements cannot ignore the mass media. They have to engage at some level, if they are to get their message across.

Another defining characteristic of new social movements is the way in which they represent a departure from previous movements and organisations.

One of the key aspects to note is that, unlike other organisations such as, for example, the workers/trade union movements, they are not simply concerned with issues such as pay and working conditions, with improving living standards and with the material conditions of our lives. They are concerned with lifestyles and values, focused upon the way we live our lives, upon how we conduct ourselves as a society. One of the key writers in relation to new social movements, Alan Scott, believes that new social movements are understood '. . . as first and foremost *social* movements' (1990: 16), clarifying this by saying they are concerned '. . . less with citizenship, and hence with political power, than with the cultural sphere, their focus being on values and lifestyles' (*Ibid.*). A pertinent example to illustrate this point is the women's movement. The women's liberation movement encouraged and enabled women to assess the way that they lived their lives. These were questions that had probably not been asked before, or at least not on such a large scale. Issues such as who does the washing up at home, whether childcare and domestic chores were shared between the sexes, whether women were entitled to be 'valued' by society as being of equal worth to men, were all brought to the forefront. Specific questions such as whether women should get married or whether that was a bourgeois institution that oppressed women were also raised. The effect of this was to encourage many women to think about their lives in ways which hitherto they would never have contemplated. This notion of 'consciousness-raising' and getting women to perceive the way in which they were oppressed in society was at the very core of the women's movement. This was a fundamental shift in attitudes and in thinking about women's role and position in society. They began to question all aspects of women's role in society. Indeed, the feminist mantra of the 'personal is political' was at the heart of this sea-change in thinking. They were able to encourage women to see that their own personal situation was not unique and that it had parallels with what other women were experiencing, all over the country and, to a great extent, all over the world. The notion of patriarchy and male domination were highlighted as being insidious and wrong. As stated, this emphasis upon lifestyles and values is one of the key ways in which new social movements differed from earlier organisations. It meant getting people to question the very core of their lives and the way that they lived those lives. Another classic example of this is the gay liberation movement. Prior to the growth and development of new social movements, homosexuality was regarded as an individual/pathological 'problem'. It was seen as there being something 'wrong' with a specific individual. The gay liberation movement was able to portray the collective nature of homosexuality and for it to be seen as a collective struggle against a primarily hostile and prejudiced society. Many homosexuals had married and this was often as a way of denying their homosexuality either to the wider society or even to themselves. With this questioning of lifestyles and values and challenging the status quo and the orthodoxy, many homosexuals were able to lead much more fulfilling, rewarding and, above all, happier lives. Without the consciousness-raising and the challenges cultivated by the movement, it is doubtful whether individuals would have had the strength and courage to take a stand against society as a whole. The women's liberation movement and the gay rights movement, therefore, are two classic examples of the way in which new social movements constituted a very different form of organisation in comparison to earlier groupings. It is precisely this direct and overt challenge to and reassessment of lifestyles and values that made them crucial parts of the societal changes that occurred in the latter part of the twentieth century. It is difficult to over-estimate the importance of new social movements to changing the world in which we lived. This radicalisation led to many people completely transforming the way that they lived. Some, for example, chose to move away from traditional nuclear family structures and instead moved to communal forms of living, with shared childcare and domestic duties being central components of creating a more equitable distribution of power and rewards. Others were even more radical and chose, for example, to shun men altogether, blaming patriarchal power relations as the root cause of societal ills. The Society for Cutting Up Men (SCUM) is a case in point!

When did new social movements emerge?

In terms of when new social movements came into being, it is generally accepted that the late 1950s and early 1960s is the key period when they began to emerge and develop. As stated, they are a phenomenon of the latter part of the twentieth century. In comparison with earlier movements, such as the trade union movement, they were not so much concerned with tinkering with the existing political system but rather they wanted to question and challenge that system as a whole. The focus upon lifestyles and values is very much symptomatic of that approach. Key examples of new social movements include the peace movement, the gay rights movement, the women's movement, the animal rights movement, the environmental movement, the student and youth movement, amongst others. In a whole host of areas of the civil sphere of life people were starting to challenge the status quo, to question those in positions of political power and to postulate alternative ways of living and organising.

Why are people more willing to protest?

It is interesting to analyse what accounts for the growth and development of new social movements. Certainly, they are a twentieth century phenomenon, even though protest has obviously existed since the beginning of time – as long as there have been disagreements between people, there has been protest. Protest, dissent and resistance remain at the heart of politics. As stated in Chapter Two, politics is about conflict, about the allocation of scarce resources and relates to the fact that difficult decisions and choices have to be made. Inevitably, some of these decisions and choices will lead to a backlash. Some people who feel they are the 'losers' in terms of these difficult decisions may not take it lying down and may feel that they should, nay must, protest and try to get their voices and opinions heard.

The growth and development of new social movements are part of this response and backlash. The ordinary person has become more willing to protest and dissent in recent years – much more so than people would have done in the early part of the twentieth century, for example. It is interesting to analyse not just what has happened, in terms of this increasing protest and dissent, but also why this has happened. What has occurred within the psyche of the British population that means that they are more willing to question and challenge those in positions of power and authority? In addition, it is also interesting to analyse whether this is exclusively a British phenomenon or whether it occurs on a global scale and, if so, whether there are certain nations and nationalities that are more willing, perhaps more suited, to protest and dissent than others.

From the late 1950s onwards, people in a number of western democracies became increasingly more willing to question and challenge those in positions of power and authority. Prior to this time, particularly in the United Kingdom, people were generally extremely deferential to those who they regarded as their social superiors. Whether this was by virtue of their birth or the fact that they were deemed to be in possession of particular qualities and attributes is debatable. What is clear, however, is that, from the late 1950s onwards, this situation started to change. This esteem for so-called 'social betters' manifested itself in such aspects as, for example, in certain communities the local doctor would be regarded as almost a God-like figure. They were in possession of medical knowledge and, therefore, alongside this went a certain amount of power, status and kudos. The Conservative Party, likewise, were regarded by many people as the born leaders in society, the natural party of government and they too benefitted from these relatively high levels of deferential attitudes. The growth of more questioning and challenging attitudes amongst the general public meant that people start to think about why they should vote or behave in a certain way. These changing attitudes can be linked to a number of wider developments in society at large. The development and expansion of the mass media meant that people were becoming more open and receptive to new ideas and opinions. Some of these new ideas and opinions led them to challenge previously held beliefs about the way in which society was organised. The 1950s and 1960s were a time of increasing affluence and prosperity. Indeed, the thirteen years of continuous Conservative rule between 1951 and 1964 came to be dubbed the 'age of affluence', following on as it did from the 1945 to 1951 period of the 'age of austerity'. During the late 1950s and early 1960s, people saw their living standards improve significantly. The so-called hungry thirties were now a distant memory and the ordinary person had disposable income and a greatly improved lifestyle from their immediate predecessors. Consumer durables were starting to be mass produced and people wanted to acquire these material possessions. Vacuum cleaners, washing machines and the television set appeared on most people's wish lists and for many became a reality. Alongside the ubiquitous radio or wireless, the development and availability of the television set meant that people were able to attain information about the wider world to a much greater extent than hitherto. Their view of the world was expanding exponentially. The educative effect of the mass media should not be underestimated. This again contributes to making people more questioning and challenging. Horizons were broadened; people could look beyond their immediate vicinity and even contemplate different ways of living and organising.

As well as the educative effects of the mass media, the education system itself expanded its reach. In particular, the growth in the numbers participating in the higher education system, with many more young people proceeding on to further and higher education, meant that young people were opening their minds to new ideas and beliefs. Allied to this greater willingness to question orthodox beliefs, participation in the higher education system meant that young people, in particular, had time on their hands and, in addition, often had spare finances to enable them to participate in protest and dissent. Whereas previously, young people entered the world of work at the earliest possible opportunity, now they were afforded the luxury of time to engage in new social movement activities. The student movement is regarded as a prime example of a new social movement. Young people started to challenge their elders, galvanised by the ideas that were being taught especially within the university sector. The pinnacle is often regarded as May 1968 when events were set in motion by students in Paris but which quickly spread to other countries and, for a while at least, it looked as though revolution was in sight. Ideas, time, space and money all converged to provide the student movement with a unique momentum. Alongside the student movement, there were also other protests spreading from the United States of America. These included the aforementioned women's liberation movement; the Anti-Vietnam protests propagated by those opposed to the War in Vietnam; and the Black Power Movement that pushed for civil rights in America. There was a wave of protest spreading across the developed world.

Young people certainly played a part in the student movement but they were also becoming active more generally. This phenomenon ties in with the growth and development of a specific youth culture. Previously, one was either a child or an adult, there was no such focus upon an in-between stage. The creation of the concept of a teenager led to the focus upon a particular stage in life, following on from childhood but prior to the onset of adulthood, with all that it entails in terms of responsibilities and restrictions. Prior to the Second World War, the notion of a teenager did not really exist; it is only during the age of affluence that young people, alongside the rest of society, begin to have access to disposable income and this, in turn, leads to the development of a clearly discernible youth culture. The music, fashion and film industries, alongside many other aspects of life, begin to grow and develop and particularly to target and focus upon cultivating a specific appeal to young people. Films such as those featuring the young Elvis Presley, Cliff Richard, James Dean or Marlon Brando were targeting a particular audience. What is more, in some cases they were featuring the notion of a disaffected or alienated youth that sought to challenge both their elders and society at large, *Rebel without a Cause* and *The Wild One* being two such movies. British films such as *A Taste of Honey*, *Look Back in Anger* and *Saturday Night/Sunday Morning* were a specific manifestation of this genre. Fashion acquired a distinctive youth angle and appeal, and designers such as Mary Quant and Ossie Clark designed for this distinctive youth cohort, producing clothing that was very different to that worn by their parents' generation. Music was revolutionised by new bands such as The Beatles and the Rolling Stones, with their distinctive sound, appearance and appeal that was very different to what had preceded it. Loud, exciting and with meaningful lyrics, young people felt that these groups spoke both to and for them. In addition to this wave of developments in relation to youth culture, there was also a significant growth in the relative affluence levels of young people. Mike Abrams's (1961) research reveals the extent to which their purchasing power increased exponentially at the end of the 1950s and early 1960s, to the extent that young people were now a significant source of disposable income, and certainly those wishing to pursue a profit would do well to focus their business acumen on this ever-expanding cohort of young people. The notion of the 'baby boomer' generation highlights the extent to which this sector of society was increasing in size in comparison to other sectors of society. For all these reasons, young people were to form a significant part of new social movement activity. They were often at the forefront of these protests and provided a direct challenge to the older generation and to the way that society was organised.

Another crucial aspect to flag up in terms of why new social movements emerged at the point in history when they did relates to the so-called post-affluence, post-materialism or post-industrialisation thesis. Much of this is associated with the work of the American political scientist Professor Ronald Inglehart (cf.: 1977a, 1977b for example). Inglehart espouses the viewpoint that as people become better off financially they are thus able to turn their attention away from basic economic survival and then they might become interested in other aspects such as animal rights or environmentalism. If, however, people are focused upon basic economic survival and are worrying about whether and indeed how they are going to be able to feed their children then they are much less likely to be concerned about the plight of the blue whale, the Natterjack toad or the Amazonian rainforest. These concerns are all luxuries that are only likely to be afforded in times of relative prosperity – as Inglehart's thesis observes. With the rise of affluence in the 1950s and 1960s, improving living standards and, generally, more of a focus upon living as opposed to mere survival, people were able to do precisely as Inglehart outlines and were able to turn their attention to matters such as animal rights, environmentalism and peace protesting. Critics of Inglehart point out that certain protests have, in fact, emerged during times of relative poverty and from groups fighting for jobs and livelihoods, such as the March for Jobs and specific riots that were linked to unemployment and rising levels of poverty. Nonetheless, Inglehart's thesis does carry a certain amount of weight amongst new social movement theorists *per se*.

One key aspect that has undoubtedly contributed to the rise and development of new social movement activity is that of the changing role of women in society. Gender roles have changed dramatically over the past fifty years or so. In the 1950s, gender roles for both men and women were clearly demarcated. Men were the breadwinners, the ones who went out to work, women were the homemakers, the child bearers and the child rearers. Clearly, they remain for biological reasons at least the child bearers (although even here technological advances have brought numerous changes to this process, IVF, neo-natal advances, etc., but have not yet eradicated the primary involvement of women). Specific gender roles have been challenged, most noticeably by the women's movement. In addition, the key medical advance that should be flagged up is the creation and widespread availability of the contraceptive pill. This meant that, for the first time in human history, women could truly control their fertility and could decide for themselves whether and when they wished to have children. The fact that women were able to limit the number of offspring that they produced meant that they could restrict the amount of time that they devoted to bringing up children and could contemplate a career and a world beyond the realm of the home. In addition, societal changes such as increasing numbers of divorces and the decline in the social stigma associated with divorce meant that women were no longer trapped in a loveless marriage. Allied to this, many more women were choosing to cohabit either before marriage or instead of marrying. In the world of work, women found it easier pursue a career especially given that legislative advances, such as the 1970 Equal Pay Act and the 1975 Sex Discrimination Act, meant that discrimination against women could be subject to legal challenge. The women machinists at the Ford Car Plant in Dagenham, Essex, were instrumental in getting the Labour Government to bring in legislation that would mean that women and men should be paid the same rate for work of a similar type. The Labour Minister Barbara Castle empathised with the women's plight and ensured that equal pay was enshrined in law prior to the Labour Government leaving office at the 1970 General Election. The 2010 feature film entitled *Made in Dagenham* is based on the strike and provides a fascinating insight into how the striking machinists were able to get their message across to Barbara Castle, in particular. What is interesting, however, is that more than forty-three years after the legislation was placed on the statute books, equal pay between men and women is still not a reality. The campaigning organisation the Fawcett Society provides regular updates and it remains the case that the gender-pay gap still exists. In 2012, for example, if comparison is made between women and men in full-time work then a 14.9 per cent pay gap existed (see http://www.fawcettsociety.org.uk/equal-pay/ for further information). On this one issue alone, the women's movement still has a role to play in raising awareness and campaigning for change.

In addition, whilst men are taking on more domestic duties than hitherto, it remains the case that women still undertake most of the household chores – even, surprisingly, when their male partner does not work (see Philipson, 2013). Gender roles have, therefore, undergone some changes since the 1950s but perhaps that difference is not so marked as one might at first think. Traditional gender roles have been challenged but have not been eradicated. New social movements have reflected and questioned these roles but have not fundamentally changed them.

Who are the protesters? What sort of people protest?

It is difficult to generalise and stereotype in terms of who are the protesters and activists within the various new social movements. Is there a typical member of a new social movement? Often they are people who have not belonged to a political party or political grouping before. There has been a tendency for them to be more middle class than the majority of the population. Again, this could be linked to Inglehart's post-affluence thesis and allied to the fact they are possibly the ones who have more time and resources to enable them to participate and protest. Scott highlights how the Anti-Vietnam protests in America saw middle class people begin to protest, as he says,

> The imminent prospect of conscription into a distant war, where neither the possibility of quick victory nor a convincing political and moral justification were at hand, led to violent clashes on American university campuses during the summer of 1968. These events hit middle-class Americans in a way in which racial conflicts could not.
>
> (1990: 13)

What actions do they undertake?

In terms of what the members of new social movements actually do, it is fair to say that they use a whole host of different methods in order to try and achieve their aims. These range from writing to Members of Parliament, through to using gimmicks to gain media attention for their cause through to utilising means that go above and beyond the law, even terrorist activities. One interesting aspect of new social movement activity is that their support and action tend to ebb and flow. They have periods of time where a lot happens and then other occasions when they might be regarded as relatively dormant. The women's movement, for example, might mount a high profile

137

campaign if there is a threat to the abortion legislation but might then seem relatively inactive for a while. Likewise, gay rights groups might protest if there is a particular issue or topic (such as gay marriage) that they wish to highlight and gain media attention for. At other times, there may be relatively little happening. This approach contrasts fairly starkly with, for example, political parties, which have a permanent organisation and structure.

Gimmicks and stunts are used by new social movements primarily to gain publicity and media attention for their cause. Recent examples include those of the group *Fathers 4 Justice*, which campaigns for fathers' rights in the event of marital and relationship breakdown. Dressing up as Batman and scaling a public building was instrumental in raising the profile of the organisation. Early examples include, in 2003, one of their supporters, David Chick, dressing up as Spiderman and climbing a crane near Tower Bridge. Another stunt, in May 2004, involved two F4J protesters, Guy Harrison and Ron Davis, throwing condoms filled with purple powder, one of which landed on the then Prime Minister Tony Blair, from the Gallery in the House of Commons. It gets the group's name known and out there in the public sphere. Similarly, the feminist group *Slutwalk* encouraged women to dress in provocative clothing to illustrate that how a woman dresses is a matter of personal choice and does not mean she is sexually available. The walks began in April 2011 in Toronto but soon spread to other countries. They were a direct response to a comment from a Canadian police officer that some women may provoke attacks by the way they dress and that they should '. . . avoid dressing like sluts' (Bell, 2011). Other groups that have been known to use gimmicks and publicity stunts are the disabled rights groups who chained themselves to the railings of the Houses of Parliament. Animal rights groups, such as PETA (People for the Ethical Treatment of Animals), were successful in getting celebrities and supermodels, for example the model Christy Turlington, to pose naked with the slogan 'I'd rather go naked than wear fur'. Subject to criticism from feminist animal rights protesters, this was undoubtedly, however, a simple, effective and definitely eye-catching campaign!

Do they achieve their aims?

In terms of whether they actually achieve their aims, it is fair to say that this is a more difficult question to answer. There is a definitely a niche here in the existing literature on new social movements and a need for scholars to pursue this area with vigour. The question of how much impact and effect new social movements have is certainly open to debate. Looking back over the past fifty years or so, it is certainly the case that society has changed a great deal and much of this change can be attributed to the actions of new social movements. The women's movement, the gay rights movement and the environmental movement amongst others have all achieved significant successes. The gay rights movement is an interesting organisation upon which to focus because, if, for example, examination is made of their aims and objectives in the mid-late 1990s, it can be seen that they have achieved virtually everything that was on their political agenda. From the lifting of the ban on gays in the armed forces to civil partnerships, gay adoption and the removal of section 28 from the 1988 Local Government Act, their aims have been met. Gay marriage, perhaps the final goal, is now a reality. Within the space of two decades, they have transformed society. And yet, as stated previously, homophobia still exists and it is difficult to change entrenched attitudes. Education will certainly help in this area but attitudinal change may take much longer to happen. Legislation is certainly on the statute books but it may be a while before there is genuine equality in this area.

Is social class a factor?

Social class does not appear to be a key factor in terms of those who get involved in new social movement activity. Whereas previous movements, in particular the workers' or trade union movement, did have a specific class angle, these newer movements draw support from all walks of life. Some groups have been labelled as more middle class than others. For example, the anti-aviation group 'Plane Stupid' that protests against the expansion of air travel was dubbed the 'Barbour Brigade' in the press. It was noted that many of its supporters came from fairly exclusive backgrounds; for example, one was identified as being the grandson of a lord. The fact that they were deemed to be unrepresentative of society as a whole led to criticism. Surely, however, the focus should be upon their aims and objectives and whether these are laudable and not the detail in relation to their socio-economic backgrounds. The media does seem to focus upon trying to portray certain protesters as middle and upper class idealists. Is it the case that they are judging this new politics by a defunct yardstick of social class or is this still an important factor in analysing political protest? Given that new social movements have a focus upon lifestyles and values perhaps it is irrelevant to focus upon class when issues such as the environment, animal rights, the propensity for peace affect the whole of society and not just specific social strata.

Previous protests that were primarily associated with the workers' or trade union movement did have a definite class base. Examination of struggles such as the 1984/85 Miners' Strike, for example, reveals the centrality of social class in this epic clash between the workers and the government. Notions of a 'them' and 'us' mentality were clearly in evidence here (*cf.* Briggs, 1998) and were exacerbated when the then prime minister, Margaret Thatcher, referred to the miners as the 'enemy within'. The miners, in 1984/85, were protesting not just for better pay and conditions, as they had done in previous strikes, but for the very survival of their communities – perhaps this was why it was such an internecine battle. It possibly marked the last great class-based struggle in British history.

Certainly, new social movement activity focuses upon creating a better world of the whole of society. Emphasis upon lifestyles and values has moved us beyond a focus upon a narrow class-based analysis. In theory at least, activities and protests such as those in support of animal rights, environmentalism or gay rights produce a narrative that is wider than one specific social class. Society as a whole should benefit from such change. Having said this, a working class person who is struggling to make ends meet may find it difficult to contemplate protesting regarding animal rights. For example, in one predominantly working class area of West Yorkshire at the end of the 1990s there was relatively little protest that took place in support of a rare species of bat. This colony was lost when disused railway tunnels (defunct since the Beeching reforms) were demolished to make way for a road bypass. It does beg the question as to whether or not this would have occurred in a more middle class area. One rather suspects that middle class protestors would have been out en masse getting the message across that this bat was threatened and that the bypass should be re-routed.

New social movements in the twenty-first century

In the early years of the twenty-first century, there remains a significant amount of new social movement activity taking place. Fathers 4 Justice, the Slutwalks and Plane Stupid have already been mentioned. On a global scale, the Occupy movement is also part of this continued level of protest. It saw a significant number of sustained protests against social and economic inequality. Occupy Wall Street began in September 2011 and quickly spread to more than ninety cities across the world. The Occupy movement was partly inspired by the Spanish Indignados Movement (which began in May 2011 in Madrid) and by the Arab Spring (which began in December 2010 but which spread across a number of Arab countries in the spring of 2011 and which saw the toppling of governments in a number of Arab countries). Most of the protest camps had been cleared by the spring of 2012 but it was clear that there was a significant amount of opposition to the global financial institutions and to giant corporations. The overarching belief was that the system worked in favour of a tiny minority of the population and there was pressure for politicians and bankers to act in a more moral and responsible way. It is debatable whether the protestors brought about significant change, but they did, at least, raise the profile of this issue and get it on to the political agenda.

One aspect to flag up in relation to the recent wave of protest activity is the way in which a great deal of the protest has been facilitated by the use of new technology. The internet and the widespread use of mobile devices have meant that protest is able to spread quickly between local groups. The use of social media sites such as Facebook™ and Twitter™ has meant that ordinary people are able to communicate with thousands of like-minded protesters and get their message out there in an instant. Whereas previous new social movement activity often relied on word of mouth or relatively slow modes of communication such as landline telephones and even letter-writing, nowadays an SMS text message or a video on YouTube™ can reach a mass audience in an instant. The immediacy of new technology heightens the potential impact of new social movements. This enables ordinary people to circumnavigate messages being expounded by governments and the other usual powerbrokers in society. A video can, in theory at least, reveal an alternative viewpoint put forward sometimes as a countervailing perspective to that espoused by the government. No longer do citizens solely rely on the traditional mass media for their information; street journalism and ordinary people can help to provide information and updates – sometimes in ways that do contradict orthodox opinion or the party line.

Another point to note in relation to new social movements is the way in which some political scientists have highlighted how more recent protests might be seen as being in direct opposition to earlier new social movements. For example, relatively recently there has been a rise of so-called men's movements, such as the men's rights movement or the Mythopoetic Men's Movement. In part, these could be seen as being a direct backlash against the women's movement. They often see themselves as trying to redress the balance in a world where the axis has tipped in favour of women and where men are often regarded as losing out in the modern world. As stated, Fathers 4 Justice is a classic example that rallies against the courts, believing that the judicial system rules in favour of mothers without giving sufficient regard to

141

the rights of fathers. Likewise, the fuel protesters who first came to prominence in the autumn of 2000 might be seen as being in direct opposition to the environmental movement, feeling that they have tipped the balance away from the motorist to such an extent that the motorist is almost regarded as a social pariah. The pro-hunting campaigners are similarly regarded as providing a direct challenge to successes achieved by the animal rights movement. (For further information and clarification on this point see the work of Garnett and Lynch, 2009: Chapter 19). As Garnett and Lynch state, '. . . all three causes can be said to be reactions *against* the success of new social movements' (2009: 518). Is it the case, therefore, that we are now in a new era of new social movement activity that is identified by 'new' or possibly second generation new social movements that counteract earlier ones?

Conclusion

New social movements constitute a phenomenon that began in the latter part of the twentieth century but that are still prevalent today in the twenty-first century. They have changed and adapted in response to changing circumstances but, nonetheless, their central identifying features remain the same. They are primarily located within the civil as opposed to the political sphere of life, they are concerned with lifestyles and values and they tend towards organising themselves in a non-hierarchical manner, shying away from traditional concepts of leadership wherever possible. They operate on a global scale and movement activity can quickly spread from country to country, as evidenced by protest movements such as that manifested under the monikers of the Arab Spring or the Occupy Movement. New social movements encourage people to question how we live our lives today. They illustrate the power and potential power that the ordinary person possesses in relation to the political élite. The notion of collective strength remains important *vis-à-vis* the powers that be. Group activity can effect change. Governments have to remember that fact. Democratically elected governments, for that matter despotic regimes too, have to remember that people power remains a potent force for change. As outlined earlier, people join new social movements and participate in new social movement activity for a whole host of reasons. One such explanatory theory, the post-affluence thesis (*cf.* Inglehart), highlights how, as people became better off financially, they were then able to turn their attention away from basic economic survival and perhaps become interested in environmentalism or animal rights, to name a couple of movements. Other theories emphasise aspects such as the growth and development of youth culture, regarding this as being a galvanising factor behind the proliferation of social protest. As illustrated, a variety of reasons have been postulated to explain why people became increasingly more willing to resort to protest and dissent. Regardless of these explanatory factors, it is certainly the case that protest has become more prevalent.

In terms of what impact, if any, new social movements have and whether or not they are successful, it is difficult to ascertain categorically whether or not new social movements achieve their aims. It is difficult to isolate a causal link; this is to say, to be able to pinpoint whether or not a particular social and political change occurs due to the new social movements actions. Did the recent changes in relation to the gay rights agenda, for example, occur because of gay rights movement activity or because there was support at governmental level? Would those changes have occurred without the activities of groups such as Stonewall and OutRage? Likewise, can the move away from testing cosmetics on animals be directly linked to protest activities emanating from animal rights organisations? There is definitely a niche here for political scientists to investigate the achievements of new social movements. New social movements are, however, here to stay. Over the last fifty to sixty years, they have provided a conduit for the ordinary person to gather together and to make their collective voice heard. A whole host of areas that were previously just accepted as being the norm have been subject to challenge and question. Issues ranging from eating meat to the institution of marriage; from using nuclear technology to how we express our sexuality; to whether we choose to live in a nuclear family or as part of a communal set-up; the way we live our lives has been examined in detail. Allied to this, the spontaneity facilitated by new technology, the internet and mobile devices means that new social movements are able to organise instantaneously and to be both reactive and proactive in the face of political change. Never before has *Doing Politics* been so immediate and so powerful!

Chapter bibliography

Abrams, M. (1961) *Teenage Consumer Spending in 1959*, London, Press Exchange.

Barker, C., Johnson, A. and Lavalette, M. (2001) *Leadership and Social Movements*, Manchester, Manchester University Press.

Bell, S. (2011) 'Slutwalk London: "Yes means yes and no means no"', http://www.bbc.co.uk/news/uk-13739876 BBC News website 11 June, accessed 10 January 2013.

Briggs, J. E. (1998) *Strikes in Politicisation*, Aldershot, Ashgate.

Dalton, R. and Kuechler, M. (eds) (1990) *Challenging the Political Order: New Social and Political Movements in Western Democracies*, Cambridge, Polity.

Della Porta, D. (1995) *Social Movements, Political Violence and the State: A Comparative Analysis of Italy and Germany*, Cambridge, Cambridge University Press.

Della Porta, D. and Diani, M. (2006) *Social Movements: An Introduction*, second edition, Oxford, Blackwell.

Diani, M. (1992) 'The concept of social movement', *Sociological Review*, Vol. 40, Issue 1: 1–25.

Dobson, A. (2007) *Green Political Thought*, 4th edition, London, Routledge.

Eder, K. (1993) *The New Politics of Class: Social Movements and Cultural Dynamics in Advanced Societies*, London, Sage.

Eyerman, R. and Jamison, A. (1991) *Social Movements: A Cognitive Approach*, Cambridge, Polity Press.

Garner, R. (2004) *Animals, Politics and Morality*, second edition, Manchester, Manchester University Press.

—— (2005) *Animal Ethics*, Cambridge, Polity.

—— (2006) *The Political Theory of Animal Rights*, Manchester, Manchester University Press.

Garnett, M. and Lynch, P. (2009) *Exploring British Politics*, second edition, Harlow, Pearson Education.

Grey, S. and Sawer, M. (2008) *Women's Movements*, London, Routledge.

Hansard Society (2010) *Audit of Political Engagement 7*, London, Hansard Society.

Hay, C. (2007) *Why We Hate Politics*, Cambridge, Polity Press.

Henn, M., Weinstein, M. and Forrest, S. (2005) 'Uninterested Youth? Young People's Attitudes towards Party Politics in Britain', *Political Studies*, Vol. 53: 556–578.

Henn, M., Weinstein, M. and Wring, D. (2002) 'A generation apart? Youth and political participation in Britain', *British Journal of Politics and International Relations*, Vol. 4, No. 2, June: 167–192.

—— (2004) 'Alienation and youth in Britain', in Todd, M. J. and Taylor, G. (eds), *Democracy and Participation: Popular Protest and New Social Movements*, London, Merlin: 196–217.

Hobson, B. (ed.) (2003) *Recognition Struggles and Social Movements*, Cambridge, Cambridge University Press.

Inglehart, R. (1977a) *The Silent Revolution: Changing Values and Political Styles among Western Publics*, Princeton, New Jersey, Princeton University Press.

—— (1977b) *Modernization and Post-Modernization: Cultural, Economic and Political Change in 43 Countries*, Princeton, New Jersey, Princeton University Press.

Inglehart, R. and Norris, P. (2003) *Rising Tide: Gender Equality and Cultural Change around the World*, Cambridge, Cambridge University Press.

Jenkins, J. C. and Klandermans, B. (1995) *The Politics of Social Protest*, London, UCL Press.

Johnston, H. and Klandermans, B. (eds) (1995) *Social Movements and Culture*, London, UCL Press.

Kolinsky, M. and Paterson, W. (1976) *Social and Political Movements in Western Europe*, London, Croom Helm.

Koopmans, R. (1995) *Democracy from Below: New Social Movements and the Political System in West Germany*, Oxford, Westview Press.

Kriesi, H., Koopmans, R., Duyvendak, J. W. and Giugni, M. G. (1995) *New Social Movements in Western Europe*, London, UCL Press.

Lovenduski, J. and Norris, P. (eds) (1996) *Women in Politics*, Oxford, Oxford University Press.

Maheu, L. (1995) *Social Movements and Social Classes*, London, Sage.

Michels, R. (1966 [1915]) with introduction by Seymour Martin Lipset, *Political Parties: A Sociological Study of the Oligarchical Tendencies of Modern Democracy*, New York, Free Press.

Offe, C. (1980) 'Am Staat vorbei? Krise der Parteien und neue soziale Bewegungen', *Das Argument*, Vol. 22, No. 124: 809–821.

Philipson, A. (2013) 'Women still do household chores even when male partner doesn't work', *Telegraph*, 24 January, http://www.telegraph.co.uk/women/9823375/Women-still-do-household-chores-even-when-male-partner-doesnt-work.html, accessed 3 May 2013.

Pugh, J. (2010) (ed.) *What Is Radical Politics Today?*, Basingstoke, Palgrave Macmillan.

Ruggiero, V. and Montagna, N. (2008) *Social Movements: A Reader*, London, Routledge.

Scott, A. (1990) *Ideology and the New Social Movements*, London, Unwin Hyman.

Todd, M. J. and Taylor, G. (eds) (2004) *Democracy and Participation: Popular Protest and New Social Movements*, London, Merlin Press.

Websites

http://www.fawcettsociety.org.uk/equal-pay/, accessed 10 May 2013.

8

Compare and contrast

An investigation into comparative politics

This chapter highlights one of the key areas of political study, namely that of comparative politics. The works of Jean Blondel and also Rod Hague and Martin Harrop are important here. The comparative approach is examined in depth and analysis is made of the fact that whilst we may not necessarily be comparing like with like when we assess differing political systems, nonetheless the comparative approach does help the student of politics to make greater sense of the political world. Many students of politics will be familiar with the way that their own country's political system operates but often they seek to enhance their knowledge by focusing upon at least one other country or supranational body, such as the European Union.

What is comparative politics?

Most students of politics usually commence by learning about their own political system. This is a logical and relatively simple approach to take given that it can be reasonably expected that an individual is likely to have some prior knowledge, albeit possibly at a simplistic level of understanding and analysis, of their own country and its governmental system. Political socialisation occurs throughout childhood as an individual becomes assimilated into the rules, regulations and morals of their native political culture. This can sometimes be on a subliminal level with an unconscious acceptance of 'this is how we do things here'. It might also be on a more overt basis, for example learning about how laws are made and finding out about the role of a politician. Either way, logic reveals that this is likely to be the case. Comparative politics, therefore, takes us to the next level of understanding. As with many aspects of life, a deeper level of understanding of concepts and phenomena is to compare and contrast with other concepts and phenomena. It is helpful to fully grasp the essence of something by being able to make a direct comparison with something else. It can be claimed, therefore, that 'X' is 'X' precisely because it differs from 'Y'; ergo, 'Y' is 'Y' precisely because it is not 'X'.

In life, whether consciously or not, we make comparisons all the time. This is often in terms of ourselves and who we are. To be able to understand the *Id* (i.e. the self) with greater clarity it is necessary to compare oneself with others around us. Comparison with peers, with colleagues and even, in contemporary society, with celebrities helps us to understand the self. The basic human problem or issue of 'difference' is at the heart of politics and political understanding. Comparison with others can be a positive aspect, It can, however, degenerate into a more negative process if those comparisons reveal feelings of inadequacy. Notions of 'keeping up with the Joneses' or, for example, people who live beyond their means by financing a lifestyle built upon unsustainable levels of credit, reveal the downside of the comparative approach. Within reason, however, comparison can be healthy. It enables a greater understanding of the self and, possibly, provides an aspirational tool too. Comparative politics, therefore, is a natural progression from what happens at the individual level. Patrick O'Neil refers to comparative politics as a '. . . subfield that compares [the] pursuit of power across countries. The method of comparing countries can help us make arguments about cause and effect by drawing evidence from across space and time' (2013: 5). Furthermore, he posits that comparative politics helps to solve a number of puzzles such as

> . . . why some countries are democratic while others are not. Why have politics in some countries resulted in power being dispersed among more people, while in others power is concentrated in the hands of a few? Why is South Korea democratic while North Korea is not?
>
> (*Ibid.*)

It can be seen, therefore, that comparative politics deal with a whole host of complicated questions and conundrums. As Patrick O'Neil, this time working alongside Karl Fields and Don Share, points out,

Comparative politics is the study and comparison of politics across countries. Studying politics in this way helps us examine major questions of political science; for example, why do some countries have democratic regimes whereas others experience authoritarianism? Why and how do regimes change? Why do some countries experience affluence and growth, but others endure poverty and decline?

(2013: 3)

These are serious questions that vex the student of comparative politics.

Why study comparative politics?

In terms of why we perhaps might want to study comparative politics, this is possibly as old as history itself. Comparisons aid our understanding. As Bingham Powell *et al.* state, 'Comparative analysis helps us develop and test explanations and theories of how political processes work or when political change occurs' (2012: 29). Despite, however, recognising that the '. . . goals of the comparative methods used by political scientists are similar to those used in more exact sciences such as physics' (*Ibid.*), the authors acknowledge the limitations of comparative politics in that those studying the discipline

. . . cannot always control and manipulate political arrangements and observe the consequences. We are especially limited when dealing with large-scale events that drastically affect many people. For example, researchers cannot and would not want to start a war or social revolution to study its effects.

(*Ibid.*)

This limitation of the comparative method is an issue to which we will return later in this chapter. Political studies/science is one of the social sciences. Unlike the natural sciences, the situation is not so simple as to be able to conduct a scientific experiment to aid our understanding and knowledge of various phenomena. It is difficult to be able to isolate all factors and set up a controlled experiment whereby the focus is just upon one key area of difference. In order to understand whether, for example, voting should be compulsory in the United Kingdom, it helps to compare with other countries, such as Belgium or Australia, where voting is compulsory but the comparisons may not be as rigorous as a controlled experiment in the natural sciences. The history and development of Belgium, likewise Australia, differ greatly from that of the United Kingdom. Political culture differs, as do the political social-isation processes in each nation. Conclusions and comparisons can be drawn but the scholar of comparative politics has to bear the natural limitations in mind when reaching any conclusions. This key issue inherent in comparative politics is precisely this notion that, quite often, one is not able to compare 'like with like' in all respects. The control mechanism is intrinsically flawed. An attempt can be made to minimise difference, for example by careful selec-tion of similar states to use as comparator sets, but it can never be ironed out completely. Using the, already cited, example of compulsory voting, it might, therefore, yield better and more comprehensive/reliable results to compare with Belgium given its similarities as a relatively small state in the northern hemisphere. On the other hand, the common language and other points of divergence might mean that comparison with Australia is a more productive and revealing route to take. The political scientist has many decisions to make in terms of careful selection of comparator sets. Selection of comparators is a key aspect of comparative politics. Explanation is required as to why country 'Y' was chosen as opposed to country 'Z'. This is a difficult process, as Rod Hague and Martin Harrop testify:

> ... [even] with nearly 200 sovereign states, it is impossible to find a country which is identical to another in all respects except for that factor (say, the electoral system) whose effects we wish to detect. For this reason, political comparison can never be as precise as laboratory experiments. We just do not have enough countries to go round.

> (2007: 96–97)

Some of the difficulties of comparative political analysis are clearly outlined by Judith Bara and Mark Pennington, whereby they reveal how '... Comparative political analysis is always constrained by the number of cases with reliable available data, which means that such analysis should always acknowledge the limitations of what it can achieve' (2009: 61). They elucidate, that this '... is especially problematic in quantitative analysis where few cases mean we can only employ a small number of variables' (*Ibid.*). Bara and Pennington proceed to point out the hazard in trying to infer too much from small-scale data, trying to over-generalise from a limited number of cases or research material. This aspect and these limitations must be borne in mind when choosing the comparative approach.

Key areas of comparison

Comparisons can be made at the international level, i.e. between countries, but they can also be made within countries, so at the intra as well as the inter country level. Within a unitary state, such as the United Kingdom (in its current format at least), comparisons might be made between the different nation states. This might involve, for example, examination of how the law operates in England when compared with Scots Law. It is also the case that comparisons and contrasts might be examined at the sub-national level, i.e. between various devolved bodies or between different local authorities, to see how they operate. Comparative politics opens up a whole host of differing possibilities for investigation.

As Rod Hague and Martin Harrop, the doyens of comparative politics, reveal, comparative politics can involve analysis of a whole host of differing areas. Key aspects amongst these include comparative political systems, political economies, political cultures, political parties, levels of political participation, comparative elections and voting behaviours, comparative governmental structures and public policies. In essence, virtually all the areas that can be looked at from the perspective of a lone state can be assessed by way of a comparative analysis. Hague and Harrop combine the various areas of investigation into three levels of analysis, which they label institution-centred (for example, a focus upon judiciaries or legislatures), society-centred (such as an analysis of electoral data and voting behaviour) and state-centred (this might involve, for example, a comparison of welfare states) (*cf.*: 2007: Box 5.2, 85). Hague and Harrop emphasise the benefits of this comparative approach by stating that the

> . . . goal of comparative politics is to encompass the major political similarities and differences between countries. The task is to understand the mixture of constraints and variability which characterizes the world's governments, bearing in mind the national and international contexts within which they operate. Given this definition of comparative *politics*, the comparative *approach* is simply the family of strategies and techniques which advances this goal.
>
> (2007: 83)

With regards to why scholars of politics ought to compare, Hague and Harrop are of the opinion that, '. . . such an approach broadens our understanding of the political world, leading to improved classifications and giving potential

151

for explanation and even prediction' (*Ibid.*; Hague and Harrop, 2010: 46). They proceed to highlight the advantages of the comparative approach as being primarily four-fold, namely,

> . . . Learning about other governments broadens our understanding, casting fresh light on our home nation; Comparison improves our classifications of political processes; Comparison enables us to test hypotheses about politics; Comparison gives us some potential for prediction and control.
>
> (*Ibid.*: Box 5.1, 84; Hague and Harrop, 2010, Box 3.3: 46)

It can be seen, therefore, that the comparative approach aids the student of politics' understanding of the world around them.

Equally emphatic on the comparative approach, Jean Blondel's work proceeds to emphasise the inherent value of comparative politics. As Blondel states,

> . . . far from being antithetical to the study of individual governments or institutions, general comparative studies constitute a major help – indeed an irreplaceable help – as they can show the direction which studies of individual governments or institutions should most profitably take.
>
> (1990: 6–7)

Comparative politics can, therefore, provide guidance for politicians and policy makers in terms of the way in which they should lead their state, in terms of the type of state that they ought to strive to attain. As Blondel states, '. . . the search for comparisons naturally becomes central to the study of government and this is why the analysis of comparative government is necessarily the cornerstone of a rigorous and scientific study of government' (*Ibid.*: 4). Leading on from this, he expounds that if

> . . . we are to understand better the way governments work, comparison is not only valuable: it is inevitable. Any judgement on the workings of a government or of an institution of that government is based in reality on some underlying notion of how similar governments or similar institutions of government work in other circumstances.
>
> (*Ibid.*: 4–5)

Jean Blondel is correct to highlight the centrality of the comparative approach as an aid to our understanding of politics *per se*. Understanding and knowledge are undoubtedly enhanced by examination of 'other' political systems. This might provide us with ideas in terms of how not to do things just as much as in terms of what to do.

In terms of how to compare, Hague and Harrop (2010) highlight a number of approaches to the study of comparative politics. These include: the institutional approach – with its focus upon comparing different institutions; the behavioural approach, whereby the focus is upon how individuals act as opposed to focusing upon institutions. The emphasis, therefore, as they state, is '. . . on voters rather than elections, legislators rather than legislatures, and judges rather than the judiciary' (2010: 28). A third strategy for analysing comparative politics is labelled the structural approach, which is where analysis is made of specific structures or groupings, so going beyond specific institutions to look at say, social class, political parties or the military, to name a few areas (*Ibid.*: 31). Other theoretical approaches flagged up by Hague and Harrop include the rational choice approach and the interpretive approach. A rational choice analysis involves focusing upon the '. . . interests of the actors as the explanatory factors' (*Ibid.*: 33), whereas the interpretive approach emphasises the notion of shared ideas, the idea being that ideas '. . . shape how we define our interests, our goals, our allies and our enemies. We act as we do because of how we view the world; if our perspective differed, so would our actions' (*Ibid.*: 39). In essence, therefore, individuals and nation states, for that matter, have a particular and partial view of the world. Under this interpretive approach, this colours our judgement. It can be clearly seen, therefore, that there are a number of approaches and perspectives from which to study comparative politics. These differing theoretical perspectives form part of the attraction of comparative politics. The fact that the subject area can be tackled from a number of different angles adds to its appeal.

In addition, comparisons may focus upon a specific aspect, for example comparison of legislatures, electoral systems or pressure group activity. Scholars of politics often find that the comparative approach enhances their understanding of their own political system. It provides a yardstick against which to cross-reference how their own political system operates in relation to others. In addition, where a state considers altering key aspects of its political system and culture, for example when the UK held its referendum (in May 2011) regarding whether or not to change its electoral system for elections to the Westminster Parliament, politicians, policy makers and academics often look to other countries for evidence and guidance. In this example, the

UK looked overseas in order to assess their experience of different electoral systems, especially in relation to the Alternative Vote system, which was the option offered to the electorate in the plebiscite. Other examples include where states focus upon other countries with regards to specific policy areas. Examples include whereby the UK has looked to other countries in relation to the question of gay marriage or youth justice policies. A comparative approach might be to examine particular phenomena; new social movements, for example, are often examined from a comparative perspective as they operate on the world stage and exist in most nation states. Hank Johnston highlights this development by illustrating that in

> . . . the US, a critical mass of social movement researchers was reached sometime around the mid-1970s, and their concepts, findings, methods, and debates took off exponentially thereafter. Today the study of protests, social movements, and contentious politics is a major research focus in both North America and Europe, and its influence continues to grow.
>
> (2014: 27)

Johnston proceeds to highlight how the study of social movements has moved beyond North America and Europe and how the focus has switched to North Africa, with the emphasis upon newer and more varied forms of political protest involving social media and other twenty-first century forms of communication. As Johnston states, the

> . . . relation between virtual and traditional protest actions has come to the forefront in research about the Arab Spring, during which social media such as Facebook, YouTube, and Twitter were used in huge popular mobilizations. The Arab Spring of 2011 was made up of several people-power uprisings against repressive regimes in the Middle East and North Africa: Tunisia, Egypt, Libya, Yemen, Bahrain, and Syria. Most important . . . are the successful movements in Tunisia and Egypt, where mass protests eventually led to regime change after national military elites intervened in support of protesters' demands.
>
> (*Ibid.*: 143)

The Arab Spring is a relatively recent phenomenon that has proved fascinating for the student of comparative politics. There is already a burgeoning literature in this area which will, no doubt, continue to grow as analysts and experts abound (*cf.*: Barany, 2011; Dalacoura, 2012; Hollis, 2012; Lynch, 2011; Masoud, 2011; Way, 2011). This is clearly one area that academics and students alike will continue to find intriguing and inspiring. On a number of levels, be that from the perspective of notions of democracy, youth movements, use of social media as a form of political participation, etc., the Arab Spring provides tremendous scope for those *Doing Politics* and is an interesting case study in terms of both qualitative and quantitative data analysis.

Indeed, the case study approach constitutes another way in which to 'do' comparative politics. Hague and Harrop (2010: 43) point out that a '. . . case study is an instance of a more general category. By its nature, to conduct such a study is to undertake an investigation with significance beyond its own boundaries'. Case studies permit a detailed investigation that will, hopefully, lead to a wider applicability. Patrick O'Neil, Karl Fields and Don Share (2013) use the case study approach to just such an effect. Their examination of thirteen different case studies from across the globe, including India, Japan, Brazil and Nigeria, furnishes an in-depth study and a wealth of data for the comparative politics undergraduate. As they state, the

> . . . inquisitive student of comparative politics will find fascinating similarities in the 13 cases that follow. The commonalities across cases give credence to the utility of the comparative enterprise and justify the analytic comparisons offered. But these countries are also diverse and always changing, reminding us of the daunting challenges facing comparative political study.
>
> (2013: 30)

This point about countries 'always changing' is a pertinent one because it emphasises the historical dimension to comparative politics too. Comparative politics has a long history; indeed, the ancient political philosopher Aristotle is said to have compared the Ancient Greek city-states (circa 400–300 BC) in order to learn lessons (*cf.*: Bingham Powell *et al.*, 2012: 30). Politics, as the infamous Harold Wilson quotation reminds us, is ever-changing and clearly, for example, the United Kingdom of today differs considerably from that of the 1950s. Certainly, older generations might hark back to and reminisce about the so-called halcyon days of the past but, if it were indeed possible to time travel, they would find it barely recognisable from today's UK. Historical comparison, therefore, might also prove noteworthy. It has to be remembered that comparative politics tends to, thus, focus upon a particular point in time as well as in space. As Hague and Harrop illuminate, however, '. . . today's

present is tomorrow's past' (2013: 53), before elucidating further, that political science

> ... can and perhaps should make more use of the past as a treasure
> trove of additional cases, whether of rare events such as genocide and
> revolution or of particular episodes that exemplify, challenge or refine
> existing theories. History can enlarge our database, enabling us to
> employ the most different design to examine the robustness of findings
> across different time periods.
>
> (*Ibid.*)

This is clearly an important aspect and serves to highlight too the inevitable
linkages between the two disciplines of politics and history. These connections are reiterated in academia by the fact that many undergraduates choose
to study for a joint degree combining these two separate but synergetic
disciplines.

It can be seen, therefore, that the comparative approach enables students to
have a more in-depth understanding of various political events and phenomena. Comparative politics might focus upon a specific aspect of the political
scene, for example Mark Wheeler's (2013) work that investigates the cult
of celebrity as far as politics is concerned and which has a comparative angle.
He furnishes, for example, '... an analysis of modern celebrity politics in
America and its exportation to other mass democracies, particularly the
United Kingdom' (2013: 60). It is interesting to note that a concept such as
'celebrity' can be examined at a comparative level. Likewise, Chris
Phillipson's work on ageing offers a comparative perspective on a specific
topic area. As he expounds,

> ... there are in fact many different paths likely to be followed by
> ageing populations. These will reflect factors such as social and cultural
> variations across different societies, contrasting levels of resources
> within and between countries, differences in the speed of demographic
> change and contrasting attitudes towards older people and the idea of
> ageing.
>
> (2013: 11–12)

This educative aspect of comparative politics is worthy of emphasis. Countries
look and learn from each other, in terms of both positive aspects that they may
wish to emulate and negative factors that they, quite logically, will seek to

avoid. Similar problems are encountered by countries across the globe, as Phillipson highlights with regards to ageing, where the

> ... so-called "oldest-old" (those aged 85 and over) are, as a group, at a greater risk of poverty than younger older people (aged 65–84) [whereby, in view of] the substantial rise in those 85 and over by 2035, designing effective income and welfare policies for this age group will become increasingly urgent.

> (*Ibid.*: 19)

The notion of a shrinking world comes to forefront yet again. Globalisation (examined in greater depth in Chapter Nine) also contributes to this phenomenon of policy transfer and political emulation, and presumably also policy avoidance.

European Union

The existence of supranational bodies, the European Union being a case in point, provides further opportunities for the comparative approach to prevail. This leads to a level of interaction and synergy that means that countries working alongside each other, in close proximity, inevitably learn from each other. The fact that such bodies 'pool' their sovereignty in order to work together can be seen in a positive light. It means that they give up a certain amount of power and independence to work within the supranational body. Such a sharing of power and responsibility leads to nations learning from each other's experiences. The European Union, first created in the 1950s as a result of an amalgamation of the European Coal and Steel Community, set up in 1951, and the European Economic Community, created in 1958 by the initial group of six countries, was intended primarily as a trading body, indeed it was known as the Common Market. In addition, it was felt that greater co-operation between European states would mean that the horrors of war that had been witnessed again during the Second World War would be less likely to occur between trading partners. The subsequent growth and development of the European Union have led to greater integration and a move beyond a mere trading block. Known as the European Union since 1993, under the terms of the Maastricht Treaty it has expanded its reach and activities so that it currently comprises twenty-eight countries and has integrated to a much greater extent than hitherto. There is legislative integration as well as much easier movement of people and trade – a development that has pleased some but that has been of grave concern to others. Opinion differs as to how much integration is necessary or, indeed, desirable. Some feel that the integration has gone too far and too fast; witness the recent surge in support for the UK Independence Party and its leader Nigel Farage, whose anti-European stance has found favour in many quarters and which looks likely to achieve further electoral successes in forthcoming elections. This is indicative of the fact that there is clearly a sector of society for whom European integration has gone too far. Andrew Gamble encapsulates this issue when he states that the '. . . British relationship with the European Union has been one of the dominant issues of British politics in the last fifty years. It has also been one of the most divisive' (2003: 113). He proceeds to expand upon this point, explaining that the

> . . . reason why the issue of Europe has been so persistent and so divisive is that there is a lot at stake. For the future of British politics there is no more important issue, involving as it does a reassessment of British identity, security and political economy, and a judgement about the relative priority to be given to Europe as opposed to other relationships, particularly those with America.
>
> (*Ibid.*: 114)

This debate and these divisions provide further scope for analysis by the student of comparative politics.

How to study comparative politics

In terms of how to study comparative politics, it is more usual that the subject will be studied as a component of a politics degree. This might be as a route or strand, i.e. a number of connected modules that have pre-requisites or co-requisites, or it might be studied as a single or more stand-alone module. Sometimes, too, students may be able to choose their comparator sets; for example, they may be able to choose which countries they will examine and investigate. Alternatively, the countries may be predetermined and obviously this will depend upon staff expertise and their specific research areas. A module entitled *Comparative Politics* may, for example, involve a focus upon a set number of countries – say, four or five across a year's duration. In the UK, there is a tendency to focus upon the politics of the United States of America, former Soviet politics (*cf.*: Anderson, 2010), the politics of France, to name a few. In addition, popular areas of focus include Chinese politics (*cf.*: Gao, 2010; Hays Gries and Rosen, 2010; Shambaugh, 2008), Middle Eastern politics, African politics, Scandinavian politics, Indian politics, Latin American politics (*cf*: Smith and Ziegler, 2008), etc. Many degree courses focus upon specific aspects such as minority integration in Central and Eastern Europe, democratic transition in specific areas, for example Africa or Eastern Europe (*cf.*: Ishiyama, 2012; Rakner and van de Walle, 2009), poverty policies, refugee policies (*cf.*: Boswell, *et al.*, 2011), healthcare policy, housing policy or education policy (*cf.*: Lewin and Sabates, 2012; Omwami and Keller, 2010), to cite a few examples. A focus upon policy areas provides an interesting and detailed approach for the student of comparative politics. Lessons can be learned across and between states and comparisons can be particularly precise. With regard to comparative politics, there is a significant amount of choice across the university sector. The prospective student needs to undertake a thorough investigation of university websites and prospectuses in order to examine in detail the variety and scope of courses on offer. Having said this, it is difficult to know, without having covered it prior to the higher education level, whether interest will be sustained in a specific area. This is, in part, why at level one it is often useful to provide a 'taster' or insight into a number of different countries. Students may then wish to choose to specialise or research in greater depth at levels two or three, dependent upon which area has whetted their intellectual appetite.

In terms of the literature on comparative politics, it is fair to say that this is a burgeoning area of investigation and there is an expanding array of texts that focus upon this important area of study. Key texts are highlighted throughout this chapter and in the bibliography; authors including Hague and Harrop, Landman and O'Neil have written extensively on a whole host of issues relating to comparative politics. In addition, there are number of leading journals that focus upon the comparative perspective. Keys ones include the *Journal of European Social Policy*, *Comparative Education Review*, *Comparative Political Studies*, *China Quarterly*, *European Political Science*, *Latin American Politics and Society*, the *European Journal of Political Research*, *Comparative Politics*, the *Journal of Comparative and Politics*, and *Government and Opposition*, to name but a few. In addition, this is a living and evolving subject area so radio, television and newspaper resources also provide a wealth of material.

With regards to how to study comparative politics, again the pedagogical approaches are similar to studying politics *per se*. Given the focus upon other countries and areas, however, there is often the opportunity for a period of time to be spent studying overseas. In the case of the United States, this might be for a whole year's duration or, where the student's studies focus upon mainland Europe by way of comparison, a semester spent studying abroad is often the norm. During the time spent abroad, where the first language is other than English, quite often the student will have the opportunity to learn the language of the host country. Once again, to be proficient in the language as well as having an understanding of the political system of that country positively enhances an undergraduate's career prospects. Immersion in the language and culture is the best way of fully understanding a different political system. Students return from the study period abroad with renewed impetus and vigour with regard to their degree course. To have experienced the country on a first-hand basis and having been able to apply and relate their theoretical underpinnings to the reality of the situation in which they now find themselves is an invaluable educative experience.

In terms of the teaching and learning processes, seminars and lectures remain the key approaches involved in teaching comparative politics. As John Craig illuminates, '. . . the predominant learning experience for most Politics students in most cases remains the lecture and the seminar, and there are different views on the efficacy of such teaching and learning practices' (2012: 32). He proceeds to state, however, that what he '. . . would argue is that lectures and seminars will by their nature be better suited to teaching some aspects of the discipline than others' (*Ibid.*). Clearly, a lecture and seminar-driven approach is not without its critics but it is a tried and tested method. Other strategies and approaches may include debates, presentations, small group work or student-led seminars. Lectures of a hundred or more students are not uncommon as far as comparative politics is concerned. Students have to focus upon active listening and note-taking in these mass lectures. There may be some level of interaction and student participation, such as for example through the tutor asking students to vote on a specific issue or to express their option based around a range of options. Voting in this manner can take place using a device known as Optivote™ which involves a contraption similar to a television remote control handset. This is linked to software whereby the tutor is able to, instantaneously, reveal the results of such votes on the screen at the front of the lecture theatre. Diagrammatic presentations make the data easily accessible and quick to decipher. More recently, there are websites that permit such voting and the students can vote using their mobile phone. Given the proliferation of mobile phones in contemporary society and especially amongst the undergraduate population, this does not prove exclusive and it is likely that such websites will grow and develop in the future.

Seminars in comparative voting constitute another key way in which students learn the subject material. These tend to be much more student-led and participatory than the lectures. Formats are many and varied but might involve, for example, a small group of students giving a presentation to the rest of their seminar group or students discussing a number of specific issues related to particular countries. In terms of how comparative politics is assessed, this is usually in a similar way to straight politics modules. There may, however, have been more innovative forms of assessment used in comparative politics modules. By way of example, poster presentations have been used as an assessment tool for a comparative politics module, with students providing a visual display of the key aspects of a specific country. Other innovative forms of assessment include role play and simulations, which, although potentially challenging in terms of how to assess, lend themselves to innovative approaches (see Chapter Nine for further information about the innovative uses of simulations and role play). In addition, the student of comparative politics will also benefit from an emphasis upon key transferable skills; these are highlighted throughout this text, but to reiterate at this juncture, they may include such aspects as presentational skills, problem-solving techniques, critical thinking, group working, interview techniques, qualitative and quantitative data analysis, to highlight a few (cf.: Marsh and Elliott, 2008; Manheim et al., 2012, for further details regarding data analysis techniques). Employers seek intelligent and self-motivated graduates who are in possession not only of the subject matter but also of these invaluable transferable skills that are necessary for the twenty-first century workplace. Indeed, before entering the world of work, job applicants may be required to give a presentation as part of the interview process. Indeed, if a graduate is unable to overcome this hurdle, their possession of the subject knowledge, however in-depth, may well prove irrelevant.

Another innovative approach to comparative politics is that propounded by Richard Rose (2008), whereby he ponders the question of what you would tell the President of the United States (in this scenario) about Iraq, if you had only three minutes in which to argue your case or to make a particular point. This is an interesting idea and encourages students to focus upon the key aspects of any given policy area. Avoiding waffle and hyperbole, the students have a relatively short amount of time in which to convey their message. A multitude of differing policy areas and situations could be used in the teaching of comparative politics as a way of encouraging students to remain sharply focused upon the matter in hand. It also prepares students who may wish to embark upon a career as a policy advisor or civil servant. Not only is it an enjoyable exercise to carry out with students doing comparative politics, it also has a number of specific objectives and learning outcomes. Based around Richard Rose's own experience of being invited to a small group discussion with President George W. Bush, the simulation provides scope for emulation. Rose's brief was to

> ... prepare a 3-minute answer to the question: What are the most important insights from [your] research about conflict societies that the President may not already have heard and what lessons could be drawn that would be relevant to Iraq right now?
>
> (2008: 79)

As Rose accurately points out, the key words were 'right now', in that immediacy and a focus upon the contemporary scenario were the essence of the advice that the President was seeking. The 'problem' or 'challenge' is in condensing the key points into a three-minute summary. This is clearly a useful skill for the politics graduate to acquire. Rose accurately acknowledges this when he states,

> Students who want to change the world can learn from the study of history and institutions that it this is easier said than done ... academics who spend a lifetime rather than just a few minutes telling others what they know can do so with clarity in public spaces as well as classrooms in efforts to further an understanding of the importance of politics.
>
> (*Ibid.*: 83)

Mike Goldsmith and Chris Goldsmith provide a lucid and detailed synopsis of political science teaching in Europe, in part covering the comparative approach. They highlight the importance of teaching *vis-à-vis* research by illustrating that '. . . teaching has always been seen as "less glamorous" than research, albeit that most professional political scientists teach more than they research' (2010: 61). The Goldsmiths outline a number of innovative approaches to teaching and learning (such as technology-enhanced learning, learning 'on the job' via placements and problem-based learning, using case studies and simulations), all of which can be applied to comparative politics. In relation to case studies and simulations, they stipulate that these

> ... require both teachers and students to change from their ordinary roles in the classroom. Greater involvement is demanded of the

student, who takes an active part in the creation and interpretation of knowledge rather than passively receiving it . . . such learning is not dependent on the tutor: it can be independent or collaborative with other students.

(*Ibid.*: 66)

It can be seen, therefore, that it is not just the subject matter that is interesting and thought-provoking but also the pedagogical methods that serve to enhance and ameliorate the learning experience *vis-à-vis* comparative politics.

Careers in comparative politics

Once again, by virtue of the fact that a graduate has attained a degree, this in itself is often a passport to a variety of career options. It testifies to the fact that a certain level of education has been attained and that any prospective employer can expect the graduate to be in possession of a certain level of key transferable skills and abilities. Beyond this, however, comparative politics links more directly to a number of specific career options. Work within various international organisations and institutions, such as the United Nations or the European Union, is eminently suitable for the graduate in comparative politics. Other students choose to work for non-governmental organisations (NGO); these bodies are generally not for profit organisations that are not connected to specific governments, such as Save the Children, the Red Cross or Greenpeace. Clearly, graduates of comparative politics, and politics *per se*, often have a strong social conscience. They are generally, by their very nature, interested in people and, presumably, harbour a desire to improve the human condition. Other career options include, for example, political journalism or related areas that rely upon the power of prose. This is understandable given the fact that the written word forms a key part of the assessment process for the social science student. Graduates are able to express themselves in a clear and concise manner. 'Political' magazines such as the *New Statesman*, *Prospectus* or *Total Politics* would all find the student of comparative politics able to bring valuable skills to their organisation. In addition, it may facilitate a move to working in another country if a graduate is able to demonstrate a grasp of that country's political system, culture and way of life. Allied to this, the student of comparative politics who also takes up the opportunity to study a language will find this a definite advantage in terms of career prospects; it will enhance their job prospects and marketability. Some students study a language as an add-on, so in addition to their degree, whereas other courses offer the opportunity to study for a language qualification as an integral part of their undergraduate degree. This may enhance a graduate's prospects of finding work in one of the large supranational organisations such as the European Union or the United Nations. Other career options may include the civil service or working at a devolved level, such as working for the Scottish Parliament located in the Holyrood area of Edinburgh, the Northern Ireland Assembly and devolved institutions at Stormont in Belfast, or the Welsh Assembly in Cardiff, or at local government level, be that at a city or county level. Certainly, the student of comparative politics, in possession of knowledge and an understanding of the intricate working of the civil service or local government institutions of another state or group of states, should prove an invaluable asset to any political body. Lessons learned from overseas can be fed into their workplace environment. Comparisons enable valuable lessons to be applied to specific policy areas. It can be seen, therefore, that the graduate of comparative politics constitutes a potentially invaluable asset to a myriad of employers and professional bodies, a valuable resource to be tapped into throughout their careers.

Conclusion

As with other areas of political study, comparative politics provides a fascinating area of investigation. Comparative politics enables us to compare like with like and to learn lessons through these comparisons and contrasts. The basic issue of difference means that human beings constantly make comparisons throughout their lives. It aids our understanding of who we are by being able to compare with others. In the realm of politics, this is also the case. Differing political systems can be compared and contrasted in order that lessons can be learned. In addition, investigation of various supranational bodies, such as the European Union, also helps to foster a greater understanding of the individual nation states and how their specific political systems and political culture operate. In situations where a state is seeking to alter, redress or tinker with some aspect of their political system, such as electoral reform, it will often look to other nations to see what can be learned from the experience of others. Emulation of neighbouring states, or even of those further afield, is a key aspect of the political landscape. The old adage of imitation being the sincerest form of flattery can equally apply at the level of statehood.

Students of comparative politics may find that their degree is enhanced by the opportunity to study abroad – whether that is for a semester or for a longer period of time. Direct immersion in the culture and way of life of another country is probably the best way to learn all about its politics and culture. The student who does spend time living, studying and working overseas is likely to have a greater understanding of politics. In addition to this greater under-standing and awareness, it is also highly likely that, in doing so, the student directly or indirectly enhances their career opportunities and available options. Employers regard the added-value of time spent abroad in a positive light. Students often return from their study abroad period with a more in-depth understanding of politics and the political system. It is generally held that travel broadens the mind and the intellectual horizons and this is certainly the case in terms of political studies. Bearing this in mind, this leads neatly into examination of a related area of study, which is international relations. International relations has a broader focus than comparative politics but, again, there is a clear synergy between comparative politics and international relations. This related discipline is examined in detail in the next chapter, Chapter Nine. The final word with regards to comparative politics can, how-ever, be left to Rod Hague and Martin Harrop, who state that, with '. . . justi-fication, the comparative approach can be regarded as the master strategy for drawing inferences about causation in any area of study' (2007: 83). They justify this conclusion by citing their observation that, 'After all, experiments and statistical analysis designed to uncover relationships of cause and effect must involve a comparison between observations; all investigations of cause and effect are by nature comparative' (*Ibid.*).

Chapter bibliography

Anderson, R. D., Jr (2010) 'When the center can hold: the primacy of politics in shaping Russian democracy', *Communist and Post-Communist Studies*, Vol. 43, No. 4: 397–408.

Bara, J. and Pennington, M. (eds) (2009) *Comparative Politics: Explaining Democratic Systems*, London, Sage.

Barany, Z. (2011) 'Comparing the Arab revolts: the role of the military', *Journal of Democracy*, Vol. 22, No. 4: 28–39.

Bingham Powell, Jr. G., Dalton, R. J. and Strøm, K. (2012) *Comparative Politics Today: A World View*, tenth edition, Harlow, Pearson Education.

Blondel, J. (1990) *Comparative Government: An Introduction*, Hemel Hempstead, Philip Allan.

Boix, C. and Stokes, S. (eds) (2009) *The Oxford Handbook of Comparative Politics*, Oxford, Oxford University Press.

Boswell, C., Geddes, A. and Scholten, P. (2011) 'The role of narratives in migration policy-making: a research framework', *British Journal of Politics and International Relations*, Vol. 13, No. 1: 1–11.

Caramani, D. (ed.) (2011) *Comparative Politics*, second edition, Oxford, Oxford University Press.

Craig, J. (2012) 'What (if anything) is different about teaching and learning in politics?', in Gormley-Heenan, C. and Lightfoot, S. (eds), *Teaching Politics and International Relations*, Basingstoke, Palgrave Macmillan: 22–37.

Dalacoura, K. (2012) 'The 2011 uprisings in the Arab Middle East: political change and geopolitical implications', *International Affairs*, Vol. 88, No. 1: 63–79.

Gamble, A. (2003) *Between Europe and America*, Basingstoke, Palgrave Macmillan.

Gao, X. (2010) 'From the Heyang Model to the Shaanxi Model: action research on women's participation in village governance', *The China Quarterly*, Vol. 204: 870–898.

Goldsmith, M. and Goldsmith, C. (2010) 'Teaching political science in Europe', *European Political Science*, Vol. 9, No. 1: 61–71.

Hague, R. and Harrop, M. (2007) *Comparative Government and Politics: An Introduction*, seventh edition, Basingstoke, Palgrave Macmillan.

——(2010) *Comparative Government and Politics: An Introduction*, eighth edition, Basingstoke, Palgrave Macmillan.

Hays Gries, P. and Rosen, S. (eds) (2010) *Chinese Politics: State, Society and the Market*, Abingdon, Routledge.

Hollis, R. (2012) 'No friend of democratization: Europe's role in the genesis of the "Arab Spring"', *International Affairs*, Vol. 88, No. 1: 81–94.

Ishiyama, J. (2012) *Comparative Politics: Principles of Democracy and Democratization*, Oxford, Wiley-Blackwell.

Johnston, H. (2014) *What Is a Social Movement?*, Cambridge, Polity Press.

Kennett, P. (ed.) (2004) *A Handbook of Comparative Social Policy*, Cheltenham, Edward Elgar.

Kopstein, J. and Lichbach, M. (eds) (2008) *Comparative Politics: Interests, Identities, and Institutions in a Changing Global Order*, third edition, Cambridge, Cambridge University Press.

Landman, T. (2008) *Issues and Methods in Comparative Politics: An Introduction*, third edition, Abingdon, Routledge.

Lewin, K. M. and Sabates, R. (2012) 'Who gets what? Is improved access to basic education pro-poor in Sub-Saharan Africa?', *International Journal of Educational Development*, Vol. 32, No. 4: 517–528.

Lynch, M. (2011) 'After Egypt: the limits and promise of online challenges to the authoritarian Arab state', *Perspectives on Politics*, Vol. 9, No. 2: 301–310.

Manheim, J. B., Rich, R. C., Willnat, L., Brians, C. L. and Babb, J. (2012) *Empirical Political Analysis*, Harlow, Pearson Education.

Marsh, C. and Elliott, J. (2008) *Exploring Data: An Introduction to Data Analysis for Social Scientists*, second edition, Cambridge, Polity Press.

Masoud, T. (2011) 'The upheavals in Egypt and Tunisia: the road to (and from) Liberation Square', *Journal of Democracy*, Vol. 22, No. 3: 20–34.

Newton, K. and van Deth, J. (2009) *Foundations of Comparative Politics*, second edition, Cambridge, Cambridge University Press.

O'Neil, P. H. (2013) *Essentials of Comparative Politics*, fourth edition, London, W. W. Norton and Company.

O'Neil, P. H., Fields, K. and Share, D. (2013) *Cases in Comparative Politics*, fourth edition, London, W.W. Norton and Company.

Omwami, E. and Keller, E. (2010) 'Public funding and budgetary challenges to providing universal access to primary education in Sub-Saharan Africa', *International Review of Education*, Vol. 56, No. 1: 5–31.

Phillipson, C. (2013) *Ageing*, Cambridge, Polity Press.

Rakner, L. and van de Walle, N. (2009) 'Democratization by elections? Opposition weakness in Africa', *Journal of Democracy*, Vol. 20, No. 3: 108–121.

Rose, R. (2004) *Learning Lessons in Comparative Public Policy*, London, Routledge.

——(2008) 'What would you tell the President in three minutes about Iraq?', *European Political Science*, Vol. 7, No. 1: 78–83.

Shambaugh, D. (2008) 'China's political elite: the party school system', *The China Quarterly*, Vol. 196: 827–844.

Smith, P. and Ziegler, M. (2008) 'Liberal and illiberal democracy in Latin America', *Latin American Politics and Society*, Vol. 50, No. 1: 31–57.

Way, L. (2011) 'Comparing the Arab revolts: the lessons of 1989', *Journal of Democracy*, Vol. 22, No. 4: 17–27.

Wheeler, M, (2013) *Celebrity Politics*, Cambridge, Polity Press.

9

The world stage

The study of Politics and International Relations has a clear synergy and intellectual linkage. This penultimate chapter analyses the connections and contrasts encountered by the student of politics *vis-à-vis* the student of international relations. Assessment is made at this juncture of how politics differs from international relations and what scope there is for collaboration between these two distinct but related disciplines. It can be seen that although the disciplines are distinct, there are clear points of convergence.

What is international relations?

International relations, as the name implies, involves the study of different nation states and an analysis of how they relate to and interact with each other. It also involves a focus upon specific regions or area studies. Some international relations scholars, for example, choose to focus upon Middle Eastern politics or upon Latin American or African politics. There are clear links and parallels with the study of politics and, indeed, many scholars of political studies choose to study international relations too. This can either be as part of a joint degree or they may choose to study international relations as a minor subject alongside their politics major or vice versa. It may also be the case that a student *Doing Politics* may decide simply to take one module as an option in the area of international relations. Either way, it is clear that those studying politics are often equally enamoured by the opportunity to investigate politics on a global scale.

Scholars recount why they studied international relations

It is interesting to ascertain what was behind certain academics deciding to pursue a career in international relations. As one senior lecturer in international relations, Dr Simon Obendorf, explains,

> My route into IR ran through the disciplines of political science and law. My undergraduate studies in these areas showed me how many of the problems confronting society resulted from politics, processes and changes that were profoundly transnational in nature.
>
> (email interview with author, April 2014)

Dr Obendorf proceeds to explain how he

> . . . studied in Australia at a time when East and Southeast Asia were becoming far more economically and politically powerful and when Australian society was undergoing changes as sources of inward migration shifted away from the countries of Europe to the economies of the Asia Pacific. This prompted what became known as the 'history vs geography' debate: a debate about the nature of Australian society and whether we should look to our (European and colonial) histories and still-dominant Anglo-Celtic cultures or to our location in a very postcolonial, economically vibrant but culturally dissimilar (Asian) neighbourhood. Through my legal training and my activism in gay and lesbian politics, I became aware both of the colonial derivation of much of the injustice facing marginalised people throughout the formerly colonised world as well as both the power and shortcomings of international human rights law as a source of potential redress. In that light, studying IR became not just a way of better understanding the processes that were impacting the world, but held out the promise of being better able to define and craft interventions to make positive change. Interestingly, as an IR scholar, I have become very critical of the discipline for its neglect of many pressing issues and its tendency to focus on 'Great Powers', but I remain convinced of its potential to be a force for good.
>
> (email interview with author, April 2014)

Obendorf's account provides a fascinating insight into what sparked his interest in international relations. It ends on a rather optimistic note with

Obendorf recognising the way in which international relations can be used in a positive way.

Another scholar who is equally passionate about international relations is Professor Steven Curtis. Similarly, Steven Curtis, Associate Professor of International Relations at London Metropolitan University, and Higher Education Academy Discipline Lead for Politics and Economics, highlights why he enjoys teaching international relations. He attributes this to the fact that the

> . . . subject changes constantly, which makes the study of world politics a deeply fascinating and engaging endeavour. Whether it is attempts to deal with the causes and consequences of global warming, trade and development issues, security threats from transnational terrorist movements to states intervening militarily in each other's affairs, striving to make sense of the nature and underlying structures of the international system is a challenging but very rewarding vocation.
>
> (email interview with author, April 2014)

He continues that he has '. . . never been very interested in party politics or domestic constitutional arrangements more generally. I suppose they lack the dynamism and the seriousness of events, developments and processes at the international level' (email interview with author, April 2014). As to the point of studying international relations, Curtis states that while

> . . . it may appear at first glance as a non-vocational subject, the knowledge and skills developed in an IR degree are highly sought after in a wide range of careers. In addition to more obvious careers in government, international organisation and other public bodies, an IR degree is also useful in the business world. For example, good political risk analysis is essential for corporations when making decisions to invest in other countries (how stable is the government in country X, what security threats does it face from abroad and at home, etc.?). Studying IR will develop knowledge and understanding of the international system and the place of individual states and other bodies within it and will develop key skills of analysis. It will also develop students' practical skills, for example through the widespread use of simulations in the discipline.
>
> (email interview with author, April 2014)

Likewise, Dr Kaisa Hinkkainen, a lecturer in international relations, reflects upon her road to studying, teaching and researching international relations. She flags up the fact that, for her,

> Two major events in history attracted me to the study of International Relations; the Cuban Missile Crisis and the conflict in Northern Ireland. I was puzzled by both how conflicts came about between states and within states as well as why they were so difficult to solve. In wanting to find an answer to these questions, I sought to study International Relations, more specifically conflict analysis. International Relations theories provide the answers to such questions that transcend space and time.
>
> (email interview with author, April 2014)

Hinkkainen reflects that such

> . . . knowledge is not only vital for individuals choosing an academic career, but also for people who choose to work for international institutions such as NATO or the UN. International Relations scholars and practitioners are key actors in future conflict resolution.
>
> (email interview with author, April 2014)

A Senior Lecturer in European Politics at the University of Leeds, Dr Simon Lightfoot, contemplates the topicality and contemporary relevance of the subject area by stating that 'Relations between states is what fills news bulletins every night on television. International Relations gives you a deeper understanding as to the underlying causes of tension and explanations for the actions of states in our interconnected world' (email correspondence with author, April 2014). Likewise, Dr Adèle Langlois, Senior Lecturer in International Relations at the University of Lincoln, reveals that she '. . . chose to study International Relations as a graduate student, as [she] wanted to explore contemporary global issues and problems more deeply', continuing that she enjoys '. . . applying theory to real world institutions and events' (email correspondence with author, April 2014). Clearly, this opportunity to apply theory to practice and to see how events pan out in the real world is a major attraction for scholars of international relations.

Why study international relations?

It is clear, therefore, that international relations is attractive for varying reasons. This ability to foster a greater understanding of global conflict is a key attraction for many scholars. Scholars of international relations presumably care about the world in which we live and want to improve the human condition. Perhaps they want to change it or at least save it from further destruction. Part of the issue here, for both academics and students of international relations, is how they can make a difference. Global conflict is a perennial issue. The casual observer might say there has not been a truly global conflict since the end of the Second World War in 1945. On the other hand, even a cursory examination of the world stage reveals that there has been war and dispute, even if on a lesser scale, at some point on the globe virtually constantly since that time. Witness, for example, the Korean War of 1950–53, the war in Algeria from 1954 until 1962, the Suez Crisis of 1956, the Hungarian Uprising of 1956. Clearly, peace did not prevail in the post-Second World War era. Likewise, the Cold War may have marked a different type of dispute but the fear felt in certain quarters and the potential threat meant that peace was far from the natural state of affairs. The notion of two global superpowers in polar opposition meant, for many commentators, that there was an uneasy truce based upon a (whether perceived or real) balance of power. The use of the newly invented atomic bomb, in August 1945 at Hiroshima and then, three days later, Nagasaki, in Japan, coming just after the end of the Second World War, highlighted for many the utter futility of a war with weapons of mass, if not total, destruction. The notion of mutually assured destruction, or MAD, meant that success in conflict would be bittersweet and extremely short-lived if one's opponents could retaliate with the flick of switch or the press of a button. What price victory if it led to the elimination of one's own society and, possibly, humankind in total? Having said this, the existence of the atomic bomb did not then result in zero conflict. In the 1960s, for example, the Cuban Missile Crisis, taking place over thirteen days in October 1962, with the world on the brink of nuclear war, posed a major threat to post-war equilibrium – and even today provides a major case study for students of international relations. The Vietnam War in the 1960s and 1970s provided a different form of conflict, one where being a major power was no guarantee of success. The notion of guerrilla warfare constituted an entirely new form of combat where having access to a virtually unlimited supply of guns and heavy artillery was not necessarily a match for a local populace familiar with the terrain, able to outsmart young recruits and conscripts from the United States. The scale of the losses on both sides and the rise of popular protest, via the Anti-Vietnam movement in the West, led to this long and protracted conflicting eventually ending in April 1975. The quadrupling of oil prices virtually overnight (from $3 to $12 a barrel), in October 1973 meant that many more people took an interest in international relations. An oil rich Middle East was able to hold to ransom a western world reliant upon the internal combustion engine and the need for petroleum. Indeed, the Middle East had long been an area of uncertainty especially with the longstanding Arab–Israeli conflict. In the early 1980s, another conflict that saw Britain embroiled in military action thousands of miles away from home was the Falklands War, which broke out in April 1982. This was when the Argentineans invaded the British-owned Falklands Islands, or Malvinas as the Argentineans called them, in the South Atlantic seas. The then British Prime Minister Margaret Thatcher ordered the dispatch of the British fleet to recapture the Islands from the Argentinean invasion. This conflict led to resignations at governmental level. Lord Carrington, for example, the Foreign Secretary, resigned over his department's failure to foresee the invasion. It was an extremely difficult time for the Conservative Government led by Margaret Thatcher and culminated in the loss of 255 British military personnel, 649 Argentinean military personnel and three islanders. The military action did, however, despite many critics, not least in the UK, restore a certain sense of national pride in the United Kingdom and led to the so-called Falklands Factor impacting on Mrs Thatcher's resounding success at the next General Election, held in 1983. This episode raises interesting questions for the student of international relations as to the factors that galvanise political leaders into taking action and how appearing as a strong, competent leader on the world stage can reap positive benefits on home territory.

Further conflict, all in the post-Second World War scenario, including the two Gulf Wars of early 1991 and March 2003, demonstrates the extent of global conflict. Likewise, the situation in the former Yugoslavia that erupted in 1992 and led to the Bosnian War (1992–1995) also provides interesting if harrowing case-study material for the student of international relations. A new era of international relations emerged after the attack on the Twin Towers in New York on 11 September 2001. The horrific events of that day are imprinted on the minds of those who witnessed what occurred first hand and, indeed, on the millions who saw the events captured on camera. These attacks on American soil demonstrated that terrorists could penetrate their homeland and nowhere, effectively, was safe from the fear of such an attack. This led the then President George W. Bush to declare a 'War on Terror'. This culminated in the invasion of Iraq by allied forces and the subsequent fall of the dictator

Saddam Hussein and, after much bloodshed, the imposition of a new regime. The fallout from 9/11 also led to the war in Afghanistan and similarly loss of life, life-threatening or life-altering injury amongst all sides. Action in Iraq and Afghanistan resulted in terrorist action on mainland Britain, for example, such as the London bombings of 7 July 2005 or the killing of serviceman Lee Rigby in May 2013, who was brutally murdered in an unprovoked attack on the streets of London. His two attackers claimed it was retaliation for British military action. More recently, the situation in the Ukraine and Russia's attempts to annexe Crimea demonstrate that conflict is as prevalent today as it has been in the past. 'War', to quote the nineteenth century German theorist Carl von Clausewitz, is said to be 'nothing more than the continuation of politics by other means' (Howard and Paret, 2007). Others regard it as symptomatic of when politics has broken down. As the wartime UK Prime Minister Winston Churchill is quoted as saying at a White House dinner in June 1954, '... to jaw-jaw is better than to war-war' (see *The New York Times*, 27 June 1954: 3). Continuing this theme, in the words of the famous quotation from the twentieth century Chinese Communist leader Mao Tse-tung, 'Politics is war without bloodshed, while war is politics with bloodshed' (Tse-tung, 1938: 153). Certainly, 'man's' oft quoted inhumanity to 'man' knows no bounds. It is likely that war will never be totally eliminated and that conflict will always exist and manifest itself in various formats. Given the basic human issue of difference, clashes, whether that be on the familial, national or, as in this case, international scale, will always exist. Politics may seek to mediate and minimise the number of conflicts but certainly if the events of the past sixty years reveal anything, it is that conflict is inevitable. Perhaps not as cynical as the quotation, often attributed to Mark Twain, that 'God created war so that Americans would learn geography', the scholar of international relations will never be short of case study material.

Having said this, international relations does not just investigate and focus upon military conflict. Other areas covered by this discipline include a focus upon issues that impact upon communities on a global scale. Population growth, for example, impacts on a global scale. With a global population of more than seven billion, some countries are affected more negatively than others by such rapid population increase. A large population can, potentially, provide personnel for the armed forces but, on the other hand, a large population requires a large amount of food to sustain it. Environmentalism, for example, is another issue of global concern. Specific issues such as acid rain or deforestation do not stop at national boundaries. Likewise health concerns such as epidemics and pandemics are not mindful of the concept of nation states. They are also affected by a range of differing factors. Patricia Campbell *et al*. emphasise how examination of health issues has to be such that any '. . . thorough analysis of how disease functions in a global context must examine the social, economic, political, climatic, technologic, and environmental factors that shape disease patterns and influence the emergence and re-emergence of diseases' (2010: 210). A multiplicity of factors, therefore, enters into the equation. The recent swine flu pandemic, or, prior to that, bird flu, did not stop at international borders or infect certain peoples as opposed to others. Our common humanity, often neglected or overlooked when focusing upon military and similar conflicts, fades into insignificance when confronted by a pandemic virus or similar. Our DNA structure shared by virtue of the fact that we are human beings renders the impact upon us similar, if not identical. In one sense, this hails the more benign aspects of international relations in that nation states often work together to fight against an external enemy – such as a virus or similar. Having said this, there has been a common struggle against HIV/AIDS (Acquired Immune Deficiency Syndrome) but it remains the case that differences in the wealth of nations mean that you are more likely to survive and manage the symptoms of the disease if you live in the global north as opposed to the less wealthy southern hemisphere. Viotti and Kauppi point out that the

> . . . global HIV/AIDS epidemic has killed 25 million people. Though curbed significantly in First World countries by access to drugs, it continues to plague the poorest countries, particularly in sub-Saharan Africa – the region accounting for some three-quarters of the global population living with HIV/AIDS.

> (2013: 441)

There is, however, some room for optimism in this otherwise gloomy scenario, for in '. . . southern Africa in 2005 the disease killed 2.1 million people. In 2009 the number dropped to 1.8 million. Approximately 5 million lives have been saved by drug treatment' (*Ibid.*). The allocation of scarce resources, bringing us back to politics again, means that money impacts upon the ability to purchase drugs that will ameliorate if not cure the symptoms of the disease. If you have the money, both on a national and an individual scale, to purchase the drugs and latest medical advances to combat the symptoms then you stand a higher chance of survival than if you are struggling at or below the poverty level. Continuing this theme, analysis of life-expectancy levels on a global scale, for example, reveals startling discrepancies even as we advance through the twenty-first century. The highest level of life expectancy, for example, is to be found in wealthy Monaco, with rates at a staggering 89.63 years. Compare this with lowest levels, currently to be found in the central African nation of Chad, where life expectancy is a paltry 49.07 years (see http://www.infoplease.com/world/statistics/life-expectancy-country.html and http://www.telegraph.co.uk/health/10561478/Countries-with-highest-and-lowest-life-expectancies-for-people-born-in-2013-charted.html). Even within localities, however, discrepancies can be huge; in 2011 the City of Lincoln, England, had a differential of 17.7 years for women living just three miles apart. In the Park Ward in Lincoln, female life expectancy is 74.6 years, compared with 92.3 years in the North Hykeham Forum Ward. International relations can, therefore, be a useful discipline for flagging up such global differences and, hopefully, trying to posit remedies for such discrepancies. It can also benefit from a focus upon the sub-global level as interesting discrepancies also provide valuable case material.

International relations can also provide a useful conduit for dealing with issues on a united front. Issues such as, for example, female genital mutilation (FGM) impact on a transnational basis and provide governments with similar dilemmas. Contemporary manifestations of slavery, the sex trade and human trafficking concern numerous nation states in equal measure. Viotti and Kauppi rightly claim that one

> . . . of the most appalling developments in recent decades has been the expansion in human trafficking. Aided and abetted by a reduction in border controls, victims end up in sweatshops, plantations and factories. The most infamous example involves the sex trade. Some countries are notorious destinations for sex-trade tourists – Myanmar, China, Cambodia, Thailand, Colombia, and the Philippines. Former communist countries such as Russia, Ukraine, Moldova, and Romania are well known for the export of sex-slaves. Recruiters promise young women a life in the West in clerical, retail or modeling work. Many, however, end up working as prostitutes in Western capitals.

> (2013: 361–362)

Shared knowledge and resourcing to tackle such transnational issues are regarded as a positive. This also relates to policy transfer, as analysed in Chapter Five on the policy making process, whereby nations learn from each other and whereby policies often cross national boundaries. Maternity policies are often cited as a case in point. Nations look to their neighbours and further afield and emulate what they regard as positive political approaches and policies. Welfare to work polices and issues in relation to youth justice, for example, have also crossed national boundaries, thereby illustrating what some commentators regard as the positive dimensions of international relations. Clearly, political ideology plays a part at this juncture but it can be seen that policies operate on a transnational basis and nations learn from each other's experiences and actions.

Global poverty is an issue which all civilised nations ought to share an interest in eradicating or at the very least ameliorating. The fact that some nations and people are wealthy beyond belief and yet others live in dire poverty is and ought to be of international concern. Shocking sights such as the plight of the street children in Mexico or famine victims in Ethiopia upset all but the most heartless of observers. Innovative charitable approaches over recent decades have proved highly popular and have enabled people to contribute and try to help. The innovative and infamous Live Aid Concert, held on 13 July 1985 and spearheaded by Boomtown Rats singer Bob Geldof, was a transnational phenomenon and attracted huge amounts of support, financial and otherwise. More recently, Comic Relief activities and Sports Relief events also raise huge amounts of money to help those in dire need. Even within nations, there are huge discrepancies in terms of wealth. In the United Kingdom, for example, it was revealed that the top five wealthiest people are as rich as the poorest 20 per cent of the population (cf.: Dutta, 2014). Many regard this as a national scandal and seek to redress such an imbalance. The extent of this division shocks most people. Issues such as these are of key concern to students of international relations and, indeed, for many it is what galvanised them and attracted them to study the subject in the first instance. A sense of injustice and a desire to bring about change inspired many IR graduates to pursue their chosen course of study. They also impact, as will be mentioned later, on the type of career upon which many of them choose to embark. Organisations that seek to improve the lot and life chances of those living in dire poverty often attract international relations graduates.

International relations becomes increasingly important and relevant when consideration is given to the concept of a shrinking world. Advances in travel, especially air travel, in terms of both speed and cost implications, mean that the world inevitably appears as a smaller place. The proliferation of foreign holidays, within the reach of even those on a moderate income, means that awareness of the plight of others is heightened. Whilst this in itself can create new problems, for example the notion of carbon footprints and using up precious resources, a more positive effect is that travel can broaden the mind and foster feelings of empathy. Air travel means that ordinary people become aware of life in other countries. No longer is understanding limited to their immediate vicinity or national state. It is possible to witness first hand life in countries that were hitherto considered too remote and too far removed from one's daily life. In addition to advances in travel, a key invention is obviously the creation and development of the internet. The creation of British computer scientist, Sir Tim Berners-Lee, the World Wide Web celebrated twenty-five years since its inception on 12 March 2014. In that relatively short time-span, the world has been transformed. The internet now permeates most households and has certainly transformed the way that we work. The click of a mouse means that communications fly across the globe. Instantaneous contact is now possible, a phenomenon that would have been unthinkable less than a generation ago. Data and information can be retrieved without leaving one's laptop. Lifestyles and locations have changed due to possibilities offered by working from home or tele-working. The daily commute has, for some, been replaced by the home-office, which though potentially physically remote can link up in an instant with colleagues on a world-wide basis. This hi-tech revolution should not be underestimated. It has certainly provided the student of international relations with plenty of scope for observation and critical analysis. Allied to this development, the expansion and proliferation of mobile phone technology at (relatively) low cost means that how we communicate has also been transformed. This also impacts upon how we receive our news and related information. No longer solely reliant upon what the news media and huge conglomerates tell us, information can also be gleaned from ordinary people who capture events as they happen and unfold using their mobile phone technology. This liberating aspect means that a countervailing viewpoint is sometimes revealed in contradistinction to that being perpetuated by the authorities. Witness, for example, the events revealed during the so-called Arab Spring of early 2011 where mobile technology resulted in a whole new understanding of people power. People, predominantly young people, were able to visually and verbally demonstrate, effectively instantaneously, that the orthodox and authoritative viewpoint was not necessarily perpetuating a correct version of events. Media outlets and corporations have found this a double-edged sword, helpful, on the one hand, in terms of furnishing an 'as it happens' version of events but, on the other hand, meaning that the media machinery has to adapt and can sometimes find itself outflanked by people journalism. In addition to the internet and mobile technology, social media sites and micro-blogging sites such as Twitter™ have also proved revolutionary or at least as having transformatory potential. Tweets, with their maximum of 140 characters, permit an edited and condensed version of events to be quickly relayed to the waiting world. Censorship proves virtually impossible with millions of Twitter™ followers on a global scale.

Supranational organisations, such as the United Nations or the European Union, also furnish a vehicle for tackling issues on a transnational scale. As well as, hopefully, trying to solve international disputes and disagreements without nations resorting to military action, such transnational organisations can also tackle problems in concert. The notion of there being strength in numbers and unity being a positive dimension also enters the debate. Countries are, statistically, more likely to achieve success if they work together and pool resources than if they seek to go it alone. This may be in terms of financial resources but it could also relate to intellectual resources or aspects such as natural resources. Either way, working together must surely be regarded in a positive light. The strength in numbers argument may also be used as a tool to stop potentially maverick or sidelined nations from acting in a way that is opposed by the majority of nations. It may make nations think twice about pursuing a solitary path if their actions are likely to be in contradiction to a majority of others. History is, however, peppered with examples where this has not been the case!

One of the key ways in which countries have preferred to work together, as opposed to against each other, is in relation to trade. As Goldstein and Pevehouse quantify, international trade '. . . amounts to a sixth of the total economic activity in the world. About \$18 trillion of goods and services cross international borders each year' (2010: 281). The sheer scale of the level of international trade is clarified by the assertion that this equates to '. . . about 12 times the world's military spending, for example' (*Ibid.*). The financial aspect is a key motivator. Countries recognise that they have a great deal to gain from fostering trading relations. The notion of import and export interactions is the cornerstone of many transnational links. By way of example, Japanese car manufacturers benefit from trading links with the United Kingdom and others. Likewise, British products such as Scottish whisky, Welsh lamb or English cider are exported to many countries across the globe. The international marketplace is a multi-billion pound industry. A key aspect of international relations involves setting up and maintaining these trading connections. Indeed, the European Union is a key example of a truly transnational business, its initial title of European Economic Community (EEC), or, as it was more colloquially known, the Common Market, being a fitting descriptor of that trading dimension. As Paul Viotti and Mark Kauppi reveal in relation to trade,

. . . it should not surprise us that anything as important as economics is also highly political. Politics is core to economics as peoples and their governments, and the international and nongovernmental organizations they form, inevitably become involved to a greater or lesser degree in the decisions they make about budgets, money, trade, investments, and other commercial matters.

(2013: 372)

The importance of trading relationships should not, therefore, be underestimated.

When did IR first begin to be taught in universities?

In comparison with the discipline of politics, the study of international relations is a more recent phenomenon. Politics has been studied for centuries. Indeed, its roots can be traced to Ancient Greece and the time of Aristotle and Plato. Moreover, wherever human interaction has taken place then a case can be made to say that politics has occurred. The allocation of scarce resources was a necessity even in hunter-gatherer societies; decisions had to be made on who got what, when and how. International relations, whilst no less important, has a more modern parentage. The study of the relations between nation states is very much a development of the twentieth century. As Jill Steans *et al.* state, 'The story of international relations usually begins with an account of the Great War (1914–18), a war so horrific that many people believed it was the war to end all wars' (2010: 1), proceeding to declare that the '. . . study of international relations grew out of the belief that war was the gravest problem facing humanity and that something must be done to ensure that there would be no more "lost generations"' (*Ibid.*). As Andrew Heywood states, it became clear that as

. . . the twentieth century drew to a close, however, there was a growing recognition that the very parameters of political life had changed. This more radically called into question the conventional distinction between a domestic realm and an international realm of politics. These complex and multifaceted changes have increasingly been referred to as 'globalization'.

(Heywood, 2007: 128)

Those studying international relations will find that the learned societies, such as the Political Studies Association of the United Kingdom, provide them with useful information, opportunities for networking and resources at their disposal. They may also find the British International Studies Association (BISA) extremely useful in supplementing their degree course and enhancing their understanding of the discipline. There are also many international relations learned societies that operate on a more overtly transnational basis, such as the International Political Studies Association (IPSA), the International Studies Association (ISA) and the European Consortium of Political Research (ECPR), all providing support for academics and students working in the field of international relations. Another organisation that benefits students through providing support for international relations lecturers in Higher Education is the Higher Education Academy (HEA). They provide financial and related support so that lecturers can attend courses and workshops centred around their discipline; topics are many and varied, such as, for example, using popular culture to teach world politics, using social media to teach international relations, or preparing the diplomats of the future, to name but a few. Many learned societies and related bodies/ charitable trusts have sections for graduates, and increasingly undergraduates, so it is worthwhile tapping into these organisations in order to discover the wealth of resources, other materials and networking opportunities that they have at their disposal. Many also have vibrant alumni groupings and these too can be invaluable for highlighting role models and possible career trajectories.

Subjects with which to combine international relations

As with politics, international relations can be studied and combined with a whole host of differing subject areas and disciplines. This can be on a major/major or major/minor basis. The most common and logical combination is usually with politics but there are links with subjects such as social policy, law, criminology, history and business, to name but a few. Indeed, data derived from the University Central Admissions Systems (UCAS) reveals some more unusual pairings such as international relations with anthropology, international relations and geography, or international relations with chemistry. Thus, the opportunities to study international relations and to combine it with a whole host of subject areas are many and varied. The potential student of international relations may well find themselves spoilt for choice given the myriad of courses on offer to those who matriculate.

What are the links between international relations and politics?

There is a clear and logical synergy between international relations and politics. Indeed, often at university level the two disciplines tend to be located within the same school or department. Both subjects involve analysis, to a greater or lesser degree, of the political system and political culture. They require an assessment of power and authority. As Roskin and Berry state,

> International relations (IR) depend a lot on power, the ability of one country to get another to do (or sometimes not to do) something. International laws and institutions are too weak to rely on them the way we rely on domestic laws and institutions. In domestic politics, when we have a quarrel with someone, we 'don't take the law into our own hands; we take him to court.' In IR, it's sometimes the reverse. There is no court, and self-help may be the only option available
>
> (2010: 3)

Concepts such as political movements and political parties are common to both disciplines. There is a theoretical dimension to both areas, with international relations theory and political thought providing the theoretical underpinning and foundations for each subject area, respectively. In addition, many of the transferable skills cross the subject divide. Key skills, such as problem-solving techniques, critical thinking and essay-writing skills, are required by both groups of undergraduates in equal measure. Likewise, presentational skills, team-building and group-working techniques, quantitative and qualitative research methods will find favour in both camps. Continuing this theme, it is also noteworthy that the relevant subject benchmarking statements produced by the Quality Assurance Agency for Higher Education cover both subject areas together such is the extent of the synergy between the two disciplines. Indeed, many politics and international relations degrees are often built around a common first year of study with students then diverging at levels two and three into a more subject-specific curriculum, often with a heavy emphasis upon theory at level two and with a move towards more options at level three based upon the research areas of specific academics.

How do politics and international relations differ?

Having outlined key points of convergence, it is also beneficial to outline where the two disciplines differ. Politics, whilst it may and often does have a comparative dimension (a subject that was covered in the preceding chapter, Chapter Eight), has a tendency in the UK to focus upon the British system of government. Politics essentially looks at the state as constituting the machinery of government and the state as an internal administrator in the first instance. International relations, on the other hand, turns the focus outwards. All states settle themselves first, meaning they have to at least try to resolve their internal differences before embarking upon an external basis. This then becomes international relations – usually based upon such aspects as trading relations or shared policies and experiences. Politics focuses upon issues that are usually related to one specific state, whereas international relations, as the title implies, concentrates upon the interactions, for example socio-economic, financial as well as political and military ones, between states. International relations places the global and transnational dimension of any given topic area at the heart of its dealings. Having an awareness of international relations provides a useful addition to the academic armoury of the politics student. As the QAA benchmarking statement for Politics and International Relations (2007) clarifies, 'Politics is concerned with developing a knowledge and understanding of government and society', before proceeding to state that 'International relations shares the concerns of politics, but its focus is the regional and global arenas' (QAA, 2007: Section 3.2, p.3). Furthermore, the benchmarking statement claims that the '. . . scope of politics and international relations is broad, the boundaries being contested . . . these differences reflect the extent to which both aspects of the discipline are taught in conjunction with one another' (*Ibid.*: Section 2.1, p. 2). Essentially, therefore, there are key differences between politics and international relations but sufficient parallels to ensure that they remain intricately entwined.

Studying international relations

In terms of topics covered when studying international relations, these vary across and within universities. In general, however, the student of international relations will cover historical background – with a focus upon key events such as the First and Second World Wars, the creation, structure and *modus operandi* of various supranational bodies, such as the League of Nations, the United Nations, the European Union and the North Atlantic Treaty Organisation. Other topics include the concepts of power, war and conflict and international security, balance of power theories, conflict resolution and peace-building, terrorism studies, international law and international relations theories such as realism (which focuses upon the sovereignty of the

nation state and the belief that international relations operates in an anarch-
istic 'state of nature' – a dog-eat-dog/survival of the fittest mentality). Further
areas encompass pluralism (whereby the focus is upon the notion of many
groups or actors in the international arena and thus pressure groups, multi-
national corporations and other organisations also play a role on the world
stage), Marxism (which can be applied not just to the nation state but also to
the international arena), and perspectives on topics such as international trade,
poverty, health issues, human rights, environmentalism, climate change,
human trafficking, or specific resources such as oil, water, land and natural
gas supplies, to name but a few. Just to flesh out one of the theoretical perspectives in slightly greater depth, realism is, as Viotti and Kauppi state,
based on four key premises: firstly, that '. . . states are the principal or most
important actors in an anarchical world' (2010: 42); secondly, that the state
'. . . is viewed as a unitary actor' (*Ibid.*); thirdly, there is an assumption that
'. . . the state is essentially a rational (or purposive) actor' (*Ibid.*: 43); and,
fourthly, there is also the assumption that '. . . within the hierarchy of issues
facing the state, national or international security usually tops the list' (*Ibid.*).
Using this one example, i.e. realism, it can be seen, therefore, that the various
theoretical perspectives are multi-faceted and founded upon a number of
premises. Students of international relations have to ensure that they fully
grasp all these aspects. Other international relations approaches involve a
focus upon particular geographical areas, such as specific regions, the Middle
East, Africa or the Pacific Rim, for example. With regard to the teaching of
international relations theory, one of the more contemporary theses is Samuel
P. Huntington's 'clash of civilisations' (1996). Essentially, he argues that conflict in the contemporary era would be cultural – as opposed to being based
primarily on ideology or on economic difference. To use Huntington's terminology, therefore, it would be between different civilisations, such as Chinese,
Islamic and Christian, to name a few. The old divisions, such as between left
and right on the ideological spectrum, would cease to be as important. Some
writers focus upon international relations from a particular perspective; for
example, Laura Shepherd brings a feminist approach to the discipline
(*cf.*: *Gender Matters in Global Politics*, 2010). There is a burgeoning literature in the area of gender and war, gender and international security and related
areas (*cf.*: Cohn, 2012; Detraz, 2012). As Christina Rowley and Laura
Shepherd argue, however, '. . . given the representational practices in the text-
books, best practice for teaching gendered IR demands careful consideration
of the ways in which the masculinism of the discipline organizes and limits
the horizons of the discipline as we teach it' (2012: 151). Given the various

perspectives and approaches, allied with the multitude of topics covered by the IR scholar, it is evident that international relations is a fascinating area of study. It concerns central questions relating to how we live our lives and, indeed, whether we live or survive at all.

The discipline of international relations, in general, is taught in much the same manner as politics (as outlined in Chapter Three). It is probably fair to say, however, that international relations lends itself to a greater emphasis upon the use of role play and simulations. Simon Obendorf and Claire Randerson's article on the Model United Nations simulation (referred to in Chapter One) provides a useful analysis of one particular simulation but there are also many others discussed in the literature on pedagogical approaches to international relations (cf.: Asal, 2005; Shellman and Turan, 2006; Simpson and Kaussler, 2009). The fact that many simulations involve students assuming the mantle of a specific nation state may make it relatively easy for tutors to assign specific roles. Another relatively novel way of teaching international relations is via the use of film. Simpson and Kaussler (*Ibid.*) analyse how films can be used to convey a multitude of messages with regards to international relations. Cinematic epics such as Richard Attenborough's 1982 film *Gandhi*, Phil Alden Robinson's 2002 movie *The Sum of All Fears*, David Lean's 1962 film *Lawrence of Arabia*, or the 1966 epic *The Battle of Algiers*, directed by Gillo Pontecorvo, alongside more contemporary works such as Steve McQueen's 2013 film *12 Years a Slave,* to name but a few, can all be used as a conduit for teaching international relations. Other devices that add to the international relations tutor's toolkit include the use of micro-blogging sites, such as Twitter™ (*cf.*: Blair, 2013). Tutors may, for example, utilise a live Twitter-feed within the lecture theatre/seminar room, enabling real time discussion and debate to occur. One of the key aspects of international relations is that, in addition to having a strong historical focus, it is alongside politics a contemporary, 'living' subject. This again is part of the appeal in that students have to keep abreast of contemporary affairs. A week may be a long time in politics. The same can be said of international relations. It is incumbent upon those studying international relations, therefore, to stay tuned to key events and happenings on the world stage. Students need to know where the current international flashpoints are and what the major issues are in relation to world affairs. Some of these, such as environmentalism or trading issues, will be perennial, but others, such as a specific act of military aggression, may be new. This notion of events unfolding in real time is certainly part of the attraction of the discipline.

Studying abroad

Many degrees in international relations have added value and attractiveness due to the fact that students have the opportunity to study for a period of time at another university in a different country. This may be for a semester but it is often the case that this is for a year. This is especially true if the student wishes to experience life and studying in America, China or Australia, by way of example. Given the distances involved, it makes sense to spend a longer period of time experiencing these educational systems and cultures. The year abroad is often added into the degree as a whole and is likely to take place after the second year of study – with the international relations student returning to complete their final year of study in the United Kingdom after the year abroad. In the case of a semester or shorter period of study, this is quite often spent in another European country. In this case, the modules studied as part of the semester abroad require parity with curricular content that would be studied had the student remained in the United Kingdom. Students gain credit for their academic success in the same way as they would do had they remained at their home institution. There is a process of credit transfer so that success during the semester abroad translates into success in the overall degree. Unless international relations students are proficient in another language, course tutors will select institutions and courses where they are taught in English. Institutions in Sweden and Holland, for example, teach in English and language is not an issue for the incoming students. Certainly, the fact that an international relations graduate has studied abroad as part of their degree must add to their marketability and enhance their skills set. In this competitive jobs market, experience of living and studying in another country is certain to enhance the curriculum vitae.

Careers in international relations

As with the student of politics, in these relatively austere times the student of international relations will be equally concerned in relation to job prospects and careers opportunities available to them due to having studied international relations. In common with any graduate, there will be a whole host of career opportunities available simply by virtue of the fact that they are in possession of a degree. This aside, however, there will also be career pathways opened up that are more specifically suited to the international relations graduate. These careers include, for example, working for an international organisation, such as the European Union or the United Nations.

Non-governmental organisations also employ many international relations alumni. The civil service and the diplomatic service, although extremely competitive in terms of entry requirements, also look favourably upon the international relations graduate. Career prospects will, no doubt, be enhanced by the acquisition of language skills and students with the ability to speak a second or even third language will find themselves more marketable than their monolingual peers. As with all graduates, there is also the opportunity to proceed to further study, such as at master's level, via a taught postgraduate qualification, or, for example, an MA by research. Proceeding to study for an MPhil or a PhD is also possible for the ablest of international relations graduates. Many may seek employment close to home or to their adoptive university town or city but, equally, a degree in international relations can represent a passport to travel on a world-wide scale.

Conclusion

In conclusion, it can be seen that there are many points of convergence between topics studied by the student of politics and the international relations undergraduate. The international dimension may enhance the marketability of a politics student. There are, however, as pointed out earlier, as many points of divergence as there are similarities. International relations students focus upon the interactions between states – be that in terms of financial, socio-economic or policy areas. Politics students are much more likely to focus upon one, or perhaps two states, to the exclusion of a wider comparative approach.

In today's shrinking world, as a result of improved transportation, such as air and other modes of travel, the international/global dimension becomes ever more important and relevant. Allied to this, relatively recent communication phenomena such as the creation, development and expansion of the world wide web, and the proliferation of mobile technology such as mobile phones and superfast broadband technology, to name but a few, mean that the spread of knowledge, ideas and information happens in an instant. Politicians and policy makers, in every nation state, know that they cannot afford to ignore the actions of their neighbours, whether near or far. Politics does not occur in a national vacuum nor in isolation. The concept of globalisation is familiar to scholars, concerned as it is with this idea that the world is getting smaller when taking into account advances in transportation and communication links. As Andrew Heywood points out,

Globalization is a complex web of interconnectedness that means that our lives are increasingly shaped by decisions and actions taken at a distance from ourselves. Economic globalization reflects the increase in transnational flows of capital and goods, destroying the idea of economic sovereignty. Cultural globalization is an homogenizing force; although globalization is by no means an entirely 'top-down' process.

(Heywood, 2007: 160)

The shrinking world syndrome is an area of interest to those studying international relations. What happens in one nation state increasingly has implications for other countries. There must be a recognition by scholars of either discipline that their relative fortunes are intertwined. Certainly, the whole gamut of international relations cannot be given sufficient coverage in a single chapter but, hopefully, this discussion has highlighted some of the key areas covered by the student of international relations, raised some of the central questions for consideration and whetted the intellectual appetite. The relevance and importance of international relations should not be ignored by the student purely focused upon *Doing Politics*.

Chapter bibliography

Asal, V. (2005) 'Playing games with international relations', *International Studies Perspectives*, Vol. 6, No. 3: 359–373.

Blair, A. (2013) 'Democratising the learning process: the use of Twitter in the teaching of politics and international relations', *Politics*, Vol. 33, No. 2: 135–145.

Campbell, P. J., MacKinnon, A. and Stevens, C. R. (2010) *An Introduction to Global Studies*, Oxford, Wiley-Blackwell.

Cohn, C. (ed.) (2012) *Women and Wars*, Cambridge, Polity.

Detraz, N. (2012) *International Security and Gender*, Cambridge, Polity.

Dutta, K. (2014) 'Britain's five richest families worth as much as poorest 20 per cent, says Oxfam', *The Independent*, 17 March, http://www.independent.co.uk/news/uk/home-news/britains-five-richest-families-worth-as-much-as-poorest-20-per-cent-says-oxfam-9195914.html, accessed 9 April 2014.

Goldstein, J. S. and Pevehouse, J. C. (2010) *International Relations*, ninth edition, London, Longman.

Heywood, A. (2007) *Politics*, third edition, Basingstoke, Palgrave Macmillan.

——(2011) *Global Politics*, Basingstoke, Palgrave Macmillan.

——(2014) *Global Politics*, second edition, Basingstoke, Palgrave Macmillan.

Howard, M. and Paret, P. (eds and translators) (2007) *Carl von Clausewitz: On War*, Oxford, Oxford University Press.

Huntington, S. P. (1996) *The Clash of Civilizations and the Making of World Order*, New York, Simon and Schuster.

Lincolnshire County Council and Lincolnshire NHS (2011) *Lincolnshire Joint Strategic Needs Assessment Overview Report*, Lincoln, Lincolnshire County Council and Lincolnshire NHS.

The New York Times (1954) 27 June: 3.

Obendorf, S. and Randerson, C. (2013) 'Evaluating the model United Nations: diplomatic simulation as assessed undergraduate coursework', *European Political Science*, Vol. 12, No. 3: 350–364.

Primoratz, I. (2012) *Terrorism*, Cambridge, Polity.

Quality Assurance Agency (QAA) (2007) *Subject Benchmark Statement for Politics and International Relations*, Gloucester, The Quality Assurance Agency for Higher Education.

Roskin, N. and Berry, N. O. (2010) *IR: The New World of International Relations*, eighth edition, New York, Longman.

Rowley, C. and Shepherd, L. J. (2012) 'Contemporary politics: using the "F" word and teaching gender in international relations', Gormley-Heenan, C. and Lightfoot, S. (eds), in *Teaching Politics and International Relations*, Basingstoke, Palgrave Macmillan: 146–161.

Shellman, S.M. and Turan, K. (2006) 'Do simulations enhance student learning? An empirical evaluation of an IR simulation', *Journal of Political Science Education*, Vol. 2, No. 1: 19–32.

Shepherd, L. J. (ed.) (2010) *Gender Matters in Global Politics*, Abingdon, Routledge.

Simpson, A.W. and Kaussler, B. (2009) 'IR teaching reloaded: using films and simulations in the teaching of international relations', *International Studies Perspectives*, Vol. 10, No. 4: 413–427.

Steans, J., Pettiford, L., Diez, T. and El-Anis, I. (2010) *An Introduction to International Relations Theory*, third edition, Harlow, Pearson Education.

Tse-tung, M. (1938) 'On protracted war', *Selected Works*, Vol. II, Section 64: 153, Peking, Foreign Languages Press.

Viotti, P. R. and Kauppi, M. V. (2010) *International Relations Theory*, fourth edition, New York, Longman.

——(2013) *International Relations and World Politics*, fifth edition, New York, Pearson.

Websites

http://www.infoplease.com/world/statistics/life-expectancy-country.html, accessed February 2014.

http://www.telegraph.co.uk/health/10561478/Countries-with-highest-and-lowest-life-expectancies-for-people-born-in-2013-charted.html, accessed February 2014.

10

Concluding thoughts on *Doing Politics*

Doing Politics is something that we all do every single day of our lives. This is true whether we recognise it or not. Those of us who *do* recognise that fact are more likely to become hooked on the subject matter and want to study the discipline. We scholars may be in a minority but greater recognition of the centrality and importance of politics would benefit society as a whole. To paraphrase the lyrics of that cheesy song, love may be 'all around us' but politics, it is possible, may actually be more prevalent. Politics is part of everything we do, from office politics to trade union politics, to negotiating contracts. It permeates our world. There is politics in the home whereby communication skills may be required or there is a political will needed to achieve desired outcomes. Anger management techniques, conflict resolution strategies, powers of negotiation, these all involve politics. Under this definition, *everything* is political. Sexual politics and the struggle for equality are embroiled in the essence of politics. Responsibility for doing the washing up at home, under this all-embracing definition, becomes a political issue. Mundane chores enter the framework of politics because it relates to notions of power and control. This is why politics is so important and so central to our lives and why, correspondingly, this book has value; why this 'story' *had* to be told.

For most of humanity, politics is not part of their daily vocabulary. Seemingly oblivious to the effect that Aristotle's 'master science' has upon their routine existence, they proceed to focus upon the minutiae of twenty-first century living. Politics would be more prevalent in the daily lexicon if people recognised and were taught to understand the importance and centrality of politics to their day-to-day lives and well-being; indeed, in some cases, to their very existence. For those of us passionate about politics, this centrality comes as no surprise. Gripped by the 'bug' of studying politics, those fascinated by politics recognise and appreciate how concepts such as power, authority, democracy and policy impact upon our routine existence. Politics is not some dry, boring, dusty old subject, confined to the history books or purely theoretical with little relevance to everyday life. It is a living, relevant, vibrant and dynamic discipline, which underpins virtually all other aspects of life. Furthermore, its ever-changing nature cements its appeal. Failure to remain abreast of contemporary affairs means it is easy to lose touch with what is happening in the political realm. The fast-moving pace of political change, be that in terms of debate or in relation to specific policies, provides a challenge for the student of political studies but it is a challenge that grips from the outset. Political debate is not a chore, it is a luxury. Political knowledge should be ours by right. Those who do not perceive the import-ance of politics may perhaps have suffered due to an education system that has traditionally sidelined political teachings, understandably perhaps, for fear of their approach being classified as indoctrination. The recent promulga-tion of citizenship classes has gone some way towards rectifying this omis-sion but there is still work to be done. In contemporary parlance, politics needs an agent, or a marketing agency, to highlight the value of studying politics and the centrality of politics to our day-to-day existence. The message in terms of what politics is and how it affects us needs to be sold; in the same way that the television advert '*You don't do politics?*' aimed to motivate voters to attend the polls, politics itself needs a crusading voice to showcase its appeal and relevance.

This concluding chapter, therefore, summarises the text and highlights what has been learned from this investigation into the study and activity of politics. Proceeding on from an analysis of key terminology and an investig-ation into why politics and politicians seem to receive such a bad press, this chapter draws all the key points together in a way that highlights the incred-ible interest gleaned through a study of politics and the overarching passion for politics that political scientists and active politicos all share.

Chapter summaries and key areas of investigation

To summarise and reiterate, the chapters were arranged in the following manner. Chapter One constituted a general introduction to the book and the topic of *Doing Politics*. This first chapter highlighted how the book constitutes a detailed guide to both the study of politics and the activity of politics. The text within provided a penetrating insight into what is involved in studying politics at university. Explanation was given as to who the book is for. What is the book intended to achieve? How should you use the book? Why should we study politics? What is involved as part of a politics degree? What topics and areas do you study on a politics degree? What sort of careers might be open to you if you study for a politics degree? Examination was made of the kinds of topics and areas that you would expect to study as part of a politics degree. In addition, reference was made to the kinds of skills you can be expected to acquire as part of your politics degree. This book gets behind the mindset needed to study politics at undergraduate level. This involves asking questions rather than just accepting what one is told. The creation and development of a 'critical thinker' is important here.

Moving on, Chapter Two focused upon the notion of if *'You don't do politics? What do you do?'* This second chapter examined the importance and the relevance of Politics. It encapsulated the key definitions of politics, including that politics is about conflict, before moving on to examine the broader definitions. What does politics mean? How does politics affect you? This chapter involved analysis of the all-pervasive nature of politics, to make us understand how politics impacts upon our lives in numerous different ways. In addition to highlighting the usual components of politics, examination was made of the broader definition of politics. This can be subsumed under the catch-all phrase 'politics is everything' but it also involved a focus upon sexual politics, office politics, etc. Widening our definition of politics so that we became aware that what goes on behind closed doors could be regarded as politics. The feminist mantra of the 'personal is political' was also highlighted at this juncture.

The third chapter examined issues involved in studying politics at university. It focused upon the question of politics and the quest for a 'right' answer. Allied to this, coverage was given to the thorny issue of bias. What topics can you expect to study at higher education level? The key areas of focus were highlighted here. The benchmarking statements for politics were illuminated. The emphasis was upon the academic study of politics, studying it as you would any other subject, history, for example. The idea is that you acknowledge and recognise the difference between fact and opinion and accept that there are occasions when we may have to 'agree to disagree' in politics. The notion of highlighting alternative viewpoints was important here; for example, some people believe X, some people believe Y, etc. We don't always need to come down on one side of the political fence or another. This chapter also investigated *how* we study politics; in particular, the use of new media in the teaching and learning of politics was assessed.

The fourth chapter concentrated upon the negativity that is often directed at politics. As a starting point, it was useful to think of why politics is often perceived in such a negative light: *Why does politics get a bad press?* [Do we hate politics?] In part, this involved analysis of Colin Hay's work and Gerry Stoker's work. This chapter examined the negativity associated with politics and politicians. Clearly, the recent expenses scandal has impacted upon the general public perception of politicians. There is a great deal of criticism levied at politicians, some deserved, some less so. Yet, this is not only a recent phenomenon. Samuel Johnson the eighteenth century writer and poet, for example, talked of politics as being nothing more than a 'means of rising in the world'; likewise, Shakespeare, in King Lear, referred to the 'scurvy politician'. It seems that politicians have always needed to be able to cope with criticism. This chapter analysed why politics and politicians are sometimes viewed in such a negative light.

Chapter Five investigated the contested concept of power and analysed where power lies in the policy making process. The policy making process was highlighted and explained. Differing models of policy making were depicted before analysing varying types of power – economic, financial, bureaucratic, etc. Students of politics need to know about how policies are made and debates centring on the locus of power. Differing ideological perspectives, concepts of left and right, were also highlighted in this chapter.

In the sixth chapter, attention turned to a focus upon the topic of the key institutions involved in the study of politics and also the key players in the process too. Analysis was made of whether these actors change over time and how much power the ordinary person in the street has in the political process. Political participation levels were highlighted here and assessment was made of whether people have real power or whether they are being placated, and whether others, higher up the political process, are paying lip-service to their views without necessarily taking any of their thoughts and observations on board.

The seventh chapter moved on to a discussion of the politics that takes place in civil society, that is to say beyond the realm of the political arena, beyond what we would usually consider as mainstream politics. Chapter Seven focused upon: *anti-politics: people, power and politics*; *new social movements*; *global civil society.* Attention now turned to less formal methods of political activity and political participation. There has been a significant amount written about involvement in formal politics and analysis made of the formal political arena as the locus of political power. This chapter sought to redress the balance somewhat by focusing upon 'other' modes of political involvement and political participation. New social movement activity and involvement via what has been termed 'global civil society' were examined in detail in this chapter. In addition, investigation was made as to whether these 'newer' forms of political activity and involvement appeal to differing sectors of society to a much greater extent than hitherto. For example, is new social movement activity more likely to appeal to younger people and those who have never had any political involvement in mainstream politics before? Contemporary protest groups such as Fathers 4 Justice (F4J) and the Plane Stupid campaign were highlighted here as examples of contemporary protest movements.

In Chapters Eight and Nine attention turned to the international sphere. Chapter Eight highlighted one of the key areas of political study, namely that of comparative politics. The works of Jean Blondel and also Rod Hague and Martin Harrop were important here. The comparative approach was examined in depth and analysis was made of the fact that, whilst we may not necessarily be comparing like with like when we assess differing political systems, nonetheless the comparative approach does help the student of politics to make greater sense of the political world. Many students of politics are familiar with the way that their own country's political system operates but often they seek to enhance their knowledge by focusing upon at least one other country or supranational body, such as the European Union. The penultimate chapter, Chapter Nine, analysed the international dimension and focused upon the inherent connections between Politics and International Relations. The study of Politics and International Relations has a clear synergy and intellectual linkage. This penultimate chapter analysed those connections and contrasts encountered by the student of politics *vis-à-vis* the student of international relations. Assessment was made at this juncture of how politics differs from international relations and what scope there is for collaboration between these two distinct but related disciplines. It was illustrated that although the disciplines are distinct, there are clear points of convergence. This leads into this final Chapter Ten, whereby the book as a whole is summarised and where thoughts turn to the future of studying politics and what that entails.

Why do politicians receive such a bad press?

As outlined in Chapter Four, politicians have recently been in receipt of negative publicity. Fuelled by the expenses scandal that first emerged in May 2009, public perceptions of their elected representatives have reached an all-time low. It will be interesting to watch what happens, as events unfold, in terms of MPs' expenses. In April 2014, Sir Ian Kennedy, chairman of the Independent Parliamentary Standards Authority (IPSA) stated, 'MPs marking their own homework always ends in scandal' (Woolf and Grimston, 2014: 1), proceeding to expand upon this point by stating that in order to '. . . avoid further damage to parliament in the future, it should have the confidence to give away powers in regulating itself and see that independent regulation is the best, most transparent way forward' (*Ibid.*). His comments were preceded by Maria Miller, the culture secretary, paying back £5,800 and making what many regarded as a rather lacklustre 32-second apology to the House of Commons. More than five years after it first erupted and entered the public's consciousness, the expenses scandal remains a key concern.

Alongside the expenses scandal, another issue that alienates the public and damages their perception of politicians is the adversarial or 'Yah-Boo' approach to politics that often occurs in Parliament. One exchange at Prime Minister's Questions was dubbed particularly confrontational and typifies this kind of behaviour. With David Cameron labelling Ed Miliband and Ed Balls 'the two Muppets' and Ed Miliband referring to David Cameron as '. . . not so much the "Wolf of Wall Street" as the "dunce of Downing Street"' (BBC News Online, 2 April 2014), the heated exchange occurred in an altercation over the pricing of shares in Royal Mail. They had both previously expressed a desire to move away from 'Punch and Judy Politics' so this episode is unlikely to find favour with an already disillusioned electorate.

Allied to these issues of the expenses debacle and the adversarial style of politics are a lack of efficacy and a belief amongst many sectors of the electorate that their vote does not make any difference; it is perhaps not surprising that politicians seem so out of favour. The Speaker's Commission on Digital Democracy might be one way in which people are encouraged to re-engage with politics, as it seeks to

> . . . consider, report and make recommendations on how parliamentary democracy in the United Kingdom can embrace the opportunities afforded by the digital world to become more effective in: making laws, scrutinising the work and performance of government, representing

citizens, encouraging citizens to engage with democracy, facilitating dialogue amongst citizens.

(see http://www.parliament.uk/business/commons/the-speaker/ speakers-commission-on-digital-democracy/terms-of-reference)

In addition, the Speaker's Commission also seeks to '. . . consider the implications for Parliament if it is to become more relevant to the increasingly diverse population it seeks to serve' (*Ibid.*). Thus, the Speaker's Commission on Digital Democracy is one way of ascertaining the wishes of the people and utilising the subsequent knowledge acquired to re-engage people with politics in the twenty-first century. In terms of political engagement *per se*, there are questions to be asked – more so in terms of young people and politics. Is there a crisis of political engagement? Without doubt, there is disquiet in certain quarters. One of the key groups that political scientists regard as being in danger of dropping off the political radar is young people. If we take student politics societies, for example, there has been some discussion as to whether they are waning in popularity. Student 'politics societies' ebb and flow in terms of their membership and often they depend upon a small group of people having the time and the inclination to galvanise their peers to action. Students are extremely hardworking and many feel that they have to ration the time that they allocate to 'other' activities. As to whether young people are interested in politics *per se*, if you use voting behaviour as an indicator then the youngest category of voters, the 18–24s, is the sector least likely to vote. At the last general election (2010), for example, only 44 per cent of this group voted – and even this figure was up 7 per cent on the previous (2005) general election. Of these, young women were less likely to vote than young men (only 39 per cent of 18–24 year old women voted compared with 50 per cent of 18–24 year old men). Studies reveal, however, that when questioned young people are not apathetic about politics but they are disillusioned with mainstream politics and political parties. They are very interested in politics with a small 'p' and concerned about issues such as environmentalism and animal rights. They are less enamoured by what the political parties are doing. Certainly, this disengagement with mainstream politics was exacerbated by the aforementioned Parliamentary expenses scandal that emerged in May 2009. Politicians were regarded as having feathered their own nests at the taxpayer's expense. Young people were just as affected by this as other age groups. The *2013 Audit of Political Engagement*, an annual survey conducted by the Hansard Society, reveals that only 12 per cent of young people say they would vote in the next general election. If this does happen there would be serious issues in relation to the absence of the voice of youth. The survey also revealed that only 23 per cent of people in general say they are satisfied with the way MPs are doing their job – 6 points lower than in 2010 just after the expenses scandal broke – and whilst this is roughly equal for young and older people, younger people are less likely than older people to be satisfied with their own MP.

Young people are often castigated for being disaffected with politics. The Scottish independence vote that took place on 18 September 2014 saw 16 and 17-year-olds being able to vote. This will, no doubt, continue to spark debate about whether this should be rolled out to Westminster elections. There are those who argue that now that the genie is out of the bottle the momentum will gather pace and it is only a matter of time before 16 and 17-year-olds will be able to vote in all elections – Ed Miliband has already laid his cards on the table, as have the Liberal Democrats. If 16 and 17-year-olds are enfranchised, it will be interesting to gauge their views too. As mentioned, William Shakespeare, in *King Lear*, talked of the 'scurvy politician', and whilst we may rate our politicians more highly than this, they still have a long way to go before people in general, and young people in particular, feel able to trust them. Is it the case that, expenses scandal aside, as well as politicians changing, people have become more questioning and challenging, less willing to accept what our politicians tell us at face value? In the 1950s and 1960s, there were surprisingly high levels of deferential attitudes towards our politicians. Nowadays, voters, young and old, have become more questioning and challenging, more willing to switch their vote and, indeed, determine whether to vote at all – witness the recent furore surrounding comments by Russell Brand *and* Jeremy Paxman. This aside, the events and debates organised by young people throughout UK universities, for example during the annual Parliament Week, reveal that young people's interest in politics remains remarkably buoyant (this section is part of an earlier piece about student politics that first appeared in the *Lincolnshire Echo*; see Briggs, 2013: 47). In addition, organisations such as Free the Children and Bite the Ballot focus upon empowering young people.

What is politics?

As outlined in Chapter One, politics can be interpreted in a number of different ways (Leftwich, 2004). On one level, it can be regarded as the study of institutions (legislature, executive, judiciary, political parties, etc.), how they operate and interact. It can also be interpreted as the allocation of scarce resources, whereby difficult decisions will have to be made and where there will inevitably be winners and losers. The famous political scientist Harold Lasswell interpreted politics in this way through his definition that politics, as the title of his book reveals, concerns *Politics: Who Gets What, When and How* (1958). Spending more on healthcare inevitably means, since resources are finite, that there will be less to spend on other areas such as education or the environment. A further, much broader, definition is an all-encompassing one that regards politics as including everything. Everything we do involves politics of one sort or another, primarily because it involves power. Under this definition, therefore, office politics and sexual politics enter the equation. Robert Leach, Bill Coxall and Lynton Robins state that politics '. . . involves far more than government and party politics. It is about power and decision-making which affect all our lives, and determines how scarce resources are allocated' (2011: 14). They proceed to declare that there

> . . . are disagreements over the legitimate scope of politics. Some distinguish between a public or political sphere and a private sphere, between the state and 'civil society'. Others would deny that politics can or should be excluded from many areas previously considered private.
>
> (*Ibid.*)

Recent debates concerning whether smoking should be banned in private cars when children are in the vehicle illustrate this issue of how far the state should intervene in the private lives of its people. Is this an example of the 'nanny state' or is it the state's duty to protect children? Leach *et al.* postulate further that although '. . . politics is clearly about power, this is difficult to define and measure. A distinction can be drawn between power and authority (or legitimate power). Those without formal power may still have influence over decisions that affect them' (*Ibid.*). Likewise, Andrew Heywood puts forward a definition of politics, claiming that

> . . . the heart of politics is often portrayed as a process of conflict resolution [. . . however . . .] politics in this broad sense is better thought of as a search for conflict resolution than as its achievement, as not all conflicts are, or can be, resolved.
>
> (Heywood, 2007: 4)

Heywood proceeds to elucidate that '. . . the inescapable presence of diversity (we are not all alike) and scarcity (there is never enough to go around) ensures that politics is an inevitable feature of the human condition' (*Ibid.*). It can be seen that the answer to the question of 'what is politics?' is multi-faceted. There are a number of differing ways in which the question can be interpreted. It is a question that has vexed political philosophers and political scientists for centuries.

In a further twist, Bernard and Tom Crick note how the '. . . word "politics" refers both to the study of Politics and to the activity of politics' (1987: 6). Those studying politics at undergraduate level analyse the subject in detail but they may also be interested in politics beyond studying it as an academic discipline. They may also want to enter politics themselves – at local, national, sub-national or other level. A degree in politics can provide a firm grounding in the theoretical perspectives, furnishing knowledge that acts as a springboard into elected office or public service. This is a point to which we will return later in this chapter in the section on careers.

Why study politics?

Aside from it being a fascinating area of investigation and research, studying politics helps us to understand the world and how it operates. Bold claims indeed, but politics is a vitally important area of investigation, centred, as it is, around how we live our lives and, as stated earlier, if we live at all. A greater understanding of how these processes operate may aid moves towards peaceful reconciliation of disagreements or may help to ensure that power and resources are dispersed more widely and shared out in a more equal manner than hitherto. There is always an element of chance and the unexpected in politics; as Andrew Gamble so rightly points out, politics '. . . often proceeds through muddle, confusion, and accident, and recent British politics has been no exception' (Gamble, 2003: 219). In part, this is what makes politics so interesting, to examine how these dilemmas are resolved.

The reasons why people decide to study politics and often follow a career path that involves teaching politics are many and varied. Professor Paul Carmichael, Honorary Secretary of the Political Studies Association of the United Kingdom and Dean of the Faculty of Social Sciences at the University of Ulster, states, for example,

> Even in childhood, I was always interested in politics. Although not from a politically active family, politics and current affairs was a frequent topic of conversation. Perhaps unsurprisingly, therefore,

in wanting to understand more about the world in which we live, the political decisions which affected our lives, and what scope there was for making a better job of it, I studied politics as part of my undergraduate degree.

(email interview with author, April 2014)

Professor Carmichael goes on to state:

The appeal was two-fold. First, the capacity of politics to change the world, hopefully for the better, represented something of a calling. Second, however, political intrigue and machinations have fascinated me just as much. Having studied the subject, my enthusiasm was such that I wanted to research and teach in the area, too, hence my decision to undertake doctoral study before entering a career in academia.

(email interview with author, April 2014)

Similarly, Claire Randerson, a Senior Lecturer in International Relations, outlines what sparked her enthusiasm for politics and international relations:

My interest in politics and more specifically international politics/relations emerged out of the experience of growing up at the end of the Cold War and in Margaret Thatcher's Britain. The decision to study a History and Politics degree and then move towards International Relations in my postgraduate studies was significantly influenced by momentous events such as the demonstrations in Tiananmen Square, the opening of the Berlin Wall, the resignation of Margaret Thatcher and the release of Nelson Mandela and the subsequent move towards democracy in South Africa.

(email interview with author, April 2014)

Claire emphasises how this '. . . potential for politics to bring about societal change was inspiring to me as a young student and stimulated a desire to learn about international relations as an academic discipline' (email interview with author, April 2014). Clearly, specific events can spark a lifelong passion for political study.

Another leading scholar who shares the factors that sparked his personal passion for politics is Professor John Benyon, Professor of Political Studies at the University of Leicester and Honorary Treasurer of the Political Studies Association of the United Kingdom. Professor Benyon reveals aspects that helped to instigate his interest in the discipline:

> I grew up in a family where we used to talk about politics a lot and we discussed the injustices in Britain and the wider world. In my teenage years, I got involved and went out canvassing and delivering leaflets and I went to a number of political meetings and even heard Harold Wilson speaking in Southampton Guildhall where we had a good knockabout with various hecklers. I went to study politics at Warwick University and really enjoyed it – I stayed on for a PhD and then became a lecturer.
>
> (email interview with author, April 2014)

Professor Benyon proceeds to highlight what politics means to him,

> Politics is about conflicts over interests, with winners and losers. It entails disagreements over ideas, and how we should live together, and politics also involves different opinions about issues and decisions and who should make them. It is the very stuff of human existence and is fascinating and gripping.
>
> (email interview with author, April 2014)

With reference, possibly, to recent issues in relation to the world of politics, Professor Benyon reflects that it

> . . . is a shame that politicians seem so out of touch with people and that the government seems so incompetent and makes so many expensive blunders. We continue to live in a country and a world where there is much inequality, unfairness and injustice.
>
> (email interview with author, April 2014)

Professor Benyon does, however, end on a positive note, stating that '. . . I am still enthralled by politics and, although it seems like an uphill struggle, I continue to think that we can change things for the better' (email correspondence with author, April 2014). Testimonies such as those of John Benyon and others provide a genuine, heartfelt insight into the appeal of *Doing Politics* and go some way towards conveying the passion that the discipline nurtures in those who choose to study it.

In terms of comparative politics, Dr Yee Wah Foo, a Senior Lecturer in Politics, explains, that there

> ... are lots of reasons why I love teaching Comparative Politics. Our particular module (it's a Level 2) is interesting because it is team-taught. This means that our lectures are delivered by colleagues who have written books or articles on the topic, and/or come from the areas/countries being discussed – which makes it even more interesting. For example, I lecture on Chinese healthcare, and China's system of government, [my colleague] speaks on democratic transition and looks at models in Latin America, Africa and Eastern Europe, [another colleague] speaks on Russia, and [a further colleague] lectures on India. In all these areas, the driving force behind the module is its emphasis on the comparative approach. So for example, we examine key concepts such as legitimacy, authoritarianism and democracy and apply them to different models and situations. We question, for example, if democracy is always desirable and suitable? Whether authoritarian government is necessarily bad? We also look at trends and developments in social and public policy. For example, should our government protect spending on foreign aid? Is China's healthcare system adequate? Is education key to eradicating poverty?
>
> (email interview with author, April 2014)

Dr Foo elaborates that as

> ... well as looking at structures and cultures of government and policy-making in selected states, we build flexibility into the programme to take account of what's happening in the world as the course is running, for example last year we included a special session on the current upheaval in the Arab world. That was lots of fun, because the students were really getting involved as the events unfolded each week on the news. I find that students not only enjoy learning and comparing different countries and how they operate – they feel inspired to think about one day travelling to these places themselves. For me this is really gratifying.
>
> (email interview with author, April 2014)

These academics provide a revealing snapshot as to why politics is so exciting as a discipline and what lies behind their passion for the subject.

Numbers studying politics

Numbers studying politics continue to be relatively buoyant. This remains the case at both 'A' level and at undergraduate level. The main examination bodies at 'A' level report a healthy level of demand for Government and Politics. In terms of numbers studying politics, for example, the entries for 'A'-level Government and Politics for the AQA Board were 10,210 in 2012 and in 2013 the figure was 9,901 – a relatively small decline of 309 (*source*: AQA Examination Board). In terms of overall numbers studying 'A'-level Politics in 2013, according to the Joint Council for Qualifications, the body that comprises the major examination boards, the provisional figures were that 15,393 UK students took 'A'-level 'Political Studies' (8,888 males and 6,505 females). The corresponding figures from 2012 were 15,260 in total (8,669 males and 6,591 females), an increase of 133 in 2013. In terms of numbers taking AS level 'Political Studies' in 2013, it was taken by 20,170 UK candidates (11,319 males and 8,851 females). The corresponding AS level figures from 2012 were 21,601 (12,087 males and 9,514 females), a decrease of 1,431 candidates taking the AS in 2013 (see http://www.jcq.org. uk/examination-results/a-levels - page 6 for 'A'-level 'Political Studies' and page 54 for AS level 'Political Studies'). These overall figures constitute a significant increase in comparison with the early days of studying politics. Derek Heater revealed how the 'A'-level in British Constitution or Government for the Joint Matriculation Board '. . . had 1,089 entries in 1966 compared with thirty-nine in 1957' (Heater, 1969: 141). Nowadays, Politics is often studied at AS level in the first instance, with students choosing to study it as a fourth subject but then becoming so fascinated by the discipline, despire never having studied it before, that many then decide to substitute it for one of their other 'A'-levels. The fear amongst many sixth-form and college tutors is that changes to AS levels may impact negatively upon this route into 'A'-level Government and Politics.

At undergraduate level, there remains a healthy number of students opting to study politics at degree level. In 2013, there were 9,105 acceptances to study politics at university (across 90 institutions). This was up from 8,407 in 2012 and 8,887 in 2011. Applications to study politics were up slightly at 19,903 in 2013 in comparison with the 2012 figure of 19,075 but down on 2011, where applications stood at 20,780 (*source*: The Universities and Colleges Admissions Service – UCAS). Figure 10.1 illustrates the trends over the past three years in terms of numbers accepting a place to study politics at undergraduate level.

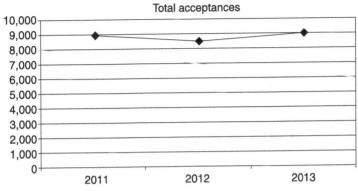

Figure 10.1 Acceptances to Study Politics at Undergraduate Level
(*Source:* Universities and Colleges Admissions Service).

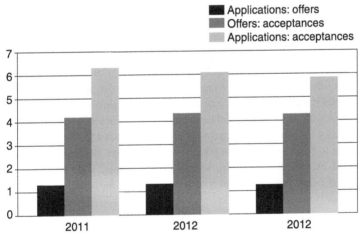

Figure 10.2 The Ratio between Applicants, Offers and Acceptances
(*Source:* Universities and Colleges Admissions Service).

Figure 10.2 depicts the ratio between applicants, offers and acceptances.

In 2013, there was an increase in the level of applications and acceptances to Politics and to International Relations degrees. Figure 10.3 reveals the trends in acceptances according to gender.

In terms of gender, politics continues to be a subject that attracts more males than females. The chart illustrates an increase of 476 females and

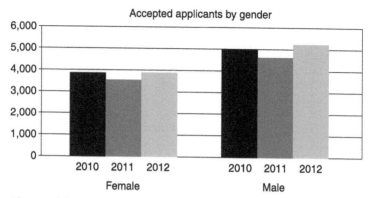

Figure 10.3 **Acceptances by Gender (*Source:* Universities and Colleges Admissions Service).**

352 males in 2013, a percentage increase of 5.45 per cent for females and 3.4 per cent for males. The 'gender gap' is, therefore, narrowing, with a higher percentage increase of female applicants (*source*: Briggs and Davies, 2014). (This detailed data is provided by UCAS, courtesy of the Political Studies Association of the United Kingdom.) It appears that the discipline has weathered the storm of the initial impact of the introduction of the new fees regime with the rise to £9,000 per annum (although it will be interesting to witness what, if anything, happens to tuition fees post-2015). The subject continues to be an attractive discipline at university level. Students, in this 9K world, are possibly more instrumental than previously with the inevitable greater focus upon assessment criteria/strategies and the career opportunities afforded by a degree in politics.

Role of the learned societies and other bodies

Learned societies, some of whose primary reason for existence is the promotion of political studies, fulfil a valuable role in providing a forum for debate and discussion and also in terms of the production of invaluable resource materials. The Political Studies Association, for example, which was established in 1950, and currently consists of around 2,000 members, including academics, retirees, graduates, teachers (and is also looking to move towards an undergraduate membership) and policy makers and politicians, exists to promote political studies. Indeed, its mission statement and *raison d'être* are to 'develop and promote the global study of politics' (see http://www.psa.ac.uk/ for the PSA's mission statement). Amongst other activities, it hosts an annual conference, an awards ceremony and contains more than forty specialist groups within its midst. It publishes a number of journals; these include *Political Studies*, *Political Studies Review*, the *British Journal of Politics and International Studies*, *Politics*, and *Political Insight*. *Political Insight* is relatively new (launched in 2010); a full-colour magazine, it comprises 'academically rigorous content in an accessible way for a wide global audience of lecturers, students, teachers and policymakers' (*Ibid.*). As well as a focus upon scholarly research, it is also increasingly concerned with pedagogical issues. One of the specialist groups is the Teaching and Learning Specialist Group. This group organises an annual conference, where the focus is upon teaching and learning concerns. It also regularly runs a number of panels at the PSA's annual conference. The Teaching and Learning Group's Chair, John Craig, has also been instrumental in creating a huge database of materials that can be used in the teaching and learning of politics. This International Political Education Database (IPED) (see https://sites.google.com/site/psatlg/Home/resources/journal-articles for further details) is a bibliographic database currently consisting of around 2,000 peer-reviewed articles on teaching and learning politics and is a veritable treasure-trove for those interested in political study. There is more material than ever out there for tutors to use in the development of innovative learning and teaching. The idea is that IPED encourages further research and enhances teaching and learning skills. Categorised into pedagogic approaches and then related and sub-fields, the database contains a wealth of information on topics as diverse as critical thinking, small group teaching, simulations, technology enhanced learning, political theory, comparative politics and political economy, to name but a few.

Other learned societies include the British International Studies Association (BISA), which was set up in 1975 and has an annual conference, as well as a journal (the *Review of International Studies*), magazine (online) and book series (Cambridge Studies in International Relations). It too focuses upon teaching and learning. As its website proclaims, it 'is a learned society which develops and promotes the study of International Studies, Politics and related subjects through teaching, research and the facilitation of contact between scholars'. It goes on to state that '. . . BISA is the leading organisation for researchers, policy makers, practitioners and students of International Studies in the United Kingdom' (see http://www.bisa.ac.uk/). BISA is slightly smaller that the Political Studies Association with a membership of circa a thousand. It regards itself as a '. . . key forum in shaping and disseminating current research in International Studies and Politics . . . [and] a dynamic and pro-active environment for more focused research into subfields of International Studies' (*Ibid.*).

The European Consortium for Political Research (ECPR) is yet another body that promotes the study of politics. Organised on a European-wide basis, it was set up in 1970 and comprises around 300 institutional members from about 50 different countries, representing '. . . the leading universities, students and senior academics engaged in the research and teaching of political science worldwide' (see http://www.ecpr.eu/AboutUs/ECPR.aspx). It was established to support and facilitate the

> . . . training, research and cross national co-operation of political scientists in a number of ways: a programme of world renowned conferences and events and a cutting edge Methods School, all with funding opportunities for members; a prestigious publishing portfolio which includes book series and three leading journals; its own publishing imprint, ECPR Press; and a range of high profile prizes celebrating academic achievement throughout the discipline, from the Jean Blondel PhD Prize to the Lifetime Achievement Award.
>
> (*Ibid.*)

It can be seen, therefore, that the ECPR supports a whole range of activities designed to promote the study of politics. Like the Political Studies Association UK, the ECPR has over forty groups covering a wide variety of sub-fields; for example, there is one on political violence. One of its journals, *European Political Science*, contains a section entitled Teaching and Training and regularly publishes articles on the pedagogy of political studies.

Further afield, the American Political Science Association (APSA) also promotes the study of politics. Set up in 1903, APSA is a truly vast organisation with more than 15,000 members in over 80 countries. APSA's core objectives include:

> Promoting scholarly research and communication, domestically and internationally [. . . and . . .] high quality teaching and education about politics and government. Diversifying the profession and representing its diversity. Increasing academic and non-academic opportunities for members. Strengthening the professional environment for political science. Representing the professional interests of political scientists.
>
> (see http://www.apsanet.org/content_1406.cfm)

Assisted by twenty-four full-time members of staff, under the guidance of three directors and its Executive Director, APSA undertakes a number of activities. These include hosting an annual teaching and learning politics conference, which takes place every February and is in its relative infancy. Under the theme of *Teaching Inclusively: Integrating Multiple Approaches into the Curriculum*, the 2014 Teaching and Learning Conference, held in the city of Philadelphia, was the Association's eleventh Teaching and Learning Conference and was attended by around 400 delegates. A comparatively minor event when compared to the main conference, held at the end of August/ early September each year, the teaching and learning conference covers a whole range of topic areas and is incredibly popular amongst those interested in pedagogical concerns. As with the ECPR's joint sessions, participants in APSA's teaching and learning politics conference are expected to attend their 'track' for the duration of the conference. This fosters a sense of group cohesion and means that topics are studied in-depth and from a variety of angles.

The now defunct body called C-SAP, which was the Subject Centre for Learning and Teaching in Sociology Anthropology and Politics, was part of the Higher Education Academy's Subject Network. It had a disciplinary-focused approach and sought to promote innovation and reform of teaching and learning in the social sciences. C-SAP is no longer in existence but many of its functions are now overseen by the Higher Education Academy. The HEA, based in York, provides support for the higher education sector. It aims to enhance the 'quality and impact' (see http://www.heacademy.ac.uk/about) of teaching in higher education. Its discipline lead for Politics, Steven Curtis, has been instrumental in encouraging scholars to engage in the creation of new and innovative ways of teaching and learning politics (and international relations). The HEA provides funding for teaching and learning projects, and is supportive of research into pedagogy. Another noteworthy organisation is the Campaign for Social Science. Set up by and allied to the Academy of Social Sciences, the Campaign is another organisation that, whilst its brief goes beyond the discipline of politics, lobbies on behalf of the social sciences *per se*. It was set up in January 2011 to promote social sciences in a number of areas, including the media, Parliament and the public at large. In early 2014, it had the support of around eighty universities, charities, learned societies and publishers. It seeks to ensure that, amongst other aspects, social science research influences public policy and that the value of a social science education is recognised and promoted. The Campaign produces briefing papers, such as one on the impact of social science research, that work towards achieving this goal (*cf*.: McAllister, 2013).

How politics is taught

In terms of how politics is taught, as outlined in Chapter Three, a variety of teaching and learning methods are used in the study of politics. These are many and varied and include a surprising number of innovative teaching methods, alongside the traditional lecture and seminar format. Case studies constitute another device that is often used as a way of teaching politics. As one of the key creators and advocates of such an approach, John Craig expands on their intrinsic value:

> Asking students to work through problem-based case studies, to each of which their group is ask to produce a response (which might be a presentation, action plan or decision), provides an effective platform to actively engage students to in the learning process. Students draw on their wider learning, seek to apply concepts, discover some of the challenges in doing so and critical reflect upon these with their peers. Where external stakeholders such as NGOs can be engaged in developing the cases, authentic dilemmas of political and public action can be brought into the classroom and support the development of students' employability.
>
> (email correspondence with author, March 2014)

Role play and simulations can be used to teach particular aspects of politics – especially in terms of comparative politics and international relations (as outlined in Chapters Eight and Nine, respectively). Students immerse themselves in a particular event or activity by assuming a character or role and trying to understand how that 'character', country or politician would or should behave. Role play and simulations are a fun and thought-provoking way in which to learn about politics. Debates are another way in which to learn about political studies. Students have to research a particular position or stance. This can be given a twist whereby students are instructed to research a position that is contrary to their own opinions. Coerced into researching the other side's standpoint, this is certain to foster greater understanding of the key issues involved in a debate. In addition, whilst the aim is not to get people to change their own opinion, it does certainly have an educative effect.

New technology also aids the teaching and learning of politics. Micro-blogging sites such as Twitter™ can be used, for example, thereby enabling students to ask real-time questions throughout the duration of a lecture or seminar (Blair, 2013). Podcasts constitute a valuable tool in the teaching and learning of politics, with significant impact (*cf.*: Ralph, Head and Lightfoot, 2010; Roberts, 2008; Taylor, 2009). The Virtual Learning Environment (VLE) can be put to great effect to enhance the teaching and learning of politics. Students can participate in online discussions, debates or write blogs or wikis (websites that allows a multitude of authors to edit a blog), to cite a few examples. In addition, online assignments may form part of the student's overall diet of assessment and feedback.

What can be gained from studying politics?

In terms of what can be gained from studying politics, clearly the love of the discipline and passion for the subject area are probably the first and foremost advantages. Increased subject knowledge goes alongside this passion. In addition to this acquisition of knowledge, be that factual, practical, theoretical, the student of politics will acquire a number of key skills. This development of transferable, key skills means that students of politics effectively enhance their marketability. Skills such as qualitative and quantitative research skills and data analysis, problem-solving techniques, critical thinking, team-working and presentational skills, are all likely to be acquired through studying politics. These were outlined in more detail in Chapter Three but it is worth reiterating at this juncture that *Doing Politics* does not just include acquiring subject knowledge and factual information but it also involves the development of a significant number of transferable skills. In these uncertain times as far as the careers market is concerned, these aspects all serve to potentially place the politics graduate in a stronger position *vis-à-vis* the world of work.

Careers in politics

Turning our attention to the world of work, a degree in politics serves as a precursor to a number of different careers. Clearly, some career destinations are more closely aligned to the actual discipline than others. Working as a political researcher, or for the civil service or in local government, all have a clear synergy with the discipline of politics and might seem obvious choices for the politics graduate (see Wyman *et al.*, 2012: 243 for a detailed list of examples. In addition, Catherine Durose *et al.* (2013) have produced a detailed and fascinating report, *Pathways to Politics*, which examines the career paths of politicians). The late Tony Benn famously stated, upon announcing that he would not be standing for Parliament again, that he wanted '. . . more time to devote to politics and more freedom to do so' (see http://www.theguardian.com/politics/2014/mar/15/10-of-the-best-tony-benn-quotes-as-picked-by-our-readers). The comment was slightly tongue-in-cheek perhaps but Benn was not wrong in that it is evident that there are a whole host of careers that, whilst less immediately obvious, may prove just as satisfying and challenging for the politics graduate. Such careers might include teaching, journalism, the public sector or private industry, by way of example. This is indicative of the fact that having obtained a degree in politics, it evidences that a student has attained a particular level of knowledge and, possibly more importantly, skills that employers find attractive. In addition, many politics courses include a more applied approach in that they look at the practical application of politics. They might also involve a period of time spent working as part of a placement opportunity (see Curtis *et al.*, 2009, for further detail on placements). As Mike and Chris Goldsmith inform us, 'As Europe drives towards a knowledge economy, universities have a key role in providing students with the skills necessary to contribute. Work placements are one way of developing these skills' (2010: 65). Wyman *et al.* make reference to the need for greater redress of the employability agenda through the politics curriculum, as they state, 'A combination of Political Science research and professionalization literature could be used more systematically to prepare our students for a range of government, public sector, media and third sector jobs' (2012: 236). They continue by stating that at '. . . the very least a more practically-oriented degree could support student interest in topical and applied politics, thereby capturing student interest when it is most passionate' (*Ibid.*). Likewise, Fidelma Ashe (2012) concentrates on the employability driver. Many degree courses have already gone down this route of a greater focus upon the employability agenda. For those that have not, this is certainly an issue for academics to ponder when they focus upon curriculum development and/or (re)validation. Dr Yee Wah Foo, a Senior Lecturer in Politics, refers specifically to comparative politics graduates and states,

> As far as careers go, students of comparative politics are well suited to any job that requires a certain amount of number-crunching – so statistical analysis, report writing. I would have thought also that comparative politics graduates might think about joining international agencies and NGOs, working with people from other countries and so on.
>
> (email interview with author, April 2014)

There is, therefore, a whole array of career opportunities potentially open to those with a degree in politics.

In addition to employment opportunities, many politics graduates choose to remain in education, either on a full-time or part-time basis, and study at master's (either taught or by research), MPhil or PhD level. This permits the continuation of their passion for research and, certainly at PhD level, allows them to add to the sum of knowledge. There is a burgeoning array of politics courses available at the postgraduate level and, whilst funding remains a perennial issue, their popularity remains unabated. Mike and Chris Goldsmith reveal how there has been an increase in the number of master's degrees on a European-wide basis, as they state,

> Master's level programmes are increasing, more are open to foreign students, more taught in English, and many developed in response to some perceived 'gap' in the market, possibly in collaboration with some other subject area [e.g. journalism and management, mainly for the public sector].
>
> (2010: 68)

Postgraduate study remains a popular option for those wishing to continue their political education.

Most universities have growing alumni organisations, which permit contact to be maintained with ex-graduates. Politics is no exception. Alongside individual institutional alumni networks, a growing number of learned societies foster and maintain links with the alumni from their disciplinary area. The Political Studies Association UK, for example, continues to build up a database of case studies of alumni and includes discussion of why these individuals decided to study politics in the first instance. These profiles demonstrate the career pathways facilitated by a degree in politics. Likewise, the Campaign for Social Science has produced detailed studies of social science graduates (including some Politics graduates) that should encourage greater take-up of social science degrees through this reiteration of their intrinsic 'value' and illustration of their practical application in the real world.

Conclusion

Moving forward, the next generation of political scientists have a great deal to be excited about. Part of the dilemma of producing a text like *Doing Politics* is that, in some respects, one is preaching to the converted. The crux of the issue is how to convey that passion so that others are likewise affected. There is, however, much work to be done. The recent episode of pollution-fuelled smog in the United Kingdom and across Europe (witness Paris and their limitations on motor vehicle usage) reiterates the ever-present threats to our planet and to life itself. Globalisation is not some theoretical concept, it is here and now. The same can be said in relation to climate change. The world continues to be a shrinking one, a global village, especially when referring to communications and travel. Messages and images fly around the globe in an instant. People power has a whole new meaning. The Arab Spring of 2011 showcased the possibilities permitted by mobile technological advances. Journalists and politicians alike recognise that their roles may be being usurped by the spread of popular news-bringers. In countries across the global reach, ordinary people can, via a revealing tweet or an evocative video diary, convey to a waiting world, hungry for information, a message that would have hitherto lain untold or been misrepresented. No longer cocooned in splendid (or not so splendid) isolation, our politicians have to focus upon the global picture. Politics is concerned with humanity and, indeed, with our very survival. Younger generations need to find ways of protecting our planet and ensuring we live together, perhaps not in harmony (that might be too much to ask) but at least in a way that will minimise conflict and spearhead the search for what the Ancient Greeks would call the '*Good Life*'; a good life that, with minimal exceptions, we surely all deserve.

The actor, writer, comedian and radio host Russell Brand reignited a debate about politics when he guest edited the *New Statesman* in October 2013. He set out his beliefs by stating,

> I don't vote because to me it seems like a tacit act of compliance . . . there is nothing to vote for. I feel it is a far more potent political act to completely renounce the current paradigm than to participate in even the most trivial and tokenistic manner, by obediently X-ing a little box.
> (Brand, 2013: 25)

Journalist Matthew Norman, analysing Brand's position and Jeremy Paxman's subsequent confession that he too had not voted in a recent election, believes that 'What we need is a change to the voting system to recognise that apathy is not the same as either Brandian revulsion at the irrelevance of any vote or Paxonian disdain for the choices on offer' (Norman, 2013: 13). Critical of our political elite, Brand's view is that we '. . . are still led by blithering chimps, in razor sharp suits, with razor-sharp lines, pimped and crimped by spin-doctors and speech-writers. Well-groomed ape-men, superficially altered by post-Clintonian trends' (Brand, 2013: 29). Despite all this, Brand ends on, for him, a positive note:

> But we are far from apathetic, we are far from impotent. I take great courage from the groaning effort to keep us down, the institutions that have to be fastidiously kept in place to maintain this duplicitous order. Propaganda, police, media, lies . . . this is the time for us to wake up.
> (*Ibid.*)

Whilst Brand has his supporters and detractors in equal measure, he may have inadvertently inspired a whole new generation to study politics. Let's hope so.

Chapter bibliography

Ashe, F. (2012) 'Harnessing political theory to facilitate students' engagement with graduate "employability": a critical pyramid approach', *Politics*, Vol. 32, No. 2: 129–137.

BBC News Online (2014) 'Dunce v Muppets' at Prime Minister's Questions', 2 April, see http://www.bbc.co.uk/news/uk-politics-26854208, accessed 3 April 2014.

Blair, A. (2013) 'Democratising the learning process: the use of Twitter in the teaching of politics and international relations', *Politics*, Vol. 33, No. 2: 135–145.

Brand, R. (2013) 'We no longer have the luxury of tradition', *New Statesman*, 25–31 October: 25–29.

Briggs, J. E. (2013) 'Passionate about their politics, not politicians', *Lincolnshire Echo*, 21 November: 47.

Briggs, J. E. and Davies, C. (2014) 'Politics: popularity persists', *PSA News*, September, forthcoming.

Crick, B. and Crick, T. (1987) *What Is Politics?*, London, Edward Arnold.

Curtis, S., Blair, A., Sherrington, P., Axford, B., Gibson, A., Huggins, R. and Marsh, C. (2009) 'Making short placements work', *Politics*, Vol. 1: 62–70.

Durose, C., Gains, F., Richardson, L., Combs, R., Broome, K. and Eason, C. (2013) *Pathways to Politics*, Report 65, Manchester, Equality and Human Rights Commission.

Gamble, A. (2003) *Between Europe and America*, Basingstoke, Palgrave Macmillan.

Goldsmith, M. and Goldsmith, C. (2010) 'Teaching political science in Europe', *European Political Science*, Vol. 9, No. 1: 61–71.

Hansard Society (2013) *Audit of Political Engagement 10*, London, Hansard Society.

Heater, D. (ed.) (1969) *The Teaching of Politics*, London, Methuen.

Heywood, A. (2007) *Politics*, third edition, Basingstoke, Palgrave Macmillan.

Lasswell, H. (1958) *Politics: Who Gets What, When, How*, New York, Meridian.

Leach, R., Coxall, B. and Robins, L. (2011) *British Politics*, second edition, Basingstoke, Palgrave Macmillan.

Leftwich, A. (ed.) (2004) *What Is Politics?*, Cambridge, Polity Press.

McAllister, F. (2013) *The Impact of Social Science Research*, London, Campaign for Social Science.

Norman, M. (2013) 'Treat me like a lab rat and I won't vote', *i-newspaper*, 6 November: 13.

Ralph, J., Head, N. and Lightfoot, S. (2010) 'Pol-casting: the use of podcasting in the teaching and learning of politics and international relations', *European Political Science*, Vol. 9: 13–24.

Roberts, M. (2008) 'Adventures in podcasting', *PS: Political Science and Politics*, Vol. 41: 585–593.

Taylor, M. Z. (2009) 'Podcast lectures as a primary teaching technology: results of a one-year trial', *Journal of Political Science Education*, Vol. 5: 135–153.

Woolf, M. and Grimston, J. (2014) '"MPs can't be trusted on expenses": angry attack by Commons watchdog', *The Sunday Times*, 6 April: 1.

Wyman, M., Lees-Marshment, J. and Herbert, J. (2012) 'From politics past to politics future: addressing the employability agenda through a professional politics curriculum', in Gormley-Heenan, C. and Lightfoot, S. (eds), *Teaching Politics and International Relations*, Basingstoke, Palgrave Macmillan: 236–254.

Websites

http://www.aqa.org.uk/, accessed March 2014.

http://www.apsanet.org/content_1406.cfm, accessed March 2014.

http://www.bisa.ac.uk/, accessed March 2014.

http://bitetheballot.co.uk, accessed March 2014.

http://www.ecpr.eu/AboutUs/ECPR.aspx, accessed March 2014.

http://www.freethechildren.org, accessed March 2014.

http://www.heacademy.ac.uk/about, accessed March 2014.

http://www.jcq.org.uk/examination-results/a-levels, accessed April 2014.

http://www.parliament.uk/business/commons/the-speaker/speakers-commission-on-digital-democracy/, accessed March 2014.

http://www.psa.ac.uk/, accessed April 2014.

http://www.theguardian.com/politics/2014/mar/15/10-of-the-best-tony-benn-quotes-as-picked-by-our-readers, accessed April 2014.

https://sites.google.com/site/psatlg/Home/resources/journal-articles, accessed April 2014.

Index

For Product Safety Concerns and Information please contact our
EU representative GPSR@taylorandfrancis.com Taylor & Francis
Verlag GmbH, Kaufingerstraße 24, 80331 München, Germany